Hervey Seaman

The expert cleaner

A handbook of practical information for all who clean houses

Hervey Seaman

The expert cleaner
A handbook of practical information for all who clean houses

ISBN/EAN: 9783337201043

Printed in Europe, USA, Canada, Australia, Japan

Cover: Foto ©Andreas Hilbeck / pixelio.de

More available books at **www.hansebooks.com**

THE EXPERT CLEANER

A Handbook of Practical Information for All Who Like Clean Homes, Tidy Apparel, Wholesome Food, and Healthful Surroundings

by HERVEY J. SEAMAN

" *With the well-advised is wisdom.*"—Solomon

NEW YORK AND LONDON
FUNK & WAGNALLS COMPANY
1899

To
Lucy,
My Wife

PREFACE

This volume has been compiled to meet the need for accurate and effective methods in every particular of household cleaning. Domestic duties should not be undertaken without due preparation, for so much depends upon their intelligent performance. Wishing to work intelligently you should not neglect what is herein offered. Often a task is approached with the impression that you remember how it should be done, when suddenly it occurs to you that you are not quite sure of the way, and can not recall the exact working of the desired method. It is difficult to retain in the memory all the details of the methods which you require, hence the necessity for a work of this kind, the first one to make a specialty of cleaning. The information here given is systematised from notes which have been gathered during a long period, from the experience of a number of successful housekeepers known to the compiler. If some of the hints given do not actually come under the head of cleaning, they are on closely allied subjects.   H. J. S.

CONTENTS

PAGE

I. THE HOME IN GENERAL.

Making a Home 11
Neatness at Home....... 15
Housework.............. 18
The Old Papers......... 21
House Cleaning......... 24

II. THE KITCHEN.

Mind in the Kitchen..... 27
Fitting Up the Kitchen . 28
Cleaning the Kitchen.... 30
Keeping Meats......... 31
Caring for Wooden Ware 32
Keeping Preserves...... 32
Keeping Eggs.......... 33
About Milk............. 35
About Salt............. 35
Saving Coal........... 36
Handy Devices......... 36
Water 38
Useful Kitchen Hints.... 40

III. THE LAUNDRY.

Washing Made Easy..... 42
Cleaning Laces......... 47
Washing Cottons....... 49
Washing Silks.......... 51
Washing Linen......... 52
Washing Flannels....... 53
Starch and Starching.... 55
Ironing 58
Blueing................ 60
Drying Clothes......... 61

PAGE

IV. SOAP.

Laundry Soap........... 62
Soft Soap.............. 62
Toilet Soap............. 64
Kitchen Soap........... 66
Care of Soap........... 66

V. REMOVING STAINS.

Removing Grease from
    Clothes.............. 68
To Remove Scorching... 73
Removing Grease from
    Silk.................. 73
Wine, Fruit, and Acid
    Stains 76
Ink Stains............. 80
Removing Mildew....... 83
Grass Stains........... 84
Iron Rust... 84
Iodine Stains.......... 86
Iron Stains on Marble... 86
Paint Stains........... 87
Cleaning Gloves........ 88
Blood Stains.......... 89
Stains on Carpet....... 89
To Clean Furs.......... 90

VI. MENDING AND MAKING.

The Apparel........... 92
Mending 96
Putting Away Apparel.. 99
Useful Sachets......... 101

7

PAGE

A Clothes Hamper...... 102
Cushions................. 103
Save the Pieces.......... 104
Table Linen.............. 105
Dish Cloths.............. 106
Odd Hints................ 106
Useful Devices.......... 109

VII. CLEANING GLASS.

To Clean Mirrors........ 111
To Clean Mica........... 112
To Clean Ivory.......... 112
To Wash Glassware..... 113
To Clean Bottles........ 114
To Clean Lamp Chimneys............... 115
To Clean Marble........ 116
To Clean Windows....... 118

VIII. TEMPERING GLASS.

Table Glass............. 120
.... 120

Lamp Wicks.......
Care of Lamps.......... 124

X. TINS AND KETTLES.

Iron Pots............... 125
New Tins 126
The Tea-Kettle.......... 126
To Mend Tins........... 126
To Mend Iron Pots...... 127
To Clean Tins........... 127

PAGE

XI. POLISHING METALS.

To Polishing Knives..... 130
To Clean Nickel......... 131
To Clean Zinc........... 133
To Clean Silverware..... 133
To Clean Jewelry....... 136
To Clean Japanned Ware 136
To Clean Bronze........ 137
To Clean Brass......... 138
The Stove............... 141
To Prevent Rust........ 142

XII. FURNITURE.

To Remove Stains from
  Furniture 145
Furniture Polish........ 146
To Clean Furniture...... 149
The Piano............... 150
Wickerware............. 152
To Repair Furniture.... 153

XIII. PICTURES AND FRAMES.

To Restore Frames...... 155
To Clean Pictures....... 158
To Transfer Pictures.... 159
To Make Frames........ 160
To Hang Pictures....... 162

XIV. CARPETS.

Carpets in General 164
To Dust Carpets........ 165
To Sweep Carpets....... 166
To Clean Carpets....... 167
To Clean Oilcloth....... 171
Carpet-Beaters 173
Padding the Steps....... 174

CONTENTS

XV. WALLS.
Selecting Paper.......... 175
To Repair Wall-Paper... 176
To Clean Wall-Paper 176
To Clean Walls.......... 177
Paste for Wall-Paper.... 178

XVI. BEDDING.
The Bed-Room.......... 180
The Bedclothes.......... 181
Feathers................. 184
To Air Beds............. 185
To Clean Beds.......... 186

XVII. BRUSHES.
To Clean Brushes....... 187
To Clean Sponges....... 189
To Clean Combs......... 189
The Care of Brooms..... 191

XVIII. PAINTS AND WASHES.
Making Paints.......... 193
Whitewash.............. 196
Ink.................... 198
Stain for Bricks......... 200
Stain for Wood 201
Varnish 201

XIX. CEMENTS AND GLUES.
Cement for China and Glassware 203
Cement for Knife-Handles 205
Cement for Bottles...... 206
Rubber Cement.......... 206
Various Cements....... 207
Liquid Glue............. 208
Mucilage............... 209
Paste 210
Paste for Leaks......... 211

XX. BOOK LEAVES.
To Take Off Grease...... 212
To Take Ink from Book Leaves................. 213
To Clean Engravings.... 214
To Restore Writing...... 215
To Prevent Mold........ 216

XXI. CLEANING WOOD.
To Remove Stains from Wood 217
To Polish Floors........ 218
Preparing to Paint...... 218
To Clean Paint 220
To Scrub Floors........ 221

XXII. CLEANING PIPES.
Stove-Pipes............ 223
Waste-Pipes 223

XXIII. DAMPNESS AND ODOR.
Sweet Odors............ 226
To Fumigate Rooms..... 229
To Fumigate Cellars.... 230
Deodorize Refrigerators. 231
To Deodorize Vessels.... 232
To Deodorize Clothes.... 232
Dampness............... 233

XXIV. CARE OF LEATHER.
To Clean Leather........ 234
Harness................. 236
To Tan Leather......... 236
Care of Shoes.......... 236

XXV. PLANTS AND GRASS.
To Keeping Flowers...... 243
To Crystalize Flowers... 243
To Destroy Weeds....... 244
Care of Plants.......... 245

PAGE

XXVI. INSECTS.

Ants...................... 247
Roaches.................. 249
Flies 250
Mosquitoes.............. 251
Bed-Bugs 251
Rats and Mice 253
Carpet-Bugs............. 254
Moths 254
Fleas..................... 258
Bugs from Vegetables... 259

PAGE

XXVII. DYEING.

Dyeing in General....... 260
Coloring Over........... 262
Various Colors.......... 264
To Set Colors........... 267
To Bleach Straw-Hats... 268
To Remove Spots in Dye-
  ing 269
Dyes for Woolens....... 269
Dyes for Cottons........ 273
Dyes for Silks........... 275

THE EXPERT CLEANER

I—THE HOME

MAKING A HOME

TASTE IN HOUSE FURNISHING.—Everybody likes a pretty, feminine-looking house. But few can help feeling disgust for a cardboard, worsted, and cheap brass establishment of about the fourth grade. It makes one feel cross to enter a woman's home and hear her lamenting that she has not the money for those things which another has, and, as it often happens, giving a sly slap at another woman of better taste for having them, "especially when everybody knows how much her husband's business has fallen off." She would probably be surprised to be told that this same result has been achieved with much less money than she herself has spent. Then, there were the many pretty childish sacrifices and indecisions that had attended every purchase. Mrs. Thomas went without candy for a month to make that splendid, big, soft, sofa pillow, while the very aristocratic couch on which the wonder-maker sits means whole season's going to social gatherings without flowers, looking sweet simplicity unadorned. When a woman makes up her mind to furnish her house at the expense of herself, it is really astonishing to note the unexpected ways by which her economies will take her. Until her object is accomplished, she is a Stoic, a Spartan, and a Buddhist—a trinity of self-sacrifice all in one.

MAKING COUNTRY HOMES ATTRACTIVE. — The well-arranged shrubbery, beautiful flowers, and nicely-trimmed lawns that adorn the homes of many who live in villages and cities are often the envy of farmers and their families. There seems to be a general impression that a home with handsome surroundings is only for those who have plenty of money and not much to do. It is also believed by some people that the things which go to make up the attractive features of home surroundings are not for the farmer, or his family. It is true, in a great measure, that people living in cities and towns do take more pains to fix up their homes than farmers. It is a fact that many country homes are wholly neglected in this respect. This is not always because the matter is lost sight of, but because of the rush of work during the season of the year when lawns and shrubbery and flowers should claim special attention. Neglect of these things is not always a sign that a family has no taste. And yet such attractiveness added to the homes of many farmers would make them really delightful. A little more time devoted to making home attractive and enjoyable might be the means of keeping the children from looking with covetous eyes upon the lives of city people, and planning to make their escape from the farm as soon as opportunity offers.

OVERFURNISHING.—Of late years there has been a sort of mild craze for filling rooms with all sorts of useless things under the notion that in this way artistic effects can be added to the home. In many cases, perhaps in most, the result has been that of overcrowding and meaningless gathering together of articles having no relation to one another, ornaments being used without any thought as to their harmony with any other furnishing, merely because they struck the fancy. Of course, pretty, dainty objects are placed in a parlor, or any room, to adorn it ; but there is no art in the meaningless and absurd articles, such as gilded rolling-pins, painted shovels, dangling ribbons stuck on everything, from chairs to coal-hod or wood-box. The men of the family will be delighted at their emancipation from "all things crazy," and will take new comfort in the air-space and floor-room that will be given them in consequence of the banishment of such useless matter. Indeed, the rooms should look more attractive and inviting than before. The one or two good engravings on the walls will be seen to better advantage since the attention is not distracted by so many small ornaments, and such a want of harmony. The two, three, half dozen good books on the table will give more pleasure to the waiting caller than any number of Japanese fans and parasols, beribboned bottles, or pieces of bad needlework. You may be sure that the general comment on your room will be as to its home-like qualities, and no one will be able to tell just where its novelty and charm lies.

FURNISHING THE PARLOR.—Of course, one must consider her purse, which we will assume to be light. Then one must make up her mind as to the color of the largest spaces; that is, the walls and floor, and see that everything harmonizes with them. If you can afford it, try to have the walls covered with cartridge paper, with a fringe or border from two to three feet in depth, according to the height of the room. A low, pitched room, of course, must not have a deep fringe. If the walls are very low, you can do without any border, and use a plain oak picture molding for the finish. If you can not afford cartridge paper, select pretty papers as low priced as twenty-five cents a roll. Avoid any widely-scattered design. You know what that means. You have seen the great bunches of flowers, separate and distinct, that repeat themselves in a tire-some way all over the wall surface. Perhaps you remember counting them, or imagining faces in them, when you have been lying sick. You should choose a paper of one color, or two shades of the same color—buff or crimson, or gray, pale terra cotta, perhaps, or old pink—if your room is dark or has a cold north light. If it is a very light, sunny room, you might venture on a sage green, or one of those pretty grayish blues. You should not have any gilding about the room, nor picture scarfs, nor very much drapery of any kind. These things catch the dust and make a room look stuffy. What to aim at in a room is a look of space and comfort, plenty of light and air, and harmonious arrangement of colors. Do not have more than two colors in a room, if you can help it, and have these in harmony rather than in contrast. For instance, try to run the scale of soft browns, yellows, russets, creams, and so on, in one room, and there will be no objection to a bit of deep red in the shape of a vase. If you can afford it, have an ingrain carpet. If not, stain the floor for about two feet all around the wall, and make the carpet that much smaller. A carpet made in that way should have a border, which can be bought to match. Or, if the floor is good enough, stain its entire space. This is not so difficult, tho it does not look well, except when kept with considerable care. It needs oiling frequently, and tracks up with dust. A painted floor is cheaper and easier to keep in order, tho not quite so pretty. Matting is cheap, and wears fairly well, and has a fresh, cool look about it that is very attractive in summer. In winter it makes a good background for rugs. Never forget that an open fire and judiciously selected pictures will make any room cheerful.

THE COZY ROOM.—There should be in every house a room where a fire can be made any time of the year, when the mornings and evenings are cool, or there is a raw, rainy day, or in case of sickness. If it is always ready, you will not care to take all the lovely autumn days for house cleaning in order that you may have the stoves ready. A nicely-blacked stove is not much of an eyesore even in summer, but you can put a screen in front of it if it worries you. You should have such a room, even tho you have to endure some slight nervousness for a while at the sight of seeming neglect.

THE MIRROR.—In the matter of selecting a mirror some caution should be used. Never choose an inordinately large mirror, with a bulbous gilt frame, planned for the evident purpose of using up as much gold-leaf as possible. Small, beveled glasses, in sconces or framed in rich plush of a color harmonizing with that of the wall-paper, are in better taste.

THE MANTEL.—The mantel-piece is now made of wood in so many beautiful forms that it should not be much trouble to decide as to the kind to use. Never permit a white marble mantel to disfigure an otherwise beautiful room. Cover it with a mantel-board. White marble has a suggestion of cemeteries. It always looks out of place in a drawing-room, even in the form of the finest sculpture work. Paint the mantel some pleasing color, and do away with its suggestiveness.

CHOOSING OILCLOTH.—Sometimes oilcloth is to be chosen for its wearing qualities rather than for its color and pattern. If you wish an oilcloth that will last well, select that which the dealer has had longest in stock, as time dries and hardens the paint and adds to the durability of it.

SELECTING FURNITURE.—One can very easily be bewildered when attempting to select furniture. There is generally such a great variety, and all so beautiful and desirable, that a selection seems hard to make. In any case let the furniture be suited to its use, solidly good in quality, subdued rather than loud in taste, and such as will give a home-like look to your apartments. Such furniture will always give satisfaction and grow into your favor, even if it does not enchant you at first.

NEATNESS AT HOME

NEATNESS.—A woman's touch is very soon discovered in the arrangement of a dining-room, the appointments of the table, though of the most ordinary kind, the neatness, the spotless purity of the table linen, the polish which the coarsest ware will show if properly washed and wiped, the arrangement of the dishes—all these tend to show the deft hands, the fine

taste of the woman whose charge it is. By fine tastes we do not
mean acquired ones. Many a girl or woman who could not
quote a line of Lowell, or use a French phrase, to save her life,
may possess a nature refined and beautiful enough to make
itself felt in all the drudgery of her daily life. In these days,
when many women are judged by their outward appearance, it
is well to look at their home life. Not that it is necessary for
every woman to make bread, and wash dishes, but the lady who
can do such things properly, should occasion require it, is far
more ladylike than she who looks upon it as menial labor, fit
only for the coarse and the ignorant.

MANAGEMENT.—If every woman would set before her,
as an object worthy of attainment and of all that is strongest
and best in her, to possess a well-ordered home, a great amount
of happiness and real beauty would be gained. It is wonderful
to see how much ingenuity is displayed by some women who,
with very little money, are always dressed in perfect taste, and
with no apparent effort keep old furniture from looking
shabby, and old carpets and curtains fresh and bright. But
these things are accomplished by much thought and a large
amount of hard work. Nothing helps one to do things so much
as doing them, and it is a fact that in time one who has an
actual distaste for housework may come to regard her kitchen as
a laboratory for the working-out of exact results. One who
sees the results only is not much to blame for thinking them
brought about in some magical way. There is a great difference in people, but many would be surprised if they were told
that the reason they can not do certain things is because they
have never really tried. A good thought to hang over the
kitchen-door is this : " Thou desirest truth in the inward parts."
The woman who, when she expected company for tea, always
went the first thing, and washed the cellar stairs, had tenden-
cies in the right direction. The best housekeeper we ever
knew used to say, "If there is any dirt in the house, let it be
where I can see it. Let it lie on the parlor tables and chairs

rather than under the beds and in corners, where it will become rich soil for the development of disease germs. When we had one of those days that aunt Lucy called 'clearin'-up times,' grandmother used to say to us, 'Girls, my grandmother used to tell me that one KEEP CLEAN is worth a dozen MAKE CLEANS.' "

HINTS ON DRESS AT HOME.—Having done our own housework for years, we know from experience that it is possible to do it and be tidy. Most women require a certain amount of neatness from their servants, and this is right. The lady of the house surely ought not to appear in a dress that she would not allow her servant to wear. Of course, we are not now speaking of " nice work." Have dark calico or gingham dresses made with short skirts, and little drapery ; button those to the throat, and have a turnover collar sewed to the band. That will insure a presentable neck without the objectionable white collar, and spare you the trouble of putting in a pin. The hair need not be curled or frizzed. Take the trouble to comb it out smoothly, and put it up closely when you rise, and you will not need to run upstairs to fix it when breakfast is ready. There is always in the kitchen a washstand with a large wash-pan—bowls are too easily broken—a clean towel, and comb. This makes it very easy to go to breakfast with a face that does not look as hot as the food ought to be. The sweeping-cap, made like a nun's cap, protects the hair, neck, and ears from dust. A housekeeper's long apron catches the stray flour, and other things that would soil the dress. A clean, white apron and white tie make the dress presentable for any emergency. Sew the buttons on at the right time, and they will be all in place at breakfast time. A woman's self-respect requires this for her, and you have heard the wise ones say it is the surest way to keep a husband's love. However, it is best to leave that subject for the wives to enlarge upon. It is well for all girls to get in the habit of dressing neatly while housekeeping cares do not press them ; then, when they have homes of their own, it will be an easy matter. Make long cloth gloves to sweep in.

They protect, and do not bind the fingers. Have a mop to wash dishes, and a large one to wash floors. The last saves many a backache and many a doctor's bill. Do not wear slovenly wrappers, and say they are good enough for home. Your brothers see them. Dress for them, instead of some other girl's brothers. Make yourself an attractive companion for them, and they will not leave home to be entertained, it may be to meet temptation which will work their ruin. It is said that "order is heaven's first law," and surely an orderly house is the nearest place to heaven on earth. These little things make or mar one's happiness to such an extent that all should give them attention.

HOUSE WORK

CLEANLINESS.—Many housekeepers have fixed seasons for brightening their tinware, and this has proved as good a plan as any ; but since enameled and other wares have come into general use it is so easy to clean such articles day by day as they are used. A little box of pumice-stone, sand, or ashes that have been sifted through a fine sieve, should be kept in readiness for use on spotted or dingy metallic surfaces, for such work is greatly quickened if the material for its performance is kept at hand. The neat housekeeper finds delight in having the tins scoured rather than in thinking they are to be attended to at some future time. The extremely neat housewife is not an agreeable person. Her nerves are too keenly alert in watching for possible defects in her own or another's housekeeping. Her sensitiveness is shown in her temper and tongue. Too much neatness, because of the anxiety attending, becomes injurious to the mental faculties, and so lessens the vitality and those energies by which the housewife should make her surroundings sweet and agreeable. Cleanliness is next to godliness, but too many enthusiastic housekeepers place cleanliness first.

THE EXPERT HOUSEKEEPER.—The expert cook has as much reason to be proud of her ability as has the skilled workman in any other occupation, because being skilled in the culinary art implies a very wide range of information and experience. If the expert cook has cause to be proud, the expert housekeeper has even more reason, for she must not only possess an intimate knowledge of cooking, but of all other arts included in the domestic economy. In addition, she must be something of a chemist, a physician, an accountant, and a disciplinarian, as well as a sanitarian. The good housekeeper sees that the food is well selected, properly prepared, cooked, and served. In cases of sudden illness she will know what simple remedies to apply before the doctor comes. She will understand the importance of keeping the house well warmed and ventilated, and free from noxious smells. She will keep the run of her household belongings, and know to exactness how many sheets and pillow-cases, towels, napkins, table-cloths, and doilies she has in use and stored away. Her watchful eye will look after the spoons, the knives and forks for the table, and see that the proper utensils for kitchen use are in the kitchen, and have their proper places, thereby saving the dining-room knives, forks, and spoons from being marred by use in scraping pots and pans. She will also keep her money accounts with such accuracy that she will know exactly how much she has laid out for household expenses, and will, therefore, be careful not to go beyond housekeeping allowance. Above all things, she will have method, fixing a routine, and insisting upon its observance to the smallest detail. The possession and practise of this varied knowledge is what makes the good housekeeper and good housekeeping. Let no one, therefore, think lightly of that occupation, that is not learned in a day, but acquired by months of study, experiment, and practise ; nor let any one enter upon it lightly, and without preparation, for upon its intelligent performance depends the happiness and health of the household. The power for good which comes from a well-regulated method of living is beyond calculation. A good breakfast well served prepares one for the day's work ; a good dinner smooths away the wrinkles caused by work, and prepares one for an evening of quiet pleasure.

HOW TO SLIGHT WORK.—Wait and see, over-particular woman. Do not faint in horror at the impious suggestion, or scornfully remark, "Everyone knows how to do that." If your life has been subject to the usual vicissitudes, you must be aware that there are times of pressure when the regular routine of work must be varied, and some things left undone; and if you are a close observer of other people, you must know that all housewives do not know what to slight and what not to neglect. Is some member of the family sick or demanding mother's care, or are you yourself feeling scarcely able to go about? Are you having some one to do your sewing, and do you wish to assist as much as possible? Is there to be a series of engagements, a gathering of former friends, or many of the proper and pleasurable things that absorb time and disturb the domestic routine? It is then of much importance to know how to slight your work without bringing it into absolute confusion. In case of sickness, the patient may demand your attention early in the morning before the work can be done. Always try, however, to clear the table first, putting away the food so it will not waste, pack the dirty dishes neatly on the wash-table, brush the crumbs from the cloth and cover, for there is nothing, unless it be a greasy, ash-covered stove, that looks more desolate and forsaken than an uncleared table. As has been hinted, the stove is another object pertaining to which your time and strength is precious. Rub it off with a piece of paper, brush the ashes from the hearth, and dust the zinc. Never neglect attending to the slops at the earliest convenient hour. Open the beds and windows, if it is not a damp day. It does no harm to let the beds lay unmade until night, but the slops must be removed early in the day. The beds can be spread smooth instead of being neatly made and tucked in, as they should be except when pressed for time. Another matter not to be neglected is the cleaning of lamps, for what is more dismal than a dirty, foggy-looking lamp! The sink and drain, or stand with its pitcher, bowl, and soap-dish, where the family wash their hands and faces, should always receive proper attention. As to cooking in times of emergency, live plainly, keep on hand plenty of good bread, plain cake, and sauce, but let the pies and puddings and extra dishes go unmade. Patronize the baker for awhile. Study to prepare dishes that will serve for more than one meal, as, for instance, roast or boiled meat, baked beans, oatmeal, and the like. Economize the washing, and, if necessary, use underwear, sheets, and pillow-cases rough dried. This has often been done when unavoidable, and that without physical pain or serious mental disturbance. Much time may be gained and strength saved by omitting the sweeping and dusting of rooms not in constant use. In the living-room and kitchen do the sweeping, and let the dust gather for a day, rather than deny yourself a ride or trip with your family, or a visit to some friend, whose stay may be limited, or neglect your children in sickness or overwork when feeling bad. Try to keep the rooms well straightened, for this gives them a tidy, homelike appearance in spite of other neglect. In time of emergency try to keep the main matters going. Have a general supervision of matters, but distinguish between the absolutely essential and the non-essential. Save your steps.

THE OLD PAPERS

FAMILY PAPERS.—"Where is last Tuesday's daily, which gives the account of Dr. Thayer's lecture?" "Where is this month's *Home Hours?*" "Where is the April *Young People?*" Such are the recurring questions in most every home. In the average house there is no place set apart for periodicals. Every member of the family makes use of each paper and magazine, for there is something in each for all members. They are used at different times and in different places. There being no regular place to which they may be returned, the periodicals are dropped where they were last used. There being so many periodicals in every family, one can not remember where he had each one last. Moreover, old copies are in the way of the search, and one often has to examine six or seven to find the most recent.

The remedy for this confusing state of affairs is very simple. It is merely a broad shelf, divided by upright pieces of board into three divisions. The central division should be used for the papers and magazines of the present date. That is, those that contain next Sunday's reading, the magazines of the month, the journals of the week, the newspapers of the day. The division on the right is for the papers that will be needed in the future—those that have references for coming weeks. The division on the left is for last week's and last month's periodicals. But two rules are required, the inflexible one that all periodicals must be returned to their place after they have been used, and by the party who has used them; the other rule that one member of the family shall examine the files every Monday morning, shifting them to the left, and taking out from the left division, either for the lumber room, to be kept, or for the cellar, to be burned, the papers and magazines more than one month old. This simple device saves endless confusion, loss of temper, and loss of time. It is incomparably easier than the present method, yet there is little doubt that many will go on in the old way.

USE FOR OLD PAPERS.—Where there are several dailies, weeklies, and monthlies taken, one soon has a large accumulation of papers, and with the exception of those relating to one's particular work or profession, they are seldom read twice. What to do with them is the question. In any case, keep them clean and neatly folded. When the papers and magazines come, perhaps on Saturday night, they might be laid on the sitting-room table, and, except when some one is reading them, kept there until the next Saturday morning, when they might be put in a closet, so that any one needing a paper could take one from there without running the risk and annoyance of carrying off those that have not been read. Twice a year the contents of this closet should be assorted, and the papers put to their various uses, those not wanted immediately being relegated to the garret. As to the daily papers, there is nothing so cheap, nothing more universally desired and watched for, even the breakfast is not so indispensable. But what is held in more contempt, and by most people so valueless as an old newspaper? And yet it has splendid possibilities to the housekeeper. It can be used to improve the appearance of the kitchen shelves. Any child can be taught to ornament old papers with scallops, and points, and stars, and bars, and be very much amused over the process. They can be put under the carpet, as they are excellent non-conductors of heat and cold. The weekly story-papers may be circulated among your friends, and sometimes exchanged, to your mutual pleasure. For the entertainment of visitors' children there is nothing better than a large picture-book, and for that purpose the illustrated papers are valuable. One large one is better than several small ones, for the children are better satisfied if they can all gather around, and all look at once, than if each had a separate book. This book is also of service to lend to a sick friend, who is too weak or too weary to read. Another purpose to which the illustrated papers may be put is to cover the walls of the room the cook occupies. She will appreciate this more than if it were done in the finest cartridge paper. The magazines can be sent to the libraries, asylums, and reformatories, or given to some acquaintance who would like to read, but is unable to purchase them. Professional books and papers that you wish to keep for reference should be bound. They will be more clumsy thus, but will be preserved in better condition. You could have them bound, buying covers, or getting some heavy pasteboard and cloth, and putting them together yourself. If there is a particular article you wish to preserve, it can be cut out and pasted in a scrap-book, which should be indexed, and have departments, so that anything can be found without having to look over the entire contents. Put the old newspapers to some useful purpose; do not destroy them, or let them get time-stained and worm-eaten.

OILED PAPERS.—Nowadays those who handle butter and lard when retailing it, cover the small packages with a kind of paper that is oiled. These papers are nice and clean, and should not be thrown away. Scrape off the particles of grease that adhere to them, and lay them away to be used in papering cake tins.

PAPER AROUND ICE.—The housekeeper is generally anxious to keep the supply of ice from melting away too fast. Wrap the ice in one or two old newspapers. Then, if you think to be doubly sure, wrap around it a piece of old carpet, or a piece of flannel. But the paper will do alone.

PAPER BAG WRAPPER.—It is surprising to note the large number of paper sacks that are used in the various lines of business of to-day. These come in no small number to your own house with the purchases you make. They should all be carefully put away, as you can make use of them in many ways. If you are going shopping, and must take a tin pail, you can put it in one of those paper bags, and it will be quite hidden from public gaze. If you are taking an old pair of shoes to be mended, drop them in one of those paper bags, and they are sufficiently wrapped. You can carry a bottle, a glass jar, or any such thing in the same way.

HOUSE CLEANING

SWEEPING. —Sweep with a long, steady stroke, taking care to form the habit of raising the broom at the end of each stroke in such a way as to prevent dust rising. Watch some people sweep, and you will see what is meant. They will work hard, and sweep as if they were digging, while a small cloud of dust follows the end of the broom every time it is raised. Be careful to go into every corner with the end of the broom, and to brush the dust from between the carpet or matting, and the skirting-board, as there the moths love to congregate. Sweep from all sides of the room to the center. This sweeping to the center instead of to the door may appear to some as an innovation, but if they will stop to consider, they will see there is no reason whatever for dragging the dust all over the room. In sweeping toward the center of a sixteen-feet square room you only sweep the dust eight feet each way, instead of carrying it before the broom the whole sixteen feet. Short, quick strokes of the broom are apt to scatter the dust, especially when the stroke ends with an upward jerk, as it often happens when the broom is in the hands of vigorous girls who imagine they are getting over the ground much more rapidly by hurried movements than they would if they took great pains. But hurry is not speed. Some persons are quick and thorough, others slow and thorough. But the one who always hurries is rarely either quick or thorough. She makes work all the time she is doing it.

Before beginning to sweep, open such windows as will not interfere with the dust—that is, those that will not let in wind to blow it about. People frequently open every window, and sweep in a sort of whirlwind. Dust can not escape through a window against which the wind is blowing. Therefore, such a window should be kept shut, unless there is an opposite one. When the sweeping is done, and the dust all carefully gathered into a dust-pan, open all windows if you wish, so that a thorough draft may carry out the particles in the air.

DUSTING.—Dust the room thoroughly. Begin at one corner and take each article in turn. Dust from the highest things to the lowest, taking up the dust in the cloth, but not knocking it off on the floor. Shake the duster frequently out of the window or door, and when through wash it, and hang it up to dry.

CLEANING HOUSE.—It seems no trouble to keep things about the house bright and shining. Only do every day or every week the same as some do only at long intervals. Once a week give the house a thorough cleaning with the broom, removing or covering everything in the room before sweeping. Then brush and rub thoroughly with a soft cloth all the furniture, pictures, and bric-a-brac before putting them in place again. Do not upset the whole house at once. Clean but one room at a time, putting everything in its place before beginning to clean another room. This is a good way for health and happiness. In cleaning an invalid's room you do not wish to make any dust or noise. Therefore, take a damp cloth to clean the room instead of a broom. This will take a little more time, but will add to the comfort of the sick.

II—THE KITCHEN

MIND IN THE KITCHEN

BE CHEERFUL.—Cheerfulness is the great element of character for success in this department. It does no good to say, "I do hate to cook. I wish we did not have to eat. I despise the kitchen." It does no good to worry about it, and dread it, and put it off as long as possible. Begin in time, so that nothing will have to be cooked hurriedly. If it is hurried, something will surely be ruined. Do not go into the kitchen with the mind full of something else than your work. While preparing a meal, do not try to make something else which should have your entire attention. For instance, you wish to make a large cake, and also have dinner to prepare. Make the cake, and put it in the stove before beginning dinner, or wait until dinner is finished, for if you hurry a cake it will not be a good one. Then, if you undertake too much at one time, you will surely be tired. Then first one and then another will come in to you, saying, "How long before dinner?" which will add to your burdens.

It is, of course, agreeable to have a neat, clean kitchen for your work. But there are times when it will get greasy and smutty. Such times require an extra amount of patience and cheerfulness, and if by accident a smut spot gets on your face, and you are laughed at, join in the laughter. A laugh will add to the fun, and we should contribute our share of fun, as well as our share of work, now and then. But, be careful. Do not send into the dining-room the smut and grease on the dishes. It detracts from the food, and the white linen cloth will be soiled. Soft soap is easily made, and is better in the kitchen than that bought at the store.

Another element of success in the kitchen is to be sure you know what you are going to do. Then have everything ready before beginning. Have plenty of fuel and water at hand, have every utensil you intend to use in its place. Decide what you intend preparing, and have everything necessary ready. Then begin. If you start without thinking of all these things, it may be that, after you have begun making something, you will find you lack some of the ingredients. Then what you have begun will be wasted, unless you are near a store, or have a good neighbor to draw upon.

FITTING UP THE KITCHEN

THE FURNISHING.—Few women are strong enough to keep a bare floor properly scrubbed, and a carpet absorbing the odors and grease of cooking is an abomination. Therefore, it is a good plan to buy brown oilcloth for the kitchen floor, as this shows the wear less rapidly than other colors, and blends better with the woodwork of the room. This seems like a small matter, but attention to details is an essential in the harmonious arrangement of a home. When buying this oilcloth, remember that your labor will be lessened, if you get enough more to cover the closet floors. Few kitchens are commodious enough. For this reason a flap-table, which, when not in use, can be folded up and fastened against the wall, is a positive boon. If not obtainable in the stores, one can be easily made by taking a dressmaker's stationary cutting-board as a model. The top of this table should be covered with white marbled oilcloth, and if the closet shelves are covered with the same material, they can be kept clean and sweet more easily. Besides the table, two chairs are needed for the kitchen. They should be made entirely of wood, as cane seats can not be used to stand on when needed. Small cooking utensils are kept in better condition when suspended. A wide, painted board, made after the model of the small keyracks so often seen in notion stores, can be hung, by means of picture hooks, back of the table. Screw on it small hooks, such as are used by upholsterers. There is no better place for knives, spoons, and small tinware. Back of the sink should hang the dish-pan, soap-rack, and small scrubbing-broom. The ordinary kitchen has two or three closets. It simplifies the work to devote each of these to some definite purpose. For instance: In one put the ironing-board, irons, tubs, and the like; in another put everything used in baking; in another the belongings of ordinary work.

THE KITCHEN SOFA.—Since so many women have to spend so much of their lives in the kitchen, it should be a place of comfort. George Eliot used to say that a "bright, clean kitchen is to me the most delightful room in the house." Be sure to have an easy chair or a lounge there. If you can not afford to buy a lounge especially for that purpose, make one. This is easily done. Get two long boxes from the dry-goods store ; place them end to end, and nail together. Make a mattress, and fill it with any desired materials. Shredded shucks are clean and excellent. Over this drape any kind of cover to suit the fancy. Be sure to get something that can be washed and ironed. Red and white bed-ticking is pretty and durable, and never fades, and when laundered looks as good as new. Make a pillow to match. Now, while you are watching the cakes, bread, pies, and the like, remember there is your lounge. *Rest.* Do not say you have no time ; you have to wait for your baking to brown. Why not rest while you wait ? You will be astonished how much it will refresh you to lie upon this sofa for even one minute.

THE PANTRY INDICATOR.—Some housekeepers have a supply-board on which is a list of groceries that are usually kept in stores. Opposite each item is a small hole with a long wooden peg to fit it. The one who takes charge of the pantry puts a peg in the hole opposite the article which is nearly gone, so that the housekeeper who does the marketing may easily see what is needed. A memorandum-book should be hung in the pantry, and the quantity and date of buying kept in this book. Where there is no pantry, a want-book, or slate, should hang in the kitchen, and the cook should be instructed to write upon this every morning the names of such groceries as are needed. Remember that the pantry should be kept light, cool, and well aired.   An arrangement like this will save the housekeeper much worry and many weary steps.

THE KITCHEN-FLOOR PAINT.—Housekeepers generally like to have some covering upon the kitchen floor. Often it is not convenient to have carpet or oilcloth, and yet a bare floor is hard to keep clean. The best thing to be done under such circumstances is to stain the floor.   Here is a composition that many have used, and speak of favorably, which is made as follows: Take three quarts of soft water, and three ounces of common glue, and dissolve the glue in the water.   When it is hot, take off the fire, and add three pounds of yellow ocher.   Paint a thick coat of this on the floor, and let it dry.   Then put on a coat of boiled linseed oil (you buy it boiled).   This soon dries.

CLEANING THE KITCHEN

AGENT FOR CLEANING.—A great saving is accomplished by the use of kerosene oil in the water in which greasy dishes, pots, and pans are to be washed.   Put a teaspoonful of kerosene oil into a small panful of lukewarm water.   It is as good as soap and hot water.   The kerosene will do away with half of the labor of washing the dishes and pans.   Kerosene is one of the purest and most effective agents for cleaning the grease and grime from any kitchen utensil.   It is a complete purifier of porcelain and other glazed wares.   Much of the dread of kitchen-work will be over as soon as the housekeeper learns the value of kerosene in her work.   You feel shocked at the thought of putting this bad-smelling element on your dishes, for you do not consider that the odor lingers but a short time on glazed goods.   A little experience will confirm you in the practise of using it.

CARE OF THE DISH-CLOTH.—The dish-cloth is an important factor in the kitchen, and great care should be taken in its use. Be careful to keep the dish-cloth clean, as many physicians claim that diphtheria has been known to start from the use of a greasy dish-cloth. Here the kerosene serves the purpose of a very good germicide.

CARE OF KNIFE-HANDLES.—How often is the house-keeper grieved at the spoiling of the nice handles of her knives. She seldom finds out the cause of this mischief until it is too late. Never put the ivory or white rubber handles in hot water. If they need cleaning, simply rub them with a damp cloth. The hot water will split them, and turn them yellow as well.

KEEPING MEATS

TO DISINFECT MEATS AND FISH.—Sometimes fresh meat, after beginning to sour, will sweeten if placed out of doors in the cool night air. Sometimes a disinfectant must be used. Here is one of the best ways. Put your meat or fish that is tainted on a nail in a box, or something that can be so closed as to keep in the fumes of the gas of this compound. Then put the cup containing the salt and acid in this tight closure, and the fumes will purify the tainted article. This will disinfect a room as well. Take one-half a teacupful of table salt. Two ounces of sulphuric acid. Put one-half ounce of acid on the salt at one time. Stir this mixture every fifteen minutes. Do this until you have used up all the acid.

KEEPING FISH.—It often happens that persons living away from market, who desire to have fresh fish, must resort to some way of keeping it. To keep fish a short time, better than it can be kept on ice, even in very hot weather, and in such a manner as will often improve its flavor, put a little vinegar on the fish, inside and out. This will keep it perfectly well.

TO KEEP MEAT FRESH.—In order to have fresh meat juicy and sweet, hang up a quarter with the cut end up. This is the reverse of the usual way. In this way the juice remains in the meat, and does not run to the cut, and dry up by evaporation.

CARING FOR WOODEN WARE.

TO PREVENT WOODEN BOWLS FROM CRACKING. —That useful article, the wooden bowl, is, as a rule, destroyed by the shrinking of its fibers. This shrinking produces cracks. In order to prevent this action in the fiber, take the wooden bowl and rub glycerine into it repeatedly, until it is soaked. This fills the fibers, and prevents the bowl from cracking.

TO KEEP BUCKETS FROM SHRINKING.—No one knows better than housekeepers how much annoyance is caused by having the water-bucket almost fall down from shrinking, not to speak of the trouble made by the leaking out onto the floor. To keep the wooden buckets from getting dry and dropping their hoops, paint these with glycerine until thoroughly saturated.

TO SWEETEN A CASK.—A cask that has had vinegar or anything sour in it, is not fit for much else until it has been cleaned. But sometimes it is difficult to know just what will effect this cleaning, so that the cask may be used without tainting the new contents. Here is a good method. Mix lime with water, and wash the cask with that. Or put in the cask hot wood coals and ashes, then put in water, and wash the cask with that. It may be necessary to let it stand in the cask, if the taint will not come out without that.

KEEPING PRESERVES

TO PREVENT MOLD.—Should you misplace the top of a Mason's jar, or have several of them without tops, even if you wish to use the common stone jars for preserves, you can very easily find tops for them. Cover them with cotton batting, for there is nothing better. Cotton batting is impervious to all life germs, and, if drawn tightly across a full jar of preserved fruit, will prevent mold and fermentation as perfectly as if the jar were hermetically sealed. Cotton batting is being used in this way by old and experienced preserve makers.

TO KEEP MOLD FROM VINEGAR.—If you experience any difficulty in keeping your pickles free from mold, take a little bag of mustard, and lay it on top of the pickles in the jar. This will prevent the vinegar from becoming moldy, that is, if the pickles have been put up in vinegar that has been boiled.

CANKER IN PRESERVES.—The time was when housekeepers used the brass kettle in making preserves, and, indeed, many still prefer the old kettle to anything else. But sometimes there is danger in the brass kettle. The housekeeper does not know when she may be called from the kitchen into the parlor, and if she is, it may be to leave the preserves in the kettle to stand for some time; there is danger, for in that way the canker from the brass gets into the preserves. Brass canker in preserves that have stood too long in a brass kettle may be detected in this way: Put one teaspoonful of preserves in a cup, and pour thirty drops of vinegar on it. Stir well with a bright, clean knitting or darning-needle. If there is any canker present, the needle will become red where it has been in the preserves. If it does not have this color at once, let it stand in the preserves six or eight hours. Then, if the needle is not red, the preserves may be used.

KEEPING EGGS

HOW TO PRESERVE EGGS.—Numerous methods of preserving eggs are in use. The idea of all of them is to exclude air from the interior of the egg, for it is by the exclusion of oxygen that decay can be arrested for a considerable length of time, especially if the eggs are perfectly fresh at the start, and are kept in a cool, dark place. The prevailing method, chiefly used by speculators and dealers, is to put the eggs in lime water. The process is as follows: Take twenty-four gallons of water, twelve pounds of unslaked lime, and four pounds of salt, or in that proportion according to the quantity of eggs to be preserved. Stir this mixture several times daily, and then let it stand until the sediment has settled, and the liquid is perfectly clear. Draw, or carefully dip off the clear liquid, leaving the sediment. Take for the above amount of liquid five ounces each of baking soda, cream of tartar, saltpeter, borax, and one ounce of alum. Pulverize and mix these, and dissolve in one gallon of boiling water. Then add to this mixture about twenty gallons of pure lime water, as made by the above directions. Put this in a forty-gallon cider or whisky barrel. Put the eggs in carefully, so as not to crack any of the shells, letting the water always stand an inch above the eggs. This can be done by placing a barrel-head, a little smaller than the barrel, upon them, and weighting it down. This amount of liquid will preserve one hundred and fifty dozen eggs. It is not necessary to wait to gather a full barrel, or a smaller package, before they can be put into the liquid. Put them in as you gather them, only they must be fresh. The same liquid should be used only once. This will preserve eggs for a long period, keeping them sweet and fresh.

STORING EGGS.—When not necessary to keep eggs any long period, and yet to store them for a few months for home use, one would find the following method very good. Eggs stored in September have been found in May to be in a perfect state of preservation by this method : Have a frame with sliding shelves ; in these shelves bore holes, one inch in size, far enough apart to keep the eggs from touching. Put them in these holes with the small end down.

ANOTHER WAY OF KEEPING EGGS FRESH.—This method has been used by one woman for twenty years with unfailing success, altho it is claimed that eggs treated in this way will not do to put under a hen, as they will not hatch. Take good fresh eggs and rub them over with melted lard, thus closing the pores in the shell. Then put a layer of oats or bran in a box, then a layer of eggs, setting them on the small end, and not allowing them to touch each other, separating them by oats or bran. Alternate these layers until the box is full.

SALT FOR KEEPING EGGS.—Here is another way of taking care of eggs, that some may prefer : Put a layer of salt in a box, then a layer of eggs, with the small ends down. Do not let the eggs touch each other. Thus alternate layers until you have packed what you want. Put the eggs in as you get them daily fresh from the nests.

ABOUT MILK

TO DETECT WATER IN MILK.—We do not like to buy water in our milk—that is, as it is mixed by man. To avoid this here is a simple means of detection: Dip a polished knitting-needle into the vessel containing the milk. If it is pure, a drop of the milk will cling to the needle ; if the least drop of water is present, the needle will be clean.

TO ARREST FERMENTATION IN MILK.—A generous pinch of borax, added to a quart of cream or milk, will keep it sweet. Sometimes milk which is a little turned, or changed, may be sweetened and rendered fit for use by stirring into it a little baking-soda.

ABOUT SALT.

ODD USES FOR SALT.—Salt thrown on burning soot will extinguish the flames. If it be sprinkled on the stove when the kettle has boiled over, it will prevent any disagreeable odor.

TABLE SALT.—Special table salts that are sold at the stores, are usually prepared by mixing a certain percentage of cornstarch with the pure salt. The starch acts as an adulterant, and while it is harmless in the salt for ordinary table use, it does not improve the seasoning qualities, and in the case of clear soup would add enough thickening to partly destroy its clearness. After all, a pure salt, dried in the oven and sifted occasionally, is the very best for all purposes. Heat the salt as hot as possible in the oven for at least ten minutes. Then crush it fine with a potato-masher, and sift it through a flour-sieve. Store it in a wooden box, and set it on a high shelf in a dry closet.

SAVING COAL

THE CINDERS.—Many people do not consider that they can use cinders to burn. A sieve for the purpose of separating the ashes from the cinders can be obtained at any house-furnishing hardware store. Make it a rule to sift the ashes at least once a week, so that they will not accumulate. Put the cinders to one side in a heap, and let them remain there until the winter breaks and you do not need very hot fires. Then use the cinders. Before putting them on the fire sprinkle them with water, which will make them burn better.

AN ASH-HOLDER.—In dumping the ashes in the ordinary way if the wind is blowing, you will raise a dust that will cover you. In order to keep your clothes clean from such dirt, take the big coarse paper-sacks that often come with your purchases. Shovel the ashes into one, then clasp the top, shutting it tight, and carry it to the ash-barrel, putting in sack and ashes in one bundle.

HANDY DEVICES

THE CHICKEN BLOCK.—In killing a chicken be careful that the blood does not scatter. Grit and dirt should be kept from the fowl's neck. You have no doubt come upon pieces of grit when eating the neck of a chicken that had been thrown to the ground when killed. You may also have seen the back fence dirty with blood at the spot where the chickens were usually killed. Here is a simple device to be used in killing chickens. Take a piece of scantling, four inches or more thick, and about three feet long. Set this on end. Take a piece of board about one inch thick, three inches broad, and two feet long, and nail this in the middle, and fasten it across the foot of the scantling, which will be in form of the letter ⊥ upside down. Now nail a piece of board, one foot long, in the opposite direction to these two projections. These will form the feet to the scantling. Now make two boxes, each with only three sides, and open at the ends. Have them two feet long, the open side wide enough to fit over the side of the scantling. Taper the sides of these boxes so that at one end there will be five inches and at the other two inches. Now take one of the wedge-shaped boxes, slip the open side on the side of the scantling, leaving an opening at the top of four inches, and at the bottom of one inch. Nail it in that position to the scantling. On the opposite side of the scantling nail the other box in the same manner. This is the chicken block. Chop the chicken's head off on the top of the scantling, then tuck the bleeding neck down in one of these boxes. You can have two boxes, if needed.

THE STOVE-LIFTER.—Sometimes the stove-lifter gets out of place and is hard to find when you need it most. Here is a good plan to keep it in place. Take a small chain, a long one, such as is used to fasten keys to your person. Fasten the lifter to one end of the chain and the stove-damper to the other end. It is always in place, and the damper may be handled by pulling the chain, thus saving your fingers.

A COOL LIFTER.—A good lifter for the stove-lids can be made of a piece of wire about an eighth of an inch in thickness and two feet long. Bend this at the middle so as to form the two corners of a square, wide enough to fit easily into the holes of the lids. Lay this flat. On the end with the corners bend up two inches of the wire. This makes it set well when using. Now twist the open ends about something round in the shape of a spiral to form the handle. Take the round piece out and tuck the ends of wire within the spiral.

A CHOPPER AND LIFTER.—Here is a convenient little device that you can easily have made. Take a piece of Russian sheet iron, three inches in width and six inches long. Round the corners of one end. Put a small hole in the rounded end to hang it by. With this you can mix cake, chop potatoes, lift pancakes, and the like.

A FISH-SCALE INSTRUMENT.—Removing fish-scales is not very pleasant work. Indeed, it is often the trouble of removing the scales that keeps you from buying fish. Here is an instrument that answers the purpose perfectly, and removes the objection to cleaning fish. Get a cheap curry-comb, such as is used for currying horses. Curry the scales the wrong way with this comb, and they will come off clean in a few minutes.

A FISH-KNIFE.—A good instrument for removing scales from fish, and otherwise cleaning them, is the following : Get an old table-knife, and with a three-cornered file make saw teeth on the back of it. With this scrape the scales the wrong way, and they easily come loose. The edge of the knife will do to cut off the head and open the fish, in order to give it a thorough cleaning.

WATER

TO CLEAN CISTERN WATER.—The cistern water often becomes black from the coal-dust or smoke settling on the roof from which the rains run into the cistern. Whenever the water becomes dirty from any cause, you could not do better than to use the following to make it clean : To fifty barrels of water take four ounces each of powdered borax and powdered alum. Mix them. Throw this mixture into the cistern, sowing it over the surface of the water.

TO CLARIFY WATER.—If your spring or reservoir gets muddy, you can clarify what water you use in the following way : Take one teaspoonful of pulverized alum and sprinkle it into four gallons of the muddy water, stirring the water before putting in the alum.

TO PURIFY PUTRID WATER.—When water smells bad in a well, or elsewhere, put into it lumps of charcoal.

SALTPETER AND PUTRID WATER.—If charcoal is not handy, perhaps saltpeter could be obtained easily. Two ounces of saltpeter should be dissolved in a quart of warm water, and thrown into the cistern or well.

TO SOFTEN WATER.—Hard water is objectionable at any time, but there are times when it can not be used at all. To make hard water soft, boil it, adding a little baking soda. After it has duly boiled, expose it to the atmosphere. It is then ready for use.

CHALK AND HARD WATER.—Boiling will soften water. To soften it without boiling, use the following : This may be put into a spring or well, if so desired. It is commonly used in a bucket or tub of water. Put into the water you wish to soften a piece of chalk. It is harmless and may be used in any amount your judgment may suggest.

ASHES AND HARD WATER.—Should one need soft water, and have nothing but hard water at hand, and have none of the usual elements to soften it with, try this : Take the required amount of wood ashes, put them in a woolen bag, and place it in the water.

BORAX AND HARD WATER.—If you wish to use only a small portion of water, as in washing your face and hands, put a teaspoonful of powdered borax into the basin.

SOFTENING WATER TO DRINK.—Hard water may be made fit to drink by boiling. By boiling the carbonic acid gas goes off with the steam, and the carbonate of lime is left as sediment, which can be removed by a filter, or by allowing it to settle, and then pouring off the clear liquid. Expose it to the atmosphere, as that will remove the flat taste boiled water usually has.

TO CLARIFY A PITCHER OF WATER.—If you are in a hurry for a pitcher of clear water, and what you have is dirty, or muddy, do this to purify it: Tie a lump of alum to a string, and swing it around in the pitcher a few times, and the sediment will settle.

USEFUL KITCHEN HINTS

TO KEEP BAKING SODA.—To have a good article of soda when needed is a great joy to the cook. Many times such an essential to good cooking is carelessly spoiled by letting it lay around exposed to the sun and air, and perhaps opened to receive the dust from sweeping. To be at its best, baking soda should be kept in a glass bottle or jar, tightly corked.   .

HOW TO USE COLD TEA.—The careful housewife is often puzzled to know what to do with the extra amount of cold tea that has been left from the supper, at which were a couple of invited friends who did not drink tea, but for whom ample supply was made. On ordinary home occasions there is often this seeming waste. It is well to remember that the cold tea should be saved for your vinegar barrel. It sours easily, and gives color and flavor to the vinegar.

TO KEEP CAKE MOIST.—Some families do not care for cake, yet they must have it for friends. So it often stands until it becomes stale. To avoid this, put an apple in the cake-box, and it will keep moderately rich cake moist for a great length of time. Renew the apple when it becomes withered. This will answer equally as well for bread that must wait before being used, as in cases of large bakings.

HOW TO TREAT CANNED FOOD.—Some people entertain a strong prejudice against canned food, constantly fearing poison, and there is ground for such fear. It is well to be careful. Canned goods are much freshened by opening and emptying them out into an open bowl, and then setting them in a cool place for a few hours before cooking. The liquid should be drained from peas and beans, and cool fresh water substituted. In this they should be soaked for two hours.

HOW TO KEEP VARIOUS ARTICLES FRESH.—Keep fresh lard in a granite vessel, or stone jar. Keep yeast in a wooden bucket, or stone jar, or granite iron ware. Keep preserves and jellies in glass. Keep salt in a dry place. Keep meal and flour in a cool dry place. Keep vinegar in wood, glass, or granite ironware, bread in a granite bucket, closed tight.

THE KITCHEN HOLDER.—The holder often seems charmed away beyond your reach, so easily does it become misplaced. When wanted in a hurry to lift a hot kettle or frying-ing pan it is sure to be under the coal-scuttle, back of the table, or just where it was dropped. Because the scissors have the same trick of making themselves invisible, the saleswoman, dressmaker, and milliner fastens them by a tape to her apron-belt. Do the same with your kitchen holder, when you are cooking, and you will not only save your apron, but your fingers, and possibly your temper.

III—THE LAUNDRY

WASHING MADE EASY

AN AID TO WASHING.—Here is a method that has been given a thorough trial, and is heartily recommended as saving half the labor of washing, besides making the clothes beautiful and white. It would be a matter of surprise should any one fail of these results when using the recipe below. Some might think this would do only for the clothes of persons who do not work, but it has been used on the clothes of those who have hoed and plowed, and the success has been unfailing. Dissolve a box, or a ball, of good lye in one gallon of water. On wash morning fill the boiler about two-thirds full of water. Into that slice one-quarter of a bar of soap, and add three tablespoonfuls of the dissolved lye. Sort the clothes. Wring the finest out of cold water, then put them into the boiler, and let them boil fifteen or twenty minutes, stirring them occasionally. Lift them out of the boiler into a tub. Have ready the rest of the clothes, put them into the boiler, adding more water, lye, and soap, and boil as before. Rub the finest clothes out of those suds, rinse them through two waters, and hang them out to dry. Warm the first rinse-water, and use it on the colored clothes.

HINTS ON LAUNDRY WORK.—"Every laundress thinks she has a superior way of doing her work," said grandmother, "but during a long life of experiment, I have learned a few easy ways of doing housework, and unless my laundress is hopelessly 'set' in her own way, I can give her some advice that will be of use to her." And here is some of her experience. It saves work, clothes, time, and trouble to put the garments to soak the evening or day before washing them. It is but little work in the morning to prepare a quantity of hot water for that purpose. Take a gallon of water, shave into it a bar of soap, and add a pint of naphtha. These should be thoroughly mixed. With that rub all the soiled portions of the clothes, and, when you have rubbed each piece, roll it tightly, and pack it into the tub. And so go over them all. The towels, especially those used about the kitchen, or those that are much soiled, should be put into a separate vessel after having been saturated with the above preparation. Take warm water, as hot as can be borne, and pour it on to the clothes until the tub is full. Then cover it with a thick cloth, and let it stand until the next day. It rarely takes more than half an hour to do the preliminary work. The next morning the least soiled pieces are rubbed out with little labor, and thrown into a suds as hot as can be handled. They are then washed lightly through that, and put into a boiler of scalding water, to which has been added a pint of the above-mentioned preparation. Do not let them boil longer than two minutes, but, of course, the water must be boiling when you put the clothes into it. The clothes are then taken out, thoroughly rinsed in two waters, and wrung as little as possible. Now put them upon the line. Have a piece of white oilcloth in the bottom of the clothes-basket, so that the water from the clothes will not run through on to the floor, as they are dripping when hung upon the line. If one can do so, it is well to put the clothes to dry on the grass in the spring. It makes them clear, and seems to freshen them for the whole season. Grandmother says, " Washing is by no means as hard as some people think, provided always that one brings brains as well as hands into the labor."

THE BRUSH IN WASHING.—You have seen experts in washing use a fiber scrubbing-brush on the very dirty spots. The brush of fiber-bristles does not become soft in the water. When washing, lay the wristband and collarbands on the wash-board, and rub them slightly with the brush. Do the same with any dirty spots on the clothes. You will find that a good device, and it saves the hands from being rubbed sore.

A WASHING-FLUID.—Housekeepers who have used the following washing-fluid value it highly. In fact, they will use nothing as a substitute for it. After you have put the soap into the water in which you are going to boil the clothes, add the following: One tablespoonful of spirits of turpentine, and one teaspoonful of water of ammonia.

TO CLEAN SOAPSUDS.—If you live where water is scarce, and so have trouble in getting enough to do the laundry, you will find the following an excellent plan: If the tub of water has been used and is dirty, and you wish to use it again, sprinkle powdered alum over the surface of the water. The sediment will settle to the bottom of the tub, leaving the water clear and fit to be used again. Pour off the water, put the sediment into another vessel, and use the water again.

A SUBSTITUTE FOR SOAP.—Water-glass is one of the best chemicals for the laundry. It has long been in use in the mechanical arts. In painting it is used for covering surfaces with a durable coat resembling glass, also as a vehicle for colors in wall-painting. Its uses, indeed, are many. In the laundry it makes the work easy and inexpensive, and does not injure the most delicate fabrics. Water-glass is a jelly-like fluid, and is made by combining alkali with sand. It is easily dissolved in water, but it must be sealed tight in whatever vessel it is kept, for, if exposed to the air, it will become hard. A Mason's jar is the best vessel to keep it in. Usually the plan is to put one pint of water-glass into three gallons of water. If the clothes are very dirty, use but two gallons of water, hot water, and one pint of water-glass. At·night put the white clothes into this mixture, and let them soak until the next morning. Then stir the clothes about, adding sufficient hot water to fill the tub. If you wish you can press or pound the clothes. Now, drain off the water, which you will find has removed all the dirt. If any spots remain, put a little soap on them, and rub slightly. They will soon disappear. Now, make a weak solution of water-glass— one pint of water-glass to six gallons of water—and rinse the clothes in that. Then boil them in clear water for a few minutes. This makes the clothes perfectly white. You need not use bluing, unless you wish. Now, hang the garments out to dry.

Wash colored cottons in the solution of water-glass made as required above for rinsing, following the same course as with the white clothes. They need no rubbing, no soap, no bluing, and less rinsing than in the old way. Treat colored flannels as you do the cotton goods, as far as the use of the water-glass is concerned.

ANOTHER WASHING-FLUID.—It is not always convenient to follow good recipes, as frequently the ingredients required are not to be had without delay and trouble. That you may not be hindered by such experience, we add the following for your convenience: Mix one pound of sal-soda, one-half pound of lime that has been air-slacked, and five quarts of water. Boil that mixture until well mingled, stirring it frequently. Then let it settle. Pour off the liquid carefully, so as not to stir the sediment. Put it into a stone jug or large glass bottle, and confine it. Then it is ready for use. Soak the white clothes in pure water over night, if you prefer it. Put warm suds to the clothes while you are getting breakfast, but soaking them over night does not hurt them. Now, take them out of that water, and soap the dirty spots. Have the boiler half full of scalding water; into that stir one teacupful of the mixture. Put the clothes in, and boil them for one half-hour. Then rub them lightly through one suds. Rinse them in bluing water, and the wash is done. This is a valuable compound, and saves half the labor of washing in the old way. It does not harm the clothes.

KEROSENE AND GASOLINE IN WASHING.—Here is a combination of chemicals that some people may find of great advantage in washing clothes. It certainly makes them white, and boiling drives off all odor of the ingredients. Put into a boiler of water one teacupful of kerosene oil and one teacupful of gasoline. Mix them well with the water in the boiler, using the usual amount of soap. Now, put the clothes in, and boil them half an hour. You need only to rinse and wring them afterward.

TO WHITEN CLOTHES.—For making the clothes nice and white, use the following, if it is not convenient to employ other agencies. Mix one tablespoonful of spirits of turpentine with one tablespoonful of powdered borax. Put the mixture into the water you intend to boil with the clothes, and let them boil until clean.

TO WASH CLOTHES WITHOUT RUBBING.—When you wish to clean your clothes without rubbing and laboring over them, use the following. When boiling, add one teacupful of coal oil, one tablespoonful of spirits of turpentine, and the usual amount of soap. Put the clothes in and boil.

THE USUAL WASH.—Put boiling water into your tubs, and to every boilerful add two tablespoonfuls of powdered borax. Soak the clothes well in the boiling borax water. Soap the parts that are soiled, and rub them on the board. After rubbing, let the clothes remain in hot borax water for twenty minutes. Do not boil them. Rinse in clear water. With the slightest wringing, hang them to dry. Press the towels, folded as usual, through the clothes wringer.

THE FAMILY WASH.—Very good results have been obtained in washing clothes by the following directions. Many have preferred this way after trying some highly recommended formula. Put as many bucketfuls of water into the tub as you desire. Into each bucketful of water put one tablespoonful of *aqua ammonia*, and add one-half the usual amount of soap. In that water soak the clothes over night. Prepare the water for the boiler in the above way the next morning. Rinse the clothes out of the first water, and put them into the boiler. Rinse in clear water, and dry them.

CLEANING LACES.

TO BRIGHTEN BLACK LACE.—You can freshen your black lace skirt in the following manner. Brush it thoroughly, to get rid of all dust, doing the dusting with a piece of crape. Take as much *aqua ammonia* as you think will be needed, and dilute it with lukewarm water. Sponge with the ammonia, and when the sponging has been thoroughly done, press the lace on the wrong side until it is dry.

TO CLEAN GOLD AND SILVER LACE.—Gold and silver lace is easily cleaned by this simple method. Take as much of the inside of a stale loaf of bread as you think will answer your purpose. Then have a quarter of a pound of powdered bluing, such as is used for the laundry. Rub the bread into fine crumbs, and mix the bluing with it. Sprinkle this mixture thickly over the lace, let it remain a short time, and it will have the desired effect. When the lace begins to look bright, brush off the crumbs with a piece of flannel, and rub lightly with a piece of red velvet.

TO REFRESH BLACK LACE.—Should you desire to renew a piece of black lace that begins to show soil, here is a good course to pursue. Take one pint of warm water, and add to it one teaspoonful of borax. Go over the lace with that mixture, using an old black kid glove as a sponge. Now pin the lace smoothly to a dry towel, and let it dry.

TO RENEW LACES.—Having washed your laces, do not experiment with them in order to get them stiff and glossy. Do not use starch in washing. Put into the rinsing water a little white sugar, and you will be pleased with the result.

TO DRY BLACK LACE.—Be careful in drying laces. Avoid putting black lace very near the fire, as heat of any kind is likely to turn it rusty. A good way is to carefully place the lace on a dry towel, then spread a towel over it; the towels will absorb the moisture.

TO WHITEN LACE.—If your lace is made of unbleached linen, and you desire to make it white, use the following. The process is good, but it may have to be repeated several times if you want the lace very white : Wash in strong soap suds and then let it remain in the suds exposed to the sun. The summer time, when the sun is hot, is the best time for this method.

TO WASH VALENCIENNES LACE.—This lace must be of good quality if it washes well. Taking that for granted, here is a good process: Have nice lukewarm suds, and wash the lace in them. When you get ready to iron it, cover with several thicknesses of flannel and iron over those.

TO WASH WHITE COTTON LACE.—White cotton laces are washed in warm soap suds. Rinse well, then boil and rinse again. Then draw between the fingers to dry. Pin smoothly to a clean dry towel. Every point of the scallops must be pinned down to the towel to dry.

TO WASH WHITE SILK LACE.—White silk lace should be soaked in milk over night, then dipped, and dipped again in warm soap suds, and finally rinsed in clear water. Draw it through the fingers to somewhat dry it, and then lay it between a clean, dry towel, and bear on to further dry. Carefully pin it down while damp, and let it dry smooth and even.

TO RENEW DELICATE LACE.—Here is direction for cleaning delicate laces that every adept will indorse. Spread the lace out on large sheets of writing paper, cover it with calcined magnesia, place another sheet of paper over it, and put it away between the leaves of a book—a Webster's unabridged dictionary would do. Let it remain there three days. Then skilfully shake off the powder, and its delicate threads will be as fresh and clean as when new.

TO CLEAN LACES.—A good way to clean laces is by winding them around a long bottle over a piece of flannel, and wrapping a piece of flannel over the lace. Then boil it in water to which you have added a little powdered borax. Remove the outside flannel, and rinse the lace in two waters, and then dip it in a weak starch or gum arabic water. Do this without removing the lace from the bottle. If it is dried in this way, it will be kept smooth, is not easily injured, and it will not need ironing.

TO WASH WHITE LACE EDGING.—Take a piece of muslin the size desired. Lay the edging on it, stretching the lace somewhat. Then make the stitch of your machine long, and run the lace on the muslin. Now, soap it well. Boil it as you would other nice goods. Rinse by plunging in clear water. Put it in the hot sun to dry. Cut the stitches, and take it off. It will be as good as new.

TO WASH CURTAINS.—Put the curtains in the tub; wet them with coal oil, and then pour on hot suds. Do not rub them, but draw through the fingers as if stripping them of dirt. Rinse once in hot water, then in cold.

WASHING COTTONS

TO SET GINGHAM COLORS.—In washing ginghams put into the tub as much cold water as is needed, then put into it as much common salt as will make it quite salty. Wash the ginghams in this salty water, and it will set the colors.

TO SET BLACK CALICOES.—Wash black calicoes in hot or cold water. To every two gallons of water add a full handful of table salt. This will prevent the color from fading.

TO SET COLORS IN SUMMER DRESSES.—When you wash the children's dresses, or your own, if they are made of light summer colors, the colors may run, and make the goods an ugly blot. To prevent this, put into the last rinsing water a teacupful of salt.

TO PREVENT RED FROM FADING.—Get the water ready for the scarlet napkins, the red-bordered towels, and the red tablecloths. Into the water put one tablespoonful of borax to the gallon. This will prevent them from fading.

TO WASH SPECIAL GOODS.—There are some goods that need a much quicker process of washing than others. The long delays of an ordinary washing would ruin them. Of this class are calicoes, ginghams, cambrics, and the like, that can not be properly washed along with the white goods. Give them a quick washing by themselves.

TO MAKE CALICOES HOLD COLOR.—You may doubt that a piece of calico will hold its color when washed. In such a case, put a tablespoonful of sugar of lead in a bucket of water, and soak the goods in that mixture for twenty minutes before washing them.

TO PREVENT FADING IN GENERAL.—Here is a good general method for preventing the fading of colors in wash goods. Make a strong solution of salt and very hot water, say one-half a cupful of salt to two gallons of water. While the solution is very hot, put the garment into it, and let it stand until cold. Wring the goods, and dry them.

TO CLEAN CHINTZ.—Chintz and other printed cottons may be cleaned in the following manner : Grate raw potatoes to a fine pulp, and add water in the proportion of one pint to a pound of potatoes. Run this liquid through a coarse sieve into a vessel, and allow it to remain until the fine white starch sinks to the bottom. Pour off the clear liquid to be used in cleaning.

Spread the soiled goods on a table covered with a linen cloth; dip a sponge into the clear liquid, and apply it until the dirt is removed. Then rinse the article several times in clean cold water.

WASHING SILKS

TO WASH SUMMER SILKS.—In washing summer silks, remove all grease, or other spots, with chloroform. Then make a solution of a teaspoonful of ammonia and a little soap in a pail of water. In this dip the silk again and again, until it looks clean. Do not wring it, but press between the hands. Rinse in water from which the chill has been taken. Hang in a shady place until partly dry, and then lay between two cloths, and press dry with a hot iron.

TO WASH A SILK DRESS.—Rip the dress apart and shake off the dust. Have ready two tubs of warm soft water. Make strong suds in one tub, and use the other for rinsing. Wash the silk, one piece at a time, in the suds, now shake it gently, rinse, shake again, smooth it out, and iron with a hot iron on what you intend to be the wrong side. So do with each piece, and when about half done, throw out the suds and make suds of the rinsing water, using fresh water for rinsing.

TO RENEW CHINA SILK.—Here is the way to have China silk to look just as good as new after it has been washed: Dust carefully and wash it in a thick suds of some good soap. Iron while quite damp.

TO WASH SILK HANDKERCHIEFS.—If you must send your handkerchiefs to the public laundry you can not help them being ruined. Wash them at home. Silk handkerchiefs should never be put into a tub with other clothes. Wash them in lukewarm water, rinse two or three times in clear, cold water, without any bluing; wring, fold, and roll tightly in a cloth, but do not let them get dry before ironing.

WASHING LINEN

TO WASH EMBROIDERIES.—To have the embroideries look nice after washing, use rain water and white castile soap. Make a thick lukewarm suds, and in the mixture wash the embroideries.

WHEN YOU LAY AWAY LINEN.—When you are about to lay away linen for any length of time, wash it, rough dry it without any bluing, and then lay it away in loose folds without much weight on it.

TO WASH TIDIES AND DOILIES.—Tidies, doilies, and tray cloths should not be put into the tub with the other laundry pieces. Wash them by themselves, using some better quality of soap. Do not boil them, and be sure to rinse thoroughly. Then spread them smoothly over a towel or sheet, and roll tightly. Begin at once to iron them on the wrong side with a very hot iron. Ironing such things while damp gives them a new look, and an effect which is not possible to obtain in any other way.

TO WASH EMBROIDERED LINEN.—If you have no castile soap, make a strong suds of some white soap and luke-warm water and wash the pieces carefully in that. The wash-board should not be used; rinse them immediately in lukewarm water, then in water slightly blued, and then hang them to dry. When half dry, lay them smoothly on a clean cloth doubled, or laid over a piece of doule-faced white canton flannel, and press them on the wrong side with a hot iron until they are dry. If the embroideries are fringed, comb the fringe out care-fully with a coarse comb.

TO WASH LINEN AND WHITE GOODS.—Some people do not take the proper care in washing certain kinds of goods separately. To keep white goods a good color, do not wash them with linen, as linen discharges a gum, or other substance that discolors white goods.

TO WASH LAWN.—A good way to wash lawns so as to cleanse and stiffen them, is as follows: Take six quarts of water, add to it two quarts of wheat-bran; boil them together for thirty minutes, and then strain. Add this to the water in which you are to wash the goods. There is no need to starch or soap the goods. Use clear water to rinse in, but do it slightly.

WASHING FLANNELS

BORAX FOR FLANNELS.—There is nothing that will cause fine, nice flannels to look so nice as borax in the water. Borax leaves flannels soft and clean without shrinking. A tablespoonful of borax to a pail of hot water is the right proportion. Use but little soap, and, if you use any, have it well dissolved in the suds.

TO WASH FLANNELS.—Here is a good method of washing flannels. First wash them with white soap in hot water, and dry them in the shade. Do not let flannel freeze, as it becomes harsh and rough after freezing. If possible, iron them while damp.

TO WASH BLANKETS.—In washing blankets one should seek to preserve their softness, also the brightness of the colored stripes. To do this, instead of using soap use *aqua ammonia* or borax, whichever is convenient.

TO WASH WORSTED GOODS.—Use a nice white soap in washing worsted dress-goods, and always wash them separately from the other laundry pieces. To wring this kind of dress-goods will not do. Shake them well and hang by the edge to dry. To iron before dry is best, as then they will look like new, and be clean, bright, and soft.

TO WASH CHALLIES.—Some housekeepers wash challies in the following manner: Boil one pound of rice in five quarts of water, and let it cool to lukewarmness. Then put in the goods anu wash well, using the rice as soap. Pour off the water, leaving the sediment. Rub the goods well in the sediment, rinsing them in the water you have poured off. Use no rinsing water, but hang the goods to dry direct from the rice water.

TO WASH ORDINARY WOOLENS.—For the ordinary woolens take soap-lye and *aqua ammonia*. They work wonders by quickly dissolving dirt from woolens. Use a tablespoonful of each to one bucket of water. Soap-lye and borax, in the same proportions, applied boiling hot, give white woolens a looseness and a dazzling whiteness which they do not often possess when new. Do not wring out your woolens, but press them between your hands; shake them well and hang out to dry. There is nothing that compares with lye and borax for washing woolens.

TO WASH FLANNELS IN GENERAL.—The best and most approved way of washing flannels, and underwear in general, is the following. It is employed by the most careful and experienced persons, and flannels washed in this way never shrink, but remain soft and last long. Put the flannels in the tub, and pour on hot suds. Do not rub them on a board, or in your hands, as to rub them makes the threads lap, and that is the shrinking you so much fear. Draw the goods through the hands again and again. If you are washing a blanket, begin at one corner, and draw it through the fingers until you get around. Repeat until the article is clean, which is very soon. Rinse in clear hot water.

A WASH FOR WOOLENS.—Get ten cents worth of pulverized soap bark (it can be gotten at any drug store), put it into a bucket of cold water, and let it stand over night. In the morning strain it, and add two-thirds of it to the water in which the goods are to be washed. If the goods are much soiled, add a teaspoonful of *aqua ammonia*. Put the rest of the soap-bark water into the rinsing water. Shake the goods well, and while yet damp, iron them on the wrong side. The soap bark cleanses, and gives body to the goods, as when new.

TO BLEACH FLANNEL.—Flannel, which has become yellow with use and poor washing, may be whitened in this way. Leave it for some days in a solution of hard soap, to which has been added strong ammonia—one pound and a half of hard soap, five gallons of soft water, and one pint of strong ammonia. If the above does not suit you, try this. Put the flannel for a quarter of an hour in a weak solution of bisulphite of sodium, to which has been added a little hydrochloric acid.

TO BLEACH FLANNELS.—Even with the most careful washing white flannels will become more or less yellow. It is very little work to bleach them. Here is an old method that leaves them soft and white. Into a large dry-goods box fasten several narrow slats across and just below the top. Get a few grains of sulphur, put in a saucer, and set on the bottom of the box, inside. Hang the flannels on the cross bars, so that they will escape contact with the saucer. Light the sulphur, cover the box so that it will be perfectly close, and let the flannels hang in the fumes for from fifteen minutes to an hour, according to their condition. The flannels must be clean and dry before doing this. Take them from the box, and hang them on a line in the open air, and the sulphur fumes will immediately disappear. The fumigating, of course, must be done out of doors.

STARCH AND STARCHING

TO POLISH SHIRTS.—Starch the shirt-fronts and wrist-bands as stiff as you can, that is, starch, then dry, then starch again. Iron the shirt with the common iron in the usual way, making the linen nice and firm, but without any attempt at a good polish. Don't lift the plait. The shirt is now ready for polishing. You ought to have a board the same size as a common shirt board, made of hard wood, and covered with one ply of plain cotton cloth. Put this board into the breast of the shirt, dampen the front very lightly with a wet sponge or cloth. Then take the polishing iron, which is flat and beveled at one end, and polish gently with the beveled end, taking care not to drive the linen up into wave-like blisters. If you are careful and persevere, in a short time you will be able to give the enamel-like finish which is so much admired.

BORAX IN STARCH. — When making starch, put one tablespoonful of borax to one pint of boiling starch. This saves the starch, and adds to the gloss without undue stiffness, and it also lessens the sticking when ironing. If you want the linen to have an extra stiffness, add one teaspoonful of powdered borax to one pint of cold starch. That is the proportion.

GUM ARABIC IN STARCH.—If you desire the shirt-fronts and wristbands, the collars and cuffs to be firm and stiff, the best way known of is to take two ounces of white gum arabic, pour on it one pint of hot water, and let it stand until melted, and then put it into a bottle, and cork it up until wanted. A tablespoonful of this in a pint of starch will produce the desired result.

GLOSS STARCH.—Chinese gloss starch is made of two tablespoonfuls of raw starch and one teaspoonful of powdered borax, dissolved in one and a half cupfuls of cold water. Dip the thoroughly dry, unstarched cuffs, collars, and bosoms of shirts in this. Roll them up tight, and let them remain for a few hours in a dry cloth. Then rub them off with a dry cloth as you iron them.

SALT IN STARCH.—Some housekeepers improve the plain starch in this way. While it is boiling they add a little table salt, or a small piece of spermaceti. This helps in ironing.

SOAP IN STARCH.—Mix the starch with soapy water, and you will find it a pleasure to do up the starched articles. The soap prevents the iron from sticking, and also makes a glossy surface.

STARCHING LINEN.—Shirt-bosoms and collars and cuffs should be dipped into boiling starch in which a small piece of lard has been melted, and then hung on the line. When dry they should be dipped into cold starch, which should be thoroughly rubbed into the article. Then they should be tightly rolled in a clean, dry cloth, and let stand a few hours before ironing. A dull finish is preferred by some to the polish.

A GOOD STARCH.—Here is an old way of starching linen, relied upon by many. To have the clothes stiff as you desire, mix two tablespoonfuls of laundry starch with a gill of cold water. Pour on that one pint of boiling water, stirring it all the time. Add to that half a teaspoonful of salt, half a teaspoonful of white sugar, and a piece of spermaceti about the size of a thimble. Boil for ten minutes, stirring frequently. Keep the starch covered while boiling. Strain through a piece of cheese-cloth, and keep covered while cooling. Have the articles to be starched nearly dry, and dip them into the starch while it is yet warm. Strike the articles between the hands that the starch may be worked into all the threads. Dry them, and then dampen with cold water. Roll them in a clean, dry cloth, and let them remain so a few hours. When ironing starched clothes, keep the unironed part damp by covering it with a wet cloth. Should that not please you, then mix two quarts of cold water with two tablespoonfuls of dry starch, and when the clothes are dry, dampen them with that instead of wetting them in cold, clear water.

THE PROCESS OF STARCHING.—Many have desired to know how to give a gloss to collars, shirts, and cuffs. Here is a tried method, but you must not expect a complete success without some practise. Make the hot starch as directed in "A Good Starch" as given above. If you have no spermaceti, use a piece of lard the same size, putting in a few drops of coal-oil or a tablespoonful of turpentine, whichever is convenient. Then set it in a cool place, and stir it now and then until quite cool; then dissolve two tablespoonfuls of raw starch in a little cold water, and pour it into the hot starch, which should be cold enough as not to scald the cold starch; stir it in thoroughly. Do not have the starch too thick. It should be the consistency of thick cream. You are reminded here that this starch is excellent for starching pillow shams, white skirts, and such things, as dampness does not affect it. Now starch the shirts; be sure to rub it in well, then dry them. Have a hardwood board a little wider than the bosom, and put several thicknesses of cloth on one side, having it tacked firmly to the edges. The other side should be made very smooth. When you have ironed the bosoms smoothly on the padded side, slip the smooth unpadded side of the board up under the bosom, and then with a six or seven pounds iron, the ordinary iron, which has the sharp edge of the heel filed off, proceed to put on the gloss by rubbing briskly crosswise of the bosom. Do not set the iron down flat on the bosom, but hold the point up, so as to use only the edge of the heel. The iron must be hot, and the bosom should be dampened by brushing it slightly with a damp cloth.

TURPENTINE IN DAMPENING.—After you have starched the linen and dried it, and are now ready to sprinkle it preparatory to immediate ironing, in the sprinkling water put in one tablespoonful of spirits of turpentine. It will help to give the linen a good gloss.

IRONING

WASH FLAT IRONS.—You can not be too careful with irons that you use on the white clothes. If they trouble you at all by dropping black specks, wash them in soap suds, and dry thoroughly before using them.

TO PREVENT SCORCHING.—You who have had experience know how easy it is to scorch the white clothes or leave on them a slight yellow tinge. The irons will not scorch if they are first rubbed on a cloth saturated with kerosene.

TO KEEP IRONS FROM STICKING.—When ironing, have lying on the table handy a piece of sandpaper, such as carpenters use. When the iron becomes sticky, rub it across the sandpaper, which will remove the stickiness of the starch from the iron perfectly with only a rub or two across the paper.

TO MAKE IRONS SMOOTH.—Here is a good old way to fix the irons when slightly rusted or defaced. Tie a small lump of beeswax in a rag. Have a paper or rag sprinkled with salt. When the irons are hot, rub them first with the wax rag, then scour them on the salt. This makes them smooth and slick, and keeps them from sticking to the clothes. If that does not answer, use a little marble dust, which may be gotten at a drug store, to polish them.

ASBESTOS HOLDERS.—Little holders for handling hot irons and pokers or dishes are made of asbestos. Asbestos cloth comes by the yard, and is a most convenient material to have at hand, a single thickness of it between squares of cloth makes the best kind of an iron holder.

IRON HOLDERS.—Here is a good iron holder used by some very wise housekeepers. It is recommended to you. Take old boots that are ready to be thrown away, and cut off the tops; cut these tops into pieces the right size, and line them with anything you wish for holders. The leather keeps the heat away from the hands.

THE CARE OF IRONS.—Flatirons should not be put into the steam of cooking, as that causes them to rust. Irons that have once been red hot never retain the heat so well afterward, and will always be rough. While losing no opportunity of using the fire, be careful not to put irons on the stove hours before they are needed, and after using them, do not set them away flat on the floor or shelf, but always on end.

THE PROPER KIND OF IRONS.—If you wish to iron well, it is necessary to have the proper kind of irons. If you wish to iron collars, cuffs, or dress-shirts, a polishing-iron must be used. Fluting-irons will improve the appearance of ruffled wear. Embroidery should be ironed on the wrong side on flannel.

IRONING TABLE-CLOTHS.—For those who are very particular about having the table-cloths look nice, the following is a good method: To iron the table-cloths without creasing them, roll them upon a long curtain-pole as fast as they are ironed dry. Begin to iron at one end of the cloth, and, when ready, roll it on the pole, proceeding in this way until the entire cloth is ironed, then unroll and fold it neatly.

BLUING

A GOOD BLUING.—You can make your own bluing as good as can be bought. Take one package of diamond dye, the blue, such as is used in dyeing cotton. Dissolve the package in one quart of hot water. In order that there may be no lumps, empty the package into a saucer, and mix it into a paste with a little water. Then put it into the hot water. When cool, bottle for use. This is to be used in the same manner as the ordinary bluing.

A BLUING LIQUID.—Take one ounce of powdered indigo, one-half ounce of powdered oxalic acid, and one quart of soft water, and mix well together. The acid is not strong, and in this connection it does no harm, but makes the bluing dissolve and spread evenly. One tablespoonful of this will do for an ordinary tub, but, of course, the quantity to be used must depend upon your judgment, as in the use of common bluing.

DRYING CLOTHES

A CLOTHES RACK.—Take a piece of wood six feet long, and two inches square. Take a piece of board an inch. thick, and two inches broad, and two feet long, and drive a nail in the center of it, and fasten it on the side of the pole at the end. Let the pole stand upright on that cross-piece. Have another cross-piece one foot long, and of the same thickness as the one above; let its end come against the first cross-piece, and nail it on the side of the pole at the same end. These answer for the feet. Take half-inch strips, three feet long, and screw them to the sides of the pole, three on each side, two feet apart. Do not screw them too tightly, as they must fall to the sides of the pole when not in use. Hold one of the strips out horizontal with the pole. Now, near the edge of the pole at the under side of the strip, bore a small hole, put in that a nail, let it slip in easy. That nail holds the arm out when the clothes are hung on it to dry. Arrange all the arms that way. When the rack is not in use, take out the nails, so that the arms may fall to the side. The rack may then be put away.

IV — SOAP

LAUNDRY SOAP

HARD SOAP.—This is a better soap than the kind usually bought as turpentine soap. The amount of material called for in these directions will make about forty pounds. When made, let it dry for two months before using. Make it this way. Take six pounds of clean fat, and four gallons of boiling water. Put into the water six pounds of washing soda, and three pounds of unslaked lime. Stir those till they dissolve. Let the water stand until clear, then drain it off from the sediment. Put the fat into this water, and boil until it begins to harden. This will take two hours, stirring all the time. On the soda and lime sediment left from draining off the above water, put two gallons of cold water, stir it, then let it stand until it settles. Drain this off, and with it thin the soap while boiling, adding it slowly when the soap threatens to boil over. Put one handful of salt into the soap before taking it from the fire. You can tell how thick the soap is by cooling a little of it on a plate, wetting the vessel you put it on to keep it from sticking. When it becomes sufficiently hard as tested, remove from the fire, or let the fire go out. Let the soap stand until solid, make into bars, and let dry as directed.

SOFT SOAP

AN EASY WAY TO MAKE SOAP.—This need not be boiled. Boiling is resorted to for the purpose of hurrying the process. This way does not require much time, however. Put grease into a barrel, or cask, and add strong lye. Continue putting the fat into the barrel, and adding lye, stirring frequently. When the barrel, or cask, is full, the soap is made. Allow time for the lye to eat the fat, if when the barrel is full, there are some traces of grease uneaten.

BORAX CURD SOAP.—One tablespoonful of the following soap will make a strong lather in one gallon of water. When making, stir it frequently. When it is cold it will make a jelly. Dissolve three ounces of borax in two quarts of hot water. Add two pounds of white bar soap, sliced thin, so as to be easily melted. Stir all together in a jar, and let it stand in a warm place until the ingredients are all melted. It is then ready to use.

A GOOD SOFT SOAP.—This is a good cheap soap, and easily made. Many a housekeeper in this way can use many a scrap of clean grease instead of throwing it away. You will be pleased with the result. Let the following mixture stand until the grease is eaten. Add water to it, if you think it is too thick. Stir the mixture often and thoroughly: Take ten pounds of grease, six pounds of washing-soda, and eight gallons of hot water, and mix them well in any vessel you prefer.

A FAMILY SOFT SOAP.—This is not an expensive way to make soap, altho it may seem so at first glace. It goes farther, and does better than the ordinary soap, as you need to use but little, and with it the washing can be done very easily. This can be made thin by adding water and more sal-soda. Take four pounds of white laundry soap; cut it into shavings, and dissolve it in four gallons of soft water. Add to this one pound of sal-soda. Let those dissolve, and mix well, then it is ready for use.

AMMONIA AS SOAP.—In washing clothes many persons use *aqua ammonia*. The best way to obtain it is to have your druggist supply you, as many inferior kinds are bottled for the general market. Take a gallon bottle, or larger if convenient, and have it filled. One or two tablespoonfuls to one gallon of water is a good proportion.

TOILET SOAP

OATMEAL SOAP.—You can make your own oatmeal soap in the following way, and you will be as much pleased with it as with any you could buy: Melt together six pounds of plain white soap, two and a half pounds of palm soap, and one and a half pounds of coconut-oil soap, and add to those one and a half pounds of oatmeal. If you have no oatmeal, a nice quality of wheat bran will do.

A NICE WHITE SOAP.—White soap is attractive. It looks clean and inviting. It may be scented, if desired. Put the scent in when the soap is off the fire cooling. Oil of caraway will give it the scent of Windsor soap, and the quality is just as good. Take two pounds of slaked lime, two pounds of sal-soda, and two pounds of tallow of any kind. Dissolve the soda by boiling it in one gallon of soft water, and then mix the lime in this water, stirring it a little. Let this mixture settle, and pour off the water for use. In this liquid boil the tallow until it is soap. You can test it as to hardness in the manner described in the directions for "Hard Soap." Pour the soap out to cool and dry.

CORN-FLOUR SOAP.—This is a good soap for the hands and face, as it does not chap or roughen the skin, and is healing to the flesh. Take what you want of barber's white shaving soap. Shave it into a vessel, and add only enough hot water to melt it. When it is melted, add one-third as much cornstarch as you have soap, adding any scent desired. Mix it well with the soap. Let it cool and dry, and it is ready for use.

SOAP BAGS.—Small pieces of toilet soap may be utilized in this way: Of Turkish toweling make a bag about nine inches square, and put into it all the small pieces of soap. When it is three-quarters full, sew up the end, and use the bag as if it were a cake of soap. Remember not to use it as a wash-rag, as it would be too soapy.

SCRAP-SOAP.—Here is an easy method with soap, the result of which will be excellent for removing stains and softening the skin. Take the small pieces of soap that accumulate in the soap-dishes, and cut them into small shavings. Dissolve them in boiling water, a cupful of water to half a cupful of the soap shavings. When this is melted, stir in ground oatmeal or cornmeal enough to make a stiff batter. Pour the mixture into any molds you desire, and let it harden and dry.

A CLEANSER FOR THE HANDS.—In the summer the hands do not require so delicate a soap as in winter. Here is a good mixture, an excellent cleansing agent for the hands in summer: Take two teacupfuls of cornmeal and one ounce of powdered borax, and mix them well.

A SOAP FOR ALL PURPOSES.—This soap is good for the skin, is better than most toilet soaps, and is also good to wash clothes with, if desired. You can scent it, if you wish, putting the scent in when cool, before it begins to harden. Take six pounds of lard, six pounds of sal-soda, three pounds of lime, and four gallons of soft water. Dissolve the lime and soda in the water and let it boil, stirring it until the ingredients dissolve. Let it settle and then pour off the liquid. Add the lard, and boil until it becomes soap. Mold it as you please, and cut it up so that it may dry.

COCONUT SOAP.—The following is a good coconut soap: Take one pound of tallow, one and a half pounds of coconut-oil, one-half pound of castor-oil, and heat them until they melt together. Add two pounds of hot caustic soda-lye, one-half pound of glycerine, and one pint of alcohol. As the alcohol evaporates quickly, the boiler should be covered closely. Boil these until they are soap. Then add one pint of heated sugar-syrup, which should be made as follows: Take one part of granulated sugar to two parts of distilled water; and when it becomes hard, upon being tested, remove from the fire, and let cool and dry. Then it is ready for use.

OATMEAL BAGS.—These are used as sponges, dipped in warm water, making a thick, velvety lather, and highly recommended for giving a velvety softness and whiteness to the skin, while the orris-root imparts a lasting fragrance. Take five pounds of ground oatmeal, one-half pound of pure castile-soap, reduced to a powder, and one pound of pure orris-root, and mix thoroughly. Cut a yard of thin cheesecloth into bags about four inches square, sewing them on the machine, taking care that no untied ends of thread be left where a break may let the contents out. Now fill these sacks loosely with the mixture, and sew up the open end. Lay them away for use.

KITCHEN SOAP

SMALL PIECES OF SOAP.—If you do not use the remnants of soap in the kitchen by means of a soap shaker, you can melt them together with very little trouble. Here is the proportion: One cupful of boiling water to one-half cupful of the soap-scraps cut into small pieces. When melted add powdered borax enough to make a paste. Then let that dry and harden before using.

SCOURING SOAP.—Take the scraps of soap left in the kitchen and melt them as described above. When melted add marble dust or a good quality of sand. Let it cool and dry. Scour with this.

CARE OF SOAP

DRY YOUR SOAP.—Always purchase soap in large quantities, if you are in the habit of buying soap. If it is in bars, while it is fresh, saw it in squares with a piece of string, as that does not break off pieces so much as a knife does. Then keep in a warm, dry place. If you do this it will last longer, as only half the usual amount will be required in use. When drying soap lay the bars across each other in an open pile in such a way as to allow the air to freely circulate among them. When thoroughly dry, the bars may be packed away to make room and for safe keeping.

TO USE SOAP PROPERLY.—It is a mistaken idea to put soap in water when using it. The approved way is to apply water to the soap. For instance, when washing your hands, dip your hands into water, then rub them over the soap, putting it back again into the dish and not into the basin. When using a rag, wet it, and rub it over the soap. The effect is perfect and does not waste soap.

TO TEST SOAP.—When upon touching a piece of soap to the tongue you experience a biting sensation, that is evidence there is too much lye in it, and will injure the skin if used.

V—REMOVING STAINS

REMOVING GREASE FROM CLOTHES

TO REMOVE MACHINE GREASE.—When washable fabrics become stained with machine grease, take cold rain-water and washing soda, or baking soda, if you have not the other. Rub the soda into the spot, and wash it in the water. Repeat until the grease is gone. Wash it also with a good soap.

TO TAKE GREASE FROM A CHILD'S DRESS.—When children's clothes get greasy, as they so often do, follow this method: Get prepared French chalk (the kind tailors use). Be sure to get that which is prepared or powdered. Thoroughly rub it into the spot. Let the chalk remain in the goods for some hours, and then it may easily be dusted out. It generally removes the grease.

ALCOHOL AND SALT.—These have been found good to remove grease from clothes, when applied with a sponge or flannel rag to the spot. Take four tablespoonfuls of alcohol and one tablespoonful of salt. Mix these and shake together until the salt is dissolved. Then use as required.

TO CLEAN A STAINED BLACK DRESS.—Take one breadth of the dress at a time, and rub with this mixture, rubbing both sides well, and stretching the goods as you go along. Afterward sponge it with clear warm water, and iron on the wrong side while damp. Make a mixture of two ounces of soft water and one ounce of alcohol. If there is any paint on the dress, add one ounce of spirits of turpentine. If any grease, leave out the turpentine and add gasoline. Dip a sponge in soap, then in the mixture, and apply.

68

TO TAKE OUT STAINS FROM BLACK GOODS.—When there are stains on a black dress, black capes, black bombazines, and the like, the following method may be just what you want in order to remove them. Dip a piece of flannel in this liquid, and rub it on the stains. Boil one handful of fig-leaves in one quart of water, continuing to boil it until reduced to one pint. It can be used at any time when reduced.

A GOOD CLEANING MIXTURE.—A useful mixture with which to clean soiled clothes is made as follows: Take one-half ounce of glycerine, one-half ounce of alcohol, one-half ounce of sulphuric ether, one-half ounce of Castile soap, and enough warm water to make a quart of the mixture. Scrape, or grate, the soap, and dissolve it first in the warm water. Then let the water cool, and add the other ingredients. Keep it in a bottle well corked, and use it with a flannel rag or sponge on the grease spots.

A GREASE REMOVER.—Sometimes one application will be more effective in removing grease than another. A great deal depends on how old and well-seated the stain has become. The following has been found so good that many have said of it, "Any grease or dirt that can not be removed with that preparation, is fixed to stay." It is one of the best mixtures for removing grease from clothing. Apply it with a piece of cloth or sponge as you would any other eradicator. It consists of two ounces of *aqua ammonia*, one teaspoonful of saltpeter, one ounce of good white soap, and one quart of soft water. Shave the soap into the water, and stir it until it dissolves. Then add the other articles, mixing them well. It is then ready for use.

TO REMOVE TAR FROM CLOTHES.—When tar, or any mixture of tar, gets on woolens and colored cotton goods, it may be treated in this way: Rub lard over the tar. Then wash the goods in warm soda-water. Then apply to the spot oil of turpentine and soap, and then wash it again. If the tar is on white goods, apply spirits of turpentine, and wash it in soap and water. If the goods are silk, apply benzine instead of the turpentine. Soap the spot, and pour water through it or on the goods.

TO REMOVE SPOTS FROM WASH-GOODS.—You can take spots from washable goods by rubbing the spots with the yellow of an egg, and then subjecting the goods to the usual washing.

TO CLEAN WOOLENS.—This is good to take out grease spots from woolen goods. One quart of boiling water, one ounce of powdered borax, and one ounce of spirits of camphor. Dissolve the borax in the water while hot, when it is cold add the camphor, and it is ready to be used. Apply it in the usual way with a piece of woolen goods.

TO CLEAN AN OLD COAT.—Take as much ground soap bark as needed, and steep it in hot water, a quart of water to the ounce of soap bark, and let it stand over night. Then strain it, and add to the liquid an equal amount of gasoline. Rub this mixture on the wristbands and collar of the coat, using a new, clean horse brush, the hair kind. Go over the grease spots that way. Wet the brush in the mixture, and go over the entire coat, wetting the brush as it gets dry, or free of the mixture. Keep the brush wet with it as you use it. If the goods has any "right way of the cloth," rub that way. Stretch the sleeves and pocket holes, and collar, and, in fact, the whole coat into shape. Spread it out smooth and flat on a clean cloth on the table. Lay a towel on the coat, and with a heated iron go over it, and in that way press it into the desired shape.

TO TAKE THE GLOSS OFF BLACK GOODS.—It is often a cause of annoyance to see a glaze appearing upon the back of your coat from the habit of leaning heavily against a hard chair. To remove this, make a saturated solution of powdered borax and water, and apply it with a sponge. Rub on thoroughly, then wash off with clear water in the same manner.

TO BRIGHTEN ALPACA.—The old alpaca coat, or dress, or anything of that goods may be brightened, and made to look well. Take the coffee that has been left from two or three meals. In that coffee wash the alpaca goods. If once washing does not bring the desired result, wash the goods again in the coffee, and then press it with a hot iron.

TO PREVENT TRICOT SPOTTING.—Here is the way to keep tricot from spotting and shrinking, also broadcloth, especially of light colors. Take a wet cloth, either a towel, or a piece of muslin, and lay it on the right side of the goods, and then iron over it with a hot iron.

TO REMOVE MUD FROM BLACK GOODS.—When you have brushed the loose particles away, and there remains a stain from the mud on your black dress, these traces may be removed by rubbing the stains with raw potato. Cut a potato in two, and rub the raw surface upon the spot.

TO REMOVE COD LIVER OIL STAINS.—Should cod liver oil get on the bedclothes, or nightclothes, it may be removed by putting a little *aqua ammonia* into the suds in which the goods are washed.

TO TAKE OUT A WHITEWASH SPOT.—To remove the stain left by whitewash that may have gotten on your clothes, rub the spot with strong vinegar.

FULLER'S EARTH AND SOAP.—An old method to remove grease is to take equal parts of Fuller's earth and soft-soap. Mix them well together, making a paste. When using, wet the grease spot with warm water; then take a piece of the mixture and rub it into the spot. Allow it to dry on the goods, then rub it well in warm water, rubbing until clean.

TO REMOVE CANDLE GREASE.—Candle grease, as well as other kinds, yield to a hot iron as follows: Place a piece of blotting-paper under the fabric, put a piece of paper also on the spot. Apply a hot iron to the paper, and as soon as a spot of grease appears, remove the paper, and repeat the operation until the spot disappears.

BENZINE TO REMOVE GREASE.—This must not be used near a light or fire, as it may catch into a blaze. Take equal parts of benzine, alcohol, and *aqua ammonia*. Apply it to the spot with a sponge or cloth, rubbing it well into the spot.

AQUA AMMONIA AND BLOTTING-PAPER.—You may find this answers the purpose, if you have tried other things without success. Wet the spot of grease with strong *aqua ammonia*, and rub with a rag; then lay on it white blotting-paper, or fold a sheet of tissue-paper into three folds, and use it instead of the blotting-paper. Hold a hot iron on the paper, being careful not to scorch the goods.

ALUM WATER FOR GREASE.—If you have tried other things to get grease out of goods, and there remains some traces of the grease, as seen in the spot gathering dust, the following will answer: Make a saturated solution of alum and water. When ready to use, put it on the stove and let it get very hot. Apply it to the spot with a sponge or brush.

TO REMOVE WAGON GREASE.—Rub lard well in on the spot of wagon grease, as if washing it. Then when it is well out, wash the spot in the ordinary way with soap and water until clean. If any grease remains, rub the spot with gasoline.

TURPENTINE AND ALCOHOL.—Some have found this convenient and effective in removing grease from any goods: Take an ounce of spirits of turpentine and an ounce of alcohol and mix them well. Rub the spot with this mixture.

A GOOD GENERAL GREASE REMOVER.—Here is a good recipe for removing grease from silks, woolens, paper, floors, and the like. Put powdered French chalk (common chalk will do) thickly over the grease spot. Cover it with a sheet of brown paper, and then set on the paper a hot smoothing-iron, and let it remain until cool. Repeat if necessary. The iron must not be so hot as to burn the paper or other article.

A GOOD CLEANING MIXTURE.—Take equal parts of chloroform, benzine, and turpentine; mix them well. Apply with a woolen rag, rubbing the grease spot with it. It would be well to be careful about using this near a light or fire.

TO REMOVE SCORCHING

EXPOSE SCORCH TO THE SUN.—When clothes are scorched, remove the stain by placing the garments where the sun can shine upon them. It will be necessary to repeat this several times.

SCORCHING.—If the sheets, pillow cases, white dresses, or any white goods should be scorched, remove the stain in this way: Get chlorine water, dip linen rags in it and rub the spot well. If colored cottons are scorched much, redye the goods. If woolen fabrics, raise a fresh surface.

REMOVING GREASE FROM SILK

A WASH FOR SILK.—For dark-colored silks there is nothing better than this: Take one ounce of alcohol, two cupfuls of water, one tablespoonful of soft soap, and one tablespoonful of honey, and mix them well. Sponge the goods well on both sides with the mixture, then rinse in a tub of cold water. Shake the goods as dry as possible, but do not wring them. Then hang them up by the edge until nearly dry. Iron on the wrong side while still quite damp.

HEAT FOR GREASE.—Lay a piece of blotting-paper on a table, press the spot on the paper right side down, lay on the other side a piece of brown paper, and put a hot iron on the brown paper hot enough to scorch it. Let the iron stay for five seconds. Then rub the spot with a piece of blotting-paper.

MAGNESIA.—Grease may be removed from silk by rubbing a lump of wet magnesia over the spot, allowing it to dry, and then brushing off the powder.

GREASE ON CHINA SILK.—If there are any grease spots on a China silk garment which you desire to wash, rub them out with an application of benzine. Then make a lather of lukewarm water and white soap, and wash the garment in it as briskly as possible. Rinse it twice through clear warm water and shake it dry. Roll it up tightly and let it stand for an hour, and then iron it on the wrong side. Do not have the iron too hot.

TO CLEAN SATIN.—If you have neckties of satin that need cleaning, or other satin articles that need to be brightened, proceed as follows: Take a weak solution of borax; carefully sponge the goods with that. Sponge moderately and lengthwise with, not across, the grain, and iron on the wrong side only. White, cream, and pink satins may be treated in the same way as cream-colored silks, but if the color has been destroyed, it must be redyed. Use benzine if there is grease on the satin.

TO CLEAN RIBBONS.—Ribbons may be cleaned by sponging them with alcohol, and then rubbing them with some nice white soap. Keep the ribbon straight during the process of rubbing. When it is clean, rinse it in alcohol. Lay it between clothes, and smooth it with a hot iron.

TO REMOVE GREASE FROM SILK.—Removing grease from silk may be found easy and satisfactory, if done in the following way: Moisten the grease spot with chloroform, and then rub it with a cloth until perfectly dry. This will not injure the most delicate color.

BROWN PAPER WILL TAKE UP GREASE.—A very simple and sure way to remove grease spots from silk is this: Take a piece of clean brown paper, and rub the spot quickly with it. Rub hard enough to cause some heat, and cause a friction. In that way the brown paper will take up the grease, the friction causing it to come out.

TO REMOVE GREASE FROM SATIN.—When machine-oil has gotten upon your satin dress, take benzine and a piece of cloth. Wet the cloth in the benzine, and rub the spot, with the nap, not against it. Repeat until the spot is gone. Be careful not to go very near a light, such as a lamp or a fire, with the benzine, as it is very explosive.

TO BRIGHTEN BLACK SILK.—Many causes may exist to make your black silk dress look dingy. When you wish to brighten its appearance this will be found useful: Take the dress and place it so as to be easily rubbed. Then take cold coffee that remains from breakfast and *aqua ammonia*, equal parts, and mix them, and with that sponge the goods.

TO REVIVE FADED PLUSH.—The articles of plush that are exposed to the sun and dust, caused by sweeping, may be renewed. Take chloroform and apply it with a sponge, brushing with it very lightly.

TO CLEAN SILK DRESSES.—After you have used any of the above ways of removing grease, and the like, let the dress become almost dry. Then take bread that is very dry, and crumble it on the goods, and rub lightly over it. The crumbs absorb any dirt that may be on the surface, having been loosened by the former rubbing.

WINE, FRUIT, AND ACID STAINS

TO REMOVE WINE STAINS.—Put milk on the fire, and while it is boiling dip the stained part of the goods in it. Let it remain in that a few minutes, and the wine stain will soon disappear.

TO REMOVE FRUIT STAINS.—Fruit stains of long standing on white goods, or fresh stains that will not yield to ordinary treatment, may be removed in this way: Dip the article into a weak solution of chloride of lime and water. Spread the article in the sun to bleach. When the stain disappears, rinse well, as the lime may injure the goods. Use soft water in the process.

CLARET STAINS.—To remove claret stains while they are yet wet, put dry salt upon them immediately, spreading it on thick. Let it stand until the salt has absorbed the wine. Then dip the article in boiling water.

BERRY STAINS.—Berry stains on the table-cloth of napkins will disappear upon being washed. First soak the spots in milk, let the article remain some time in the milk, and then send it to the laundry.

BOILING WATER AS AN ERADICATOR.—Take the material that has been stained by fruit, and place it over a basin, and pour boiling water through it. Continue this until the stain disappears.

RED WINE STAINS.—To remove red wine stains from white goods, put them in a closed box over sulphur fumes, or use a good quality of chlorine water, well rubbed in. If the wine stains are on colored cottons, or woolen goods, wash them with the usual solution of soap-lye. If that is not at hand, use *aqua ammonia*. Should the article be silk, touch very little of either of the above liquids to the spot, and remove quickly; apply it again. Have the soap-lye lukewarm when used.

RED THREAD STAINS.—This is good to remove any vegetable colors or fruit colors. Should you use red thread on white goods, as sheets and the like, even after they have been in the wash, the stains may be removed. Use the sulphur fumes as above advised. If that is not convenient, make a saturated solution of oxalic acid and water, and apply. If more convenient, the chlorine water will answer. Should a child put red thread, or a scrap into its apron pocket, and it be not found until in the wash, and the dye begins to run, the stain may be removed by using any of the above methods.

FRUIT JUICE STAINS.—When linen has been stained with fruit juice of any kind, it should at once be washed in hot water, in which a little soda has been dissolved. If the stains are old, and hard to remove, place the article over a basin of boiling water until thoroughly steamed, and then rub salts of lemon upon the stains until they are removed. Place the article in hot water, and let it soak. Should that not accomplish your purpose, make a weak solution of chloride of lime and water, and dip the stains in it; then wash it well in cold water. Do not let the goods remain long in the solution.

OXALIC ACID STAINS.—When oxalic acid gets on black clothes, or any goods, it may be completely removed, restoring the color of the goods. Make a strong solution of baking soda and water, and apply it to the spots with the fingers, until the stain disappears. Repeat the application, if needed.

TO REMOVE ACID STAINS.—When acid has been dropped on any article of clothing, *aqua ammonia* will destroy it. Should the color not come out as bright as you desire, then by applying chloroform you will, in most cases, restore the color. Chloroform usually removes spots without injury to color, but it will not bring back lost tints. Ammonia is safe only upon colors that are known to be fast.

ACID STAINS IN GENERAL.—Stains that are made by vinegar, sour wine, must, or sour fruits, may be removed from white goods by proceeding as follows: Wash the article in clear water, and then dip it in chlorine water. Colored cottons and woolens and silks are slightly moistened in diluted ammonia with the ends of the fingers. If the colors are delicate, make some prepared chalk into a thin paste with water, and apply it to the spots. Brush it off when dry.

TANNING STAIN.—This is the way to remove tanning stains that are made by chestnuts, green walnuts, or leather. When the stains are on white goods, dip the stained part in hot chlorine water, letting it remain but a short time. Then apply to the stain a solution of concentrated tartaric acid. You need not be afraid of the acid, it is not strong enough to hurt the goods. It neutralizes the chlorine alkali. When the case is that of colored cottons or woolens and silks, apply diluted chlorine water cautiously to the spot. Slightly wet the tip of your fingers in the chlorine water, and touch them to the stain. Wash it from the goods, and then reapply it several times.

TEA STAINS.—Tea stains are hard to get out if neglected. They should be soaked in milk or warm water as soon as possible, and then soaped and rubbed out. The next washing will not leave any trace of them.

BOILING WATER FOR TEA STAINS.—Tea stains may be removed easily and quickly if taken immediately they get upon the fabric. Hold the stain over a basin or pail, then take clear boiling water and pour it through the stain. That drives it out of the goods, and prevents it from spreading over the fabric.

SUGAR FOR TEA STAINS.—Tea stains may be removed from a table-cloth by immersing the stained part in a strong solution of sugar and water. Let it remain for a few minutes, and then rinse the spots in soft water.

STAINS ON TABLE-CLOTHS.—Sometimes when by accident the tea is spilled on the table-linen, it is not convenient to remove it, and apply some of the above remedies, as, for instance, when company is sitting at the table, it would be awkward to remove the table-cloth. In such a case, take powdered starch and apply it immediately, heaping it upon the stain.

COFFEE STAINS.—Coffee stains are sometimes hard to remove when allowed to stand any length of time. In such cases moisten the spots with water. Put a small piece of sulphur in an iron pot and set fire to it. Then hold the stains down over the mouth of the pot, and let the fumes from the sulphur come in contact with them. When the stains disappear, dip the part on which the sulphur acted in a strong solution of baking soda and water, if you have it convenient. *Aqua ammonia* will do in place of the soda. The sulphur fumes are acid, and may affect colored goods, if not treated with soda. Should the stain be small, strike a few sulphur matches, drop them into a tin cup and hold the stain over the fumes. Repeat this if once does not have the desired effect. If the fumes fade the color of the goods apply *aqua ammonia* or soda to the faded spots, and the color will return.

STAINED HANDS.—Paring apples or, indeed, any acid fruit, will cause the hands to stain. Such stains are unsightly and it is desirable to remove them. Rub the hands well with lemon juice, and then apply salt until the stains disappear.

FRUIT-STAINED FINGERS.—If one remedy does not answer, another one will. Some of these elements you may have at hand, some you may not have. But if your hands are stained with fruit juice, and you have oxalic acid at hand, it will speedily take away the stains. Make a weak solution of oxalic acid and water, and use that freely on the stains. If you have a sore on your hands, or cut places, be careful about getting the acid into them, as it may inflame them.   The acid is as mild on the hands as lemon juice, so that you need not be afraid of using it for that purpose.

INK STAINS

INK ON WHITE GOODS.—It is easy to take black ink from white goods. Wet the ink spot with clear water, then take powdered salts of lemon (you can get it at any drug store), cover the ink spot with it and let it remain a few minutes, and the stain will disappear.   Then wash the article with soap and rinse it in clear water.

INK ON GINGHAM.—Ink stains that are freshly made, or those that are of long standing, may be removed from ginghams by this method: Wet the spots in sweet milk, then cover them with table-salt.   It may be necessary to repeat the treatment.   It should be done before the garment is washed, if you would have real success with it.

INK AND SOUR MILK.—This method applies to any kind of fabric from which you desire to remove ink stains. When the stains are fresh, wash them in sour milk, and let it soak thus over night.

INK AND SALT. — Ink stains are entirely removed from anything by the immediate application of dry salt before the ink has dried.   When the salt becomes discolored by absorbing the ink, brush it off and apply more.   Wet the spot slightly on the second application of salt, and continue until the ink is all removed.

INK ON A TABLE-COVER.—This is a good way to take ink stains from a table-cover without injury to the fabric: Take a teaspoonful of cream of tartar, and a teaspoonful of powdered citric acid, and mix them well.   Heat a dinner-plate.   Lay the stained part in the plate, and simply moisten it with hot water.

Now rub the powder into the stain. As the plate and fabric are hot, use the bowl of a spoon to do that, continuing to apply the powder until the stain disappears. ·You may have to use the powder freely. When the stains are removed, wash the article in clear water and dry it.

INK STAIN ON CARPET.—Here is a method of removing ink stains from carpet, that has been highly praised. Cover the stain thickly with salt, and then simply moisten the salt with sweet milk. Let this remain until dry, and then rub it off. If there is any stain remaining, repeat the process.

INK ON WHITE LINEN.—When ink stains get on the white table-cloth, and you have nothing else convenient to apply, use a ripe tomato. Squeeze the juice from the tomato on the spot of ink, and work the juice into the spot, applying the tomato liberally. Pour clear water through the stain. Apply the juice again, and continue until the stain disappears. This will remove other stains as well as those of ink.

TO REMOVE RED INK STAINS.—To remove any kind of red ink, use this method. In the case of white goods, make the spot damp with clear water, and then rub tartaric acid into it. If the stain is of long standing, have the acid concentrated. For colored cottons, woolens, and silks, dilute the tartaric acid and apply it cautiously—that is, apply very little, and repeat it as often as necessary until the spot has disappeared.

TO REMOVE BLACK INK STAINS.—For black ink stains on white goods, here is another good way. Make a saturated solution of water and oxalic acid. Heat it quite hot, and apply. Should that not give the desired result, take diluted muriatic acid; put into it a few small pieces of tin, and when they have further diluted the acid, apply it. Wet the stain in clear water first, and then use the acid as you use the other acids recommended.

INK ON COLORED COTTONS.—On fast-dyed cottons and woolens that are stained with ink, you can use citric acid. Make a saturated solution of citric acid, and moisten one or two fingers in it, and touch the stains with it. Of course, the acid should be dissolved in clear water before applied.

TO REMOVE INDELIBLE INK.—It is sometimes desirable to remove what is called indelible ink. A spot accidentally made where it will look unsightly, may be removed. Make a saturated solution of cyanuret of potassium and water, and apply it with a camel's hair brush to the spot. When the ink mark disappears, wash the goods well in cold water. Be careful, for cyanuret of potassium is a poison.

INK ON THE HANDS.—When everything else fails to remove ink stains from the hands, try this. Take acid phosphate and rub it well into the stain. It will surely remove it, and do no harm.

INK ON THE FINGERS.—For a simple remedy when nothing else is at hand, and it is too late, or too far to send for the usual one, this will accomplish your purpose. Take the head of an ordinary match, moisten it, rub the inky fingers on it, and it will remove the spots.

INK ON MAHOGANY.—Ink-stained mahogany may be freed from such stains. Wash the ink off. If the stain is old, it matters not, the remedy will do. Take spirit of salt (you get it at the drug store), which is diluted hydrochloric acid, dissolved or diluted in water, and apply it to the ink stain until removed.

INK ON WOOD IN GENERAL.—After rinsing the wood with water to remove whatever ink is on the surface, take muriatic acid, and apply with a stick having a rag tied to it. If you think it too strong, put into it a small piece of tin, which will dilute it.

INK STAINS AND BRINE.—Perhaps you will have this within easy reach, when nothing else can be had at the time needed. Wash the ink stains in strong brine. Then rub them well with lemon juice until they disappear.

INK AND PUMICE STONE.—A small piece of pumice stone is one of the best things for erasing ink spots or other stains from the hands. Keep a piece in the soap dish, and when you have tested it, you will always keep it at hand. If your finger tips are rough, so that you can not handle sewing or embroidery silk, use the pumice stone on them. This does not apply to chapped hands, but to rough spots, such as are made by continuous pricking of the fingers when sewing, or calloused places made from sweeping or paring fruit. Should you care to do so, you could dip the stone in soap, and with it rub the stained spots, which would help remove them.

TO REMOVE MILDEW

STAINS OF MILDEW.—Take two ounces of chloride of lime, one quart of boiling water. Put the lime into the boiling water and let them stand for a little while. In a few minutes add three quarts of cold water. Steep the stained article in this preparation for ten or twelve hours; then remove it and wash out the lime.

MILDEW ON LINEN.—Among the ways of removing mildew from linen, the following may be found convenient: Wet the linen and put soap on the stained part. Then rub lemon juice well into the goods, and salt into the same spots. Do this on both sides of the goods. Then apply finely-powdered pipe-clay, or Fuller's earth, or powdered chalk. After that expose the article to the sun and air for several hours.

ANOTHER WAY TO REMOVE MILDEW STAINS.— To remove mildew stains, the following may be used. Wash the article thoroughly. Then rub soap well into the stain. Also rub powdered chalk quite plentifully on the spot. Then place the article on the grass in the sun. While the garment is yet damp, apply the treatment again, and sun it again, and so on until the mildew has disappeared.

MILDEW IN GENERAL.—Here is a method frequently tried: After the garment has been carefully washed, soak it over night in buttermilk, and then spread it on the grass to dry in the sun. You may have to repeat this several times before the stains come out. As it is always at hand, you might use salt in connection with the buttermilk, rubbing it into the fabric repeatedly. Salt contains a large per cent. of chlorine, a powerful bleaching agent.

GRASS STAINS

TO REMOVE GRASS STAINS.—There need be no difficulty in removing stains made by grass. The means to be used with white dresses or other white goods, also with ginghams, is as follows: As soon as the stain is discovered, and it is convenient, rub lard well into the spot. Then wash in the usual way, and the stain will be removed.

ALCOHOL FOR GRASS STAINS.—From the children's white or other colored dresses, you can remove the stain very easily. Wash the spots in as much alcohol as needed. Wash them well, and the spots will disappear. Should there be any ugly trace of green left, let the spot soak in the alcohol for a few hours, and then rub it again, as in washing. Then put the goods through the usual process of washing with soap and water.

IRON RUST

TO REMOVE IRON RUST.—This is recommended for iron rust, but it is equally good for removing ink stains, fruit stains, and mildew. Take salts of lemon, which you make yourself in this way: One-half ounce of cream of tartar, and one-half ounce of powdered salt of sorrel. Mix well and apply by first wetting the iron stain, and then putting the salts of lemon on the spot. Let it remain until the spot has gone. Then wash in clear water to remove the salts. As salts of lemon is a poison, do not put it in the mouth.

RUST STAINS.—Take an ounce of cream of tartar and one-half ounce of oxalic acid, powdered fine, and put it in a bottle, keeping it well corked. Mix it well. You will find by applying a little of the powder to the rust stain, while the article is wet, that the result will be much quicker and better. Wash the goods in clear, warm water, to prevent any injury to the fabric.

NEW RUST STAINS.—If the article has been recently stained, two or three applications of this will do to remove it. Mix equal parts of cream of tartar and salt, and wet the goods that are stained. Then sprinkle the mixture on the spot. When somewhat absorbed, cover the spot with enough of the mixture to hide it. Wet the stain every half hour. If it can be seen yet apply the mixture again, and continue until the spot disappears.

IRON STAINS.—Here is a simple and quick way to remove iron rust from white goods of any kind: Put a tablespoonful of clear water in a saucer, add as much oxalic acid as the water will dissolve, and apply to the spot with the fingers (it will not hurt the hands). When the spot disappears, dip the goods in clear water to wash out the acid, as it might affect the fabric if allowed to remain. Ammonia will restore the color of the goods.

DISCOLORATIONS FROM RUST.—When iron rust is discovered on a piece of white goods, apply lemon-juice to the stain, saturating it well. Then put the goods in the sun, on the grass if possible.

IODINE STAINS

IODINE ON LINEN.—If iodine stains should get upon the linen, dip the spots in cold water, then hold over the fire until dry. Repeat this process until the stain is removed.

FRESH IODINE STAINS.—Dilute ammonia with tepid water, put the stained article into it, and let it remain until you see the spot fading out. The stains must have been freshly made for this method to work properly.

IODINE STAINS ON COTTON GOODS.—Take hyposulphite of soda and dilute it with clear water, only slightly. Then let the stain stand in it until it disappears, or apply the drug until the same result is reached. This is for cotton or linen.

IODINE STAINS ON WHITE GOODS.—You can not always prevent iodine stains from getting on the bed clothes where a sick person lies, and sometimes it gets upon the night-clothes, making a most unsightly mark. This is what to do: Make a solution of warm water and *aqua ammonia;* dilute it slightly. Then soak the garment in this for an hour, rubbing the spot now and then. After that, if the stain is not all removed, take bicarbonate of potash, and rub it well into the stain, until the least trace of the iodine is removed.

IRON STAINS ON MARBLE

TO REMOVE IRON STAINS FROM MARBLE.—Should iron stains get upon the marble-top table or sideboard, or any marble, use one of the following drugs: Take oil of vitriol and dilute it slightly in alcohol. If that is not convenient, take oxalic acid, diluted in alcohol. Or you can use clear lemon-juice. Wet the spot with any of these, and after a quarter of an hour rub the marble dry with a soft linen cloth. Repeat operation if necessary.

SALTS OF LEMON FOR IRON STAINS.—When a piece of marble becomes stained with iron, you may employ the following means of making it clean: Take salts of lemon, being careful not to put it in the mouth, as it is poison, and put it on the iron spot, moistening it slightly with clear water, just enough to melt it. Let it stand until the stain fades away. To help along the process, you may rub the spot with a piece of pumice-stone while the acid is being applied.

PAINT STAINS

VARNISH ON THE HANDS.—If your hands are stained with black varnish, and it is hard to remove, proceed as follows: Put kerosene oil on the stain, and rub until the varnish is soft. Repeat the application of kerosene. Then wash with soap and water. You will be surprised how easily the varnish comes off.

BENZINE STAINS.—Benzine will remove paint from clothes, but it leaves its own stain. To remove that, take powdered French chalk and rub it into the spot. Lay some of the chalk upon it, and let it stand over night. The chalk brushes out easily, so you need not fear to use it.

PAINT ON CLOTH.—Turpentine will remove paint from cotton goods very quickly. Use the spirits of turpentine, and use it on any fabric. Apply it to the paint spot until it becomes soft; then wash it out in the ordinary way. You might mix equal parts of *aqua ammonia* and turpentine. Paints or varnish can be removed by that.

GASOLINE FOR PAINT STAINS.—One of the best things to remove paint stains from clothes of any kind is gasoline. Saturate the discolored part with it, rubbing it in with a flannel rag. Repeat this until the flannel has absorbed the paint, and finish off with a clean rag.

CLEANING GLOVES

KID-GLOVES.—Put the gloves on. Put gasoline in a saucer. Then wash in the gasoline as if washing your hands. Take a flannel rag and wipe and rub the gloves. Let them dry on your hands, but do not go near a fire or flame, as the gasoline may ignite. When the gloves are quite dry, take them off and sun them.

INK ON GLOVES.—It is not always easy to remove ink from kid-gloves. This is a good method: Make a weak solution of oxalic acid and water, moisten the tip of a finger in it, and touch it to the stain, being careful not to put enough on the spot to spread. You might find it best to take a crystal of oxalic acid, and touch it to water. Then shake off the water. With that crystal touch the ink spot carefully. Should the color disappear, apply *aqua ammonia* or wet baking-soda, repeating until the color returns.

INK ON KID-GLOVES.—This answers the purpose sometimes, altho it is never an easy matter to remove stains from kid-gloves. Dip the stained part in melted tallow of any kind. Then lay warm pipe-clay on that, and press it for a time. You may have to repeat this before the stain comes out.

CLEANING WHITE KID.—With this you can take off almost any stain or dirt, except ink marks. Dip a woolen rag in benzine, and then allow it to become almost dry. When it is simply damp, it is just right. Rub that over the goods. Now take bread-crumbs and rub lightly over the gloves, shoes, or suede goods, repeating the operation as required.

CLEANING WHITE SUEDE GLOVES.—White suede gloves may be cleaned by using dry pipe-clay, and an old toothbrush. White cloth, such as is used on many uniforms, may be cleaned in the same way. Put the dry clay on the article, then wet it, and rub it vigorously with the tooth-brush. It will look unsightly at first, and you may think you have ruined the goods, but rinse out the brush, and scour the cloth with clear water, and it will look all right.

BLOOD STAINS

REMOVING BLOOD STAINS. — It becomes necessary sometimes to remove blood stains from carpet, curtains, and such goods. Take lukewarm water, and add *aqua ammonia* sufficient to make the solution quite strong. Let the curtain or other fabric soak in this until the stain can be removed by rubbing. In the case of the carpet, rub the spot with the mixture, using a woolen rag.

PEPSIN FOR STAINS OF BLOOD. — Steep the stained part in lukewarm water until the spots are softened. Then get pepsin (the scales are best), and place some of it on the stain. It will digest the blood so that it can be easily washed out.

STAINS ON CARPET

WHITEWASH STAIN. — Do not worry about the whitewash stain on the carpet; while it is unsightly, it can be removed. If the color has been taken out of the carpet, or clothes, by whitewash, sponge the spot with very strong vinegar, or any other simple acid.

KEROSENE STAINS. — The stains from kerosene may be removed from the carpet. As soon as the oil is spilled, or discovered on the carpet, spread corn-meal thickly upon the spot, and let it stand.

KEROSENE AND BLOTTING PAPER. — To remove kerosene from a carpet, lay blotters of soft brown paper over the spot, and press them with a warm iron. Repeat the process with fresh papers until the spot is removed.

GREASE ON CARPET.—Grease on carpet, if not left too long, can be readily removed in the following manner : Take a gallon of hot water, and with it make soap-suds; add to this half an ounce of borax. Use a clean cloth to wash it with. Rinse with warm clear water, and wipe dry.

AMMONIA AND GLYCERINE FOR GREASE ON CARPET.—For this use a sponge, or piece of clean flannel. Take two ounces of *aqua ammonia*, two ounces of white castile soap, one ounce of glycerine, and one ounce of ether. Shave the soap fine, pour on it one pint of water, and put it on the stove to dissolve. Add two quarts of cold water. Put in the other material. Mix well, and apply.

TO CLEAN FURS

A WHITE GOAT-SKIN RUG.—White goat-skin rugs are quickly made dirty, but as quickly cleaned. You need go to no extra trouble about it. Get the required amount of gasoline (naphtha will do), and wash the rug in it. If it is too volatile, mix pure soap-suds with it.

WHITE FUR.—To clean white fur of any kind, take heated bran. Do not brown it. Oatmeal of nice quality is better. Take a clean flannel, and dip it into the heated meal or bran, and rub the fur with it.

DARK FURS.—Brown wheat bran or oatmeal in an oven. Take a nice piece of flannel. Lay the fur on a table where you can conveniently rub it. While the bran is hot, dip the flannel in it, and rub the fur, and repeat until the fur, tho dark, begins to look nice. It can then be shaken free of bran.

RENEWING LUSTER.—The following method will renew the natural luster of the fur: Put rye-flour into a pan, and brown it on the stove, stirring to keep it from burning. When the flour is so hot that you can not put your hand into it safely, it is ready to use. Take a spoon and sprinkle it over the fur, and with a flannel rub it in. The flour is easily removed by beating the fur gently or brushing it with a soft, clean brush.

CLEANING GOAT-SKIN RUGS.—Remove the lining from the rug. To four gallons of lukewarm water add half a pint of *aqua ammonia*. Stir the rug about in this preparation several times for half an hour; then rinse it thoroughly in warm, clear water, and hang it in the shade to dry. When dry, the rug will be stiff. Give it a vigorous rubbing between your hands to soften it.

VI—MENDING AND MAKING

THE APPAREL

MAKING DRESSES.—One of the small, but important, things in making dresses is that of sewing on the hooks and eyes so that they will not come unfastened, and make an ugly and unsightly gap.   Trouble about this is obviated by adopting the method of leading dressmakers, and sewing on hooks and eyes alternately, and quite close together, the space being only about three-quarters of an inch between each hook and eye.   The fashion of sewing first a hook and then an eye will be found most efficacious; and whoever tries the experiment once, will never again take up with the old way of putting the hooks all on one side, and the eyes all on the other.   Another matter that is worthy of consideration is the sewing of whalebones into dresses.   Some people have a way of sewing the seams of a waist together to make a place for the whalebones, but one can never get a smooth fit in that way.   The proper way is to open every seam in the dress-waist, overcast the edges, or, better than that, finish them with binding-ribbon, then press them open so that they will stay in place.   Put the case for the whalebone down each seam, so that there will be an equal distance on each side of the seam.   Fasten the bones securely at both top and bottom, and the waist will have a smoother appearance, and by that means should be free from wrinkles.   These may seem to be insignificant matters, but they are the little things that constitute the difference between a well-made dress, and one that is carelessly made.

92

TYING SHOE-LACES.—If the laces of the children's shoes or your shoes come untied often, and are annoying, wax the strings with beeswax. They will then stay tied until you untie them.

REMOVING ODORS FROM CLOTHES.—When any article of wearing apparel becomes affected with an unpleasant odor, and you can not conveniently put it out in the sun, treat it in this way: Lay it down in some clean place, and put pieces of charcoal on it. The charcoal absorbs the odor in a day or two. You fold the charcoal up with the clothes, and let it remain until all odor has disappeared.

WRINKLES IN LACE.—Hold the lace over a basin of steaming water; as the steam comes through, remove the lace to a new spot, and so on, until it has been all steamed. While the lace is still damp, fold it as you want it, and lay it under something heavy and flat until dry. Then you will find it renewed.

PERFUMED GARTERS.—Perfumed garters are among the most dainty of devices. They may be made in any color desired to suit the color of the hosiery worn, from watered ribbon an inch and a half wide. The ribbon is doubled over a layer of cotton that has been scented with sachet powder. The buckles are secured to the ends, if the garter is only linked. White frilled elastic may be covered in that way for special wear, as in a bridal outfit.

TO RENEW VELVET.—For velvet that has been crushed, or wet so that it looks dingy and unsightly, you can not do anything better than this: Heat a flat iron, put a wet, clean rag over its face, and then lay the velvet wrong side down on the cloth. The steam from the wet cloth rises through the nap and lifts it up. While steaming, brush the velvet.

TO CLEAN VELVET.—This is for silk velvet of fast colors. It will take two persons to properly manage the cleaning. Take gasoline and sponge the velvet until clean, and then hold it down tight over a basin of steaming water, so that the steam must escape through the article. Brush it lightly with a whisk or brush, the way the nap lays. Continue to steam the goods until the nap raises evenly over the surface of the article. The second person holds the article.

TO RENEW SILK.—Silk that has become dingy and dusty, needing to be cleaned and brightened, should be treated in this way: Take ground soap-bark (you can get it at any drug store), and put as much in cold water as you require the strength of the decoction to be. Let it remain and soak over night, and if you can use it without stirring up the sediment, you need not strain off the liquid; otherwise strain it. Sponge the goods on the right side with this liquid, and afterward, just before it dries, iron it on the wrong side.

TO SMOOTH SILK.—If a piece of silk is very much wrinkled and flimsy, and you wish to give it a body and smooth it, take gum arabic and put enough of it in the water you are to use in sponging the silk, so as to have just a suspicion of the gum. With this gum-water sponge the right side of the goods. When almost dry, iron the silk on the wrong side.

TO CURL FEATHERS.—To expose feathers to rain or heavy fog will take the beauty out of them; the curls will come out. Should your hat feathers become wet and straightened, hold them over a heated stove, being careful not to burn them. Remove them from the heat now and then, and shake out the matted down. Go through this process until the feather is curled.

POCKETS IN APRONS.—Most housekeepers know how the pockets of aprons catch every protruding object within reach, and how annoying this is. The pockets should not be on the outside. The following is a good way to manage the pockets: In making the apron use two widths of gingham, cutting them long enough to come to the bottom of the dress when finished. Make two side gores of one width, and gore the full front breadth slightly. In each seam leave a pocket hole, as you used to in your dress skirts. Instead of setting the pockets in, make them by stitching pieces of goods on the under side of the apron, extending all around and below the pocket holes. Face the openings neatly, and the pockets are invisible.

CHILDREN'S MITTENS.—The children are very apt to lose their mittens when in a hurry, and at play. This you can prevent by fastening a long string to them, or a long black tape, sewing the middle of this to the inner side of the coat-collar, passing the tape down each arm of the coat inside. If the string is long enough, it does not in the least interfere with the free play of the hands, while the mittens, being securely fastened to the coat, are never lost. The children find that a great convenience, and it saves the mother many a step and annoyance in looking for the misplaced mitten.

APRON GOODS.—Shirting gingham makes a good, lasting apron. The prettiest pattern is a small plaid of brown and white, with narrow lines of red to brighten it. This will not fade like the blue, which, moreover, has an unpleasant smell when damp.

WHALEBONE.—Whalebone, by being constantly bent, becomes fixed in that shape, and loses its power to hold any goods straight. It may be restored so that you can use it again by soaking in water for a few hours, and then laying under something heavy until dry.

HOUSE-WRAPPERS.—In making wrappers to be worn about the house, ease and comfort should be considered. The wise ones advise cutting the necks low or open, and then having the sleeves short, or about the elbows.

MAKING OVER.—In almost every household the old-fashioned dress is made over into some new fashion. It is not every one who knows how to do this to the best advantage. It does not depend so much upon the form into which the dress is altered, as upon the care in preparing the goods. The cleaning must be thorough, or the truth will be very apparent; the article is simply made over. Rip the garment entirely apart, leaving no two pieces joined. Then pick out every thread very carefully. Should the material be found to have faded, have it dyed. Black dresses that are not worn, but are faded, will look like new ones after they have been dipped in dye. If you redye the article, put the new pieces of the material also in the dye, as you may use them on the dress. Remember, that any color will take black dye. Some goods are faded on one side. Turn these goods, and make them up, leaving the bright side out. Black cashmere and silk may be thoroughly dusted, and then put into a tub, and washed in the usual way. Any fabric of a dark shade may be treated in the same way. Those should be ironed on the wrong side before they dry and ironed until dry. If you put wheat bran in the water in which you wash black goods, it will improve them. In using ammonia to get out grease from any of those articles, should the ammonia take out the color, you can restore it by using a saturated solution of water and oxalic acid, applied carefully. Stop as soon as the color returns. Light-colored goods, and figured fabrics, may be sponged with warm water, alcohol, and gasoline. If the color is very light, do the sponging on the wrong side of the goods, seeing that every fiber is thoroughly dampened. Go over every piece carefully.

MENDING

MENDING TOWELS.—If your towels are of good material, and you do not care to throw them away because they are worn in the middle, treat them after this fashion: Cut them in two, lengthwise through the center. Sew the two outside edges together, and hem the new sidès, which were formerly the center.

MENDING WHITE GOODS.—When mending any white goods, such as sheets or skirts and the like, have the pieces with which you mend large enough, so that when the article is washed, the patch will not tear out or give way.

STOCKING GUARDS.—Stockings are more or less trouble, for they seem at times to break into holes of their own accord. That tendency can be lessened by running the toes and heels with cotton or worsted, the color of the stockings, or line the toes and heels with a piece of stout cotton, cut the proper shape and sewed neatly in place.

HEEL PROTECTORS.—Heel protectors are a great saver to the stocking. They may be bought ready made, or you can make them in the following way: Get a piece of white sheep leather or chamois skin; cut a piece of it so as to fit the heel, letting the top edge come to an angle with the edge that comes up by the side of the heel. Sew a narrow binding to these edges to hold the protector in shape. Sew an elastic strap from point to point of the protector. This elastic comes over the instep, and holds the article on the heel. They go on the foot over the stocking, but, being held tightly by the elastic, they do not rub nor wear the heel.

A GOOD DARN.—To secure a good, smooth, and durable darn in a woolen stocking, remember this: When going over the break the first time, make the threads of stout, coarse cotton. Then make the cross layer of good woolen yarn.

ON IRONING DAY TAKE NOTE.—On ironing day set aside the pieces that need mending, and mend them before you put them away. When you put them away be careful to put the apparel of each member of the household where it can be found by the owner without requiring your help.

PANTS KNEE.—The pants that are worn every day after awhile need mending. Perhaps they are somewhat worn at the knee. Cut the pants' leg off above the knee; turn the back of the leg to the front, and sew it to the part from whence it was cut. Press the seam with a hot flat-iron. If the seams in the pants' leg do not fit, make the outside seam match.

MENDING GLOVES.—The stitches of gloves will break as they become worn. Instead of mending them with silk, as is usual, use a good cotton thread the color of the gloves.

STOCKING FOOT PATTERN.—This cut is a reduced size pattern of a stocking foot. When a pattern is made from this drawing, make it the size needed. This is a perfect success. It has been tried for many years. When the hose is worn out, heel and toe, and you would like to put a new foot to the top, you will find this pattern of assistance: Flatten the foot of the hose continuous with the top, as if you laid the foot and leg on the side. Now fold the pattern down the center, as indicated by the dotted line. Then lay the folded pattern on the hose foot, with the part marked A toward the sole, and pin it in place. Then cut away the worn part, following the line of the pattern. Now unfold the pattern, and by it cut the material for the new foot. Old hose tops will do for that. Where you have many that are worn, take the tops of some to mend the feet of others. Pin the new foot in place, and lay one edge to the other. That must be run together with

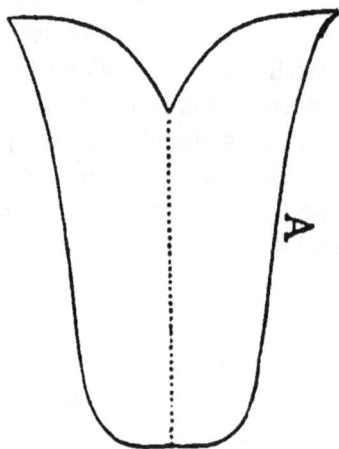

the hand. Begin sewing at the heel, and do not knot the thread, but leave an end of two inches out loose where the first stitch is taken, so as to stretch to the foot. Stretch the seam as you go. Do not take back-stitches. If the new foot is too long, shorten it at the heel, when you come around to the heel, in sewing it on. Take a day to get together the mending, and do not hurry.

PUTTING AWAY APPAREL

PACKING WINTER GOODS.—When putting away flannel and heavy winter clothing, to have it out of the way during the summer, you would do well to try this: Take pieces of camphor gum, wrap each piece separately in paper, and put these among the goods as you pack them.

PREPARE FOR PACKING.—Never put away, for the summer, a woolen garment of any kind that is spotted with grease, or soiled with mud. Grease is remarkably attractive to moths, and all the unbrushed clothes get old very rapidly.

SILK AND WHITE PAPER.—Silken fabrics should never be kept folded for any length of time in white paper. The chloride of lime which is used to bleach the paper causes a chemical change in the silk, and impairs the color.

PACK WITH BEESWAX.—In putting away an article of silk, or woolen, there is danger that it will become yellow. It is desirable to prevent that. Take genuine beeswax, break it into pieces, and place them about with the goods, to prevent them turning yellow.

TO PREVENT CREASING.—It is often annoying to find your clothes creased after being folded and put away. To prevent this in some measure, take old newspapers, and lay them, just as they are without opening, in the goods, and fold them up together, or place paper between the folds. In packing a trunk, or valise, ready to take a trip, if there are clothes therein you are particular about, this method is what you want in order to keep the garments from getting wrinkled or crushed. If there are few things in the trunk, the vacant space can be filled with crushed paper.

PACKING SUMMER GOODS.—With these precautions the summer garments will look like new apparel when you take them out in the spring. All your light-colored dresses should be well brushed and hung out in the air for a few hours, until they are free from dust and odor. Take the arm-shields out, and give them a washing; dry them out in the sun, and then lay them away for further use. Have a large box lined with blue paper, or take your trunk so lined, and use that to pack in. Fold the skirt carefully, so that it will be as smooth as possible, making but few folds. Fold the waist, as nearly as you can, as a dressmaker does. Stuff the sleeves and bust with tissue paper, and put paper under the shoulder ruffles, if the dress has them. Now pin the skirt and waist in muslin, lay them in the box, placing a fold of blue paper over them. The blue paper should be wrapped directly around a white dress of any kind, before the muslin cover is put on. This is especially true in the case of a nice white bridal dress, the whiteness of which you wish to preserve. There is something in the blue paper that will prevent the white goods from turning yellow while packed away. Summer wrappers or jackets should be well brushed, and neatly folded, before being put away in the box. Summer hats should be carefully dusted, then loosely wrapped in tissue paper, and put into a bonnet box, with tissue paper around them to fill in the vacancy, so that they will not be crushed out of shape.

RESTING CLOTHES.—Clothes last longer and look fresher if not worn too long. An old dress that looks dusty and worn out, if hung up and left to hang some days, when taken down again will look new; the wrinkles are gone, the color seems to have come back, the odors are not perceptible, and you feel like wearing it again. Take off the dress you have worn all day, shake it free from dust, and turn it inside out. If the sun is shining, hang the dress out in it for a few minutes to be aired.

Take off the shoes you have been wearing all day, dust them, pull them into shape, and set them where they may be aired. Next morning put on another dress, and other shoes. Keep two sets of garments in use in this way, if you would have them free from soil, and looking fresh when you wish to wear them. Have several house-dresses that you can wear about the place while engaged in the work of housekeeping. Air them, and let them rest after one day's wear. Brush the work-day dresses when taken off, and again when put on.

USEFUL SACHETS

THE SILVER BAG.—These are simple enough, yet when properly used they are of great aid in housekeeping. The silver bag is made to hold silver spoons, forks, and knives. It is usually of a double-faced canton flannel of a fine soft nap, either unbleached or of some pretty color. Make it oblong, furnished with pockets by sewing canton flannel across the width and left open at one end, and bind all the edges with braid or ribbon. It may be fitted with small brass rings on the top edge, so it can be hung up against the inside of the closet door.

BAG FOR SOILED LINEN.—This bag is both useful and ornamental, being just the thing in which to collect the soiled linen. Make it of a strong brown or unbleached linen; a prettily-flowered chintz will do as well. That should be made in the form of a double pocket, having one opening across the middle of the bag, leading, on both sides of it, into a large bag-like receptacle. This slit should be bound with braid, as should also the edges. If desired, the lower edge could be trimmed with worsted-balls or colored tassels. Small brass rings could be fastened to the upper edge so as to hang the bag up while in use.

A SHOE BAG.—The usefulness of this device is at once apparent. It may be made of heavy brown linen or a nice piece of chintz of any color desired. Make the shape oblong. Take

the material longer than it is wide, and fold the lower edge up
as deep as you want the pockets, then run seams from the bottom up, having them as far apart as you desire the pockets to
be wide.   Make six or eight of the receptacles for shoes, slip-
pers, and overshoes.

A DUSTING BAG.—This is a very useful article.   Every
housekeeper should have at least three of them, so that a clean
one will always be at hand.   Make it of canton flannel, with a
hem at the top to receive a drawing-string.   It must be made
big enough to slip over the brush of a broom.   Draw the bag
over the broom, tie it around the handle, then use it for dusting
down the walls after sweeping.

TRAVELING BAGS.—These can be made like the one
described as bag for " soiled linen," or in any other shape desired, of linen, or other goods preferred.   A woman who has
traveled extensively, and lives in her trunks, has large sachets
of different patterns, in which she rolls up her body linen, each
kind in a tight roll by itself.   In that way it takes but little time
to find what she wants, and there is no confusion, while it keeps
her trunks always tidy.

A CLOTHES HAMPER

A BARREL HAMPER.—A clothes hamper is a great convenience to a housekeeper.   Here is a home-made one, and,
while it may not be quite so attractive as some, it is just as convenient, more durable than many, and pretty enough for any
hall or bedroom.   It is made of a small barrel, with a cover.
Clean and scald the barrel, allowing it to become thoroughly
dry.   Take a piece of old calico, wash it and starch it a little,
and with it line the barrel smoothly on the inside.   Sew the
breadths together as you would a skirt, and then put a circular
piece for the bottom.   Tack this to the bottom of the barrel,
inside, pull the top edge up over the outside of barrel, and tack

it down, so that the edge will be hid by the outside covering, which should be of figured cretonne. As you put it on, full it evenly all around the barrel. The top, or cover, is covered with the same material as that used for covering the outside of the barrel. It may be trimmed as desired.

A BOX HAMPER.—This would be convenient in the bathroom, as it is both a seat and hamper for soiled clothes. Take a plain box of whitewood, and remove all the dark and rough places from it with sand paper. Let the top project over the edges of the box on the two sides and front. Cover the top with a padding, and cover that with a figured piece of cretonne. Fasten the top to the back edge of the box with neat, small hinges. The cretonne can be nailed with round-headed brass tacks, which will add to its looks. When you have cleaned the box, give it a coating of shellac inside and out. Openings in some fancy design should be made in the side of the box for ventilating. The design shown in the above drawing is good. Draw that on the box with a pencil, then take an inch bit and make the holes, following the lines you have drawn. You can ornament that in any way your fancy may suggest.

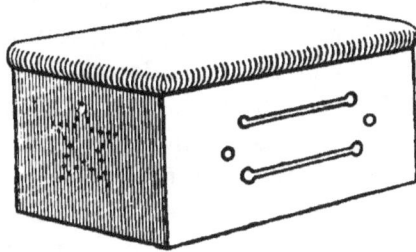

CUSHIONS

A LOUNGE COVER.—A very attractive lounge cover can be made of odd pieces of single zephyr. If the worsteds are of many bright colors, so much the better. If not, get a few shades of red, blue, orange, and green, to mix with what you have. Commencing with any color you choose, crochet a chain the desired length of the cover, and work back and forth on that, in star stitch, making a few stars of one color, interspering the other colors according to fancy.

A FOOTSTOOL.—From strong unbleached muslin cut two round pieces, each thirteen inches in diameter. Sew a strip of the same goods nine inches wide around one of these, and fill the bag as full as possible with excelsior, or anything that will answer the purpose. Now sew the remaining round of muslin over the top, and the footstool will be ready for the cover, which may be made of blue denim of some decorative design, with heavy, soft white cord ; or of common crash, figured with the heaviest Turkey red cotton. To make the cover, cut a circular piece of the denim thirteen inches in diameter, and sew on that a strip of the same goods twenty inches wide, after you have hemmed it on the upper edge. Place the cover on the stool, and with strong doubled thread gather it up in the center on the top, leaving a frill for a finish. The cover can be easily taken off and washed when it becomes soiled. If a hem is made at the base of the frill, and a draw-string inserted, it may be drawn up like a shopping bag. If the cord be tied into a bow with small tassels on the ends, it would make the cover prettier. White bolton sheeting, embroidered with heavy yellow wash linen floss in different shades, would make a dainty and serviceable cover, as it could be laundered without injury. Any combination of colors or materials, indeed, that will harmonize with the furnishings of the room, may be used.

FLOOR CUSHIONS.—These take the place of hassocks. They may be made very luxurious of velvet, a soft quality of silk, or any nice material desired. They may be thrown in an easy chair, on a divan, on the floor at the feet, or any place needed. They are made like an ordinary pillow, stuffed with hay, straw, or any material suitable.

SAVE THE PIECES

FLOUR SACKS.—These very common things may be made to do excellent and valuable service. We have known persons who have made flour and sugar sacks into underwear for their children. Flour sacks make first quality dish cloths, also good dish-towels. They are easily kept white, and last better than the towel stuffs that are bought. Some housekeepers use the best quality of them for special purposes. When the new bread has a thick, hard crust, take one of the sacks and dip it in hot water, and lay it over the bread, then cover that with a dry one, or two, and let the bread steam in that way until the crust is tender. They are also used for making linings for quilts, the sacks being first washed until all marks are removed, and then dyed any color preferred.

ODDS AND ENDS.—The foolishness of throwing away all that is not of immediate use, need not be commented on; it should be self-evident. The bits and scraps that are valuable are often allowed to go to waste through carelessness, or else permitted to become an annoyance because of their gathering dust and moths, and littering the room in which they are stored. The best plan is to provide large bags for all pieces and patches, the different kinds of goods being kept separate—cotton in one bag, silk in another, and so on.

TABLE LINEN

DOILIES.—The linens used for doilies that are to have borders of drawn work should be very fine, or of linen cambric lawn. The difficulty of drawing the threads from such linen is much lessened, if a piece of fine dry white soap is rubbed carefully over the threads.

TABLE-COVER.—Always put under the damask tablecloth a sub-cover of thick Canton flannel, if you can not afford the heavier table-felt sold for that purpose, or an old blanket, darned, washed, and kept for that use only. The upper cover will then lie smoother, look like a better quality of goods, and keep cleaner longer than if spread over the bare table top.

DISH-CLOTHS

GRASS TOWELING.--Very good dish-towels are made from grass toweling. When they are much worn, use them for dish-cloths. They make the best cloths, being coarse and open, and so not holding the grease and water.

FLY NETTING.—Do not throw away old mosquito and fly netting. Wash them and, when dry, fold several times to get into the size you want; then stitch, as you would a quilt, to make dish-cloths.

CHEESE CLOTH.—Dish-cloths, dish-towels, and the very best of dusters are made of cheese cloth. Get the quality that sells for five cents a yard, cut them one yard long, and hem them neatly. Always have several on hand.

DISH-CLOTH.—A good dish-rag is made from a growth called the dish-rag gourd, the seed of which can be obtained from any seed house. It has a strong grassy fiber, clean and lasting.

ODD HINTS

FITTING KEYS.—Sometimes it is necessary to make a new key to replace an old one. Perhaps an old key may answer with a little fitting. To find where the key strikes against a ward in fitting, light a match, and hold the locking part of the key in the flame. This leaves the key blackened. Now insert it in the lock, and where it hits a ward the black will be rubbed off. Withdraw the key, and you can see where to file to make it fit.

REMOVING GLASS STOPPERS.—It is very troublesome to remove a glass stopper when it once gets fixed. The following method for removing it is the best and most successful: Pass a strong string once around the neck of the bottle over where the cork appears. Have some one to hold the bottle, or secure it in some way; then take hold of the string, one end in each hand, and pull it back and forth rapidly for a moment. Then try the stopper, it will come out. The glass expands by the heat of drawing the string over it, and so loosens the stopper.

LUBRICATING OIL.—A lubricant which will neither gum nor corrode, and which has lasting quality, which may be used for watches and delicate machinery of all kinds, is made by putting pure olive oil into a glass bottle, and then dropping in a few strips of sheet lead. Expose the bottle and its contents to the sun for two or three weeks. After that you may drain it off and bottle it for use. If it stays on the lead four weeks, it will be that much better in quality.

MENDING THE STOVE.—To have ashes falling upon the bread, cake, and whatever you are cooking, is certainly annoying, but this is what is sure to happen when the back of the stove is cracked. The remedy is easy. Mix a handful of salt, with a pint of ashes (wood ashes is better, but coal ashes will answer), then pour water on the mixture, enough to make it into a stiff paste. When the stove is cold, plaster this thickly over the break. It will soon get hard.

ASBESTOS.—As asbestos is absolutely fireproof, it is the only sure protection for any portion of the woodwork endangered by the heat of the stove. It may be tacked up wherever wanted. Many a pretty lamp shade of silk, or crape tissue, has been ruined at the first using for want of the asbestos collar on the underside of the frame. It need not be heavy, as you can split it to any required thinness.

FEATHER BRUSHES.—To make feather brushes, boil the wing feathers of a turkey or chicken for five or ten minutes. Then rinse them in tepid water, and tie them up in bunches, to be used in greasing pans, for brushing egg over tarts and pastry, and for dusting in corners and small spaces.

DOOR STOPS.—The slamming of doors is a great annoy-ance, and can be stopped by any simple little device. Here is a good one. Always have three or more bricks about the house, neatly covered with carpet, or any other material. Place these against the doors to keep them open.

CREAKING DOORS.—A creaking door should not be tol-erated. To remedy it, dip a feather in oil, and apply it to the hinges thoroughly.

SHRINKING THREAD.—The thread is often to blame for the puckering and drawing that is seen in seams. This can be avoided in goods that have been washed. Soak the spool of thread in water over night, let it dry, and it is ready for use. Colored thread, when used on wash goods, may be made strong and easier to work, if you soak it in olive oil. Let it drain well.

CORKS.—If in need of a good stopper, and a glass one can not be had, use the common cork in this way. Put sweet oil on the stove in a heater, and when it is hot, drop the corks into it. They will then equal glass stoppers.

POLE RINGS.—To have the pole rings catching and hang-ing, when you attempt to slide them along the pole, is very trying. To make the rings slip easily, rub the pole with a rag dipped in kerosene oil until it is thoroughly smooth.

DRIVING SCREWS.—If you find a screw hard to get into a piece of wood, or likely to split it, soap it before you put it in, and you will find the work easier and better. If soap is not handy, put the screw into your mouth, and allow it to become thoroughly wet with saliva.

SOAP THE HINGE.—A creaking hinge awakes the baby, disturbs your slumbering, and arouses ire, and there is no need for it, as the remedy is easy and quickly applied. A piece of soap rubbed on the hinge will prevent the creaking.

A PEN FOR MARKING.—Marking linen is a very particular undertaking, and should be done carefully. After selecting a good quality of indelible ink, the next thing in importance is a very fine steel pen, as it is the best for marking. The ink affects the pen, and if it is but a steel one, it can be thrown away after it has been used.

USEFUL DEVICES

A NEW VARIETY OF DUST-PAN.—Take the tin top of a kettle. Have it lay flat on the carpet when placed there. If need be bend the edge, so that it will lay flat and even all around where it slopes to the carpet. Place it where you wish. You do not have to stoop to use it. Lay it on the floor as described, and sweep the dust on it. When ready to lift it, do so by the ring or center piece.

COAL-SCUTTLE.—Here is an excellent way to lengthen the life of the coal-scuttle. Take a thick piece of board and fit it to the bottom of the scuttle inside; then put a small screw into the center of it, from the under side, which holds the board in place. An old scuttle can be mended that way, and made to do service a long time. If preferable, put the block of wood on the bottom of the scuttle on the outside, and put the screw from the inside into the block.

TABLE OF THE STOVE.—To dispose of the stove in summer when you have no packing room, is easily managed in the following manner: Make a light wooden frame with a solid top—an old packing frame for a sewing machine could be made to answer the purpose—make the frame large enough to slip over the stove, covering it with some kind of goods you may desire by the way of drapery, thus making a pretty stand. Remove from the stove all ornaments or obstructions, slip the frame over it, and you have a useful stand for books or anything else.

CLOTHES BOX.—If you are limited in closet room, and the dresses and coats are overcrowded when hung on the hooks, get a common packing box, about five feet long, and two or two and a half feet wide, and the right depth for a couch. Of the top make a hinged cover, then pad it, and cover it with some nice goods. Cover the sides of the box with cretonne, chintz, or some upholstering material. Add two or three pillows, and you have a desirable resting-place and a good receptacle for the overcrowded garments.

A GOOD WARDROBE.—Take two strips of wood, as long as desired, four inches wide and one inch thick, and screw them in the angle of the wall, six feet from the floor. Cut boards to fit in the corner, and rest them on the strips to form the top or roof of the closet. If preferred, a heavy piece of goods may be drawn across for the top, tacking it to the strips. A wooden pole is put across in front, resting the ends from wall to wall on the strips. This is for curtains. Cretonne, chintz, or any such material will serve the purpose. Now screw upon the strips as many hooks as wanted, and if the top is wood, put hooks into it also. A shelf may also be put in.

SCREENS.—The doors and windows may be screened at a small cost. Get netting of any color you wish. There is a stiff black netting that lasts well, which is preferable. Cut this to fit the window opening, allowing enough to tack it to the sides. If the house has blinds, allow four inches below the bottom of the lower sash; if there are no blinds, allow only enough to come to the window-sill. Tack this on the facing of the window opening outside. Tack it at the top and sides, leaving the bottom open, if there are shutters, otherwise tack it to the sill. For the doors, have frames made, and cover them with the same material.

VII—CLEANING GLASS

TO CLEAN MIRRORS

A CLEANING MIXTURE.—Take as much whiting as you think you will use at one time, and add enough cold tea to make a thin paste. Rub the fly specks from the mirror with warm tea, then dry it. Then smear a little of the paste on the glass, rubbing it with a dry cloth.

CARE OF MIRRORS.—The looking-glass may be polished with a soft cloth, wet with a few drops of *aqua ammonia*. It injures a mirror to allow the sun to shine full on it. In some way the sun's rays affect the metallic coating on the glass, causing it to lose its brightness, and often cracking the reflecting surface, but always making it a poor reflector.

CLEANING WITH PAPER.—This is true only of the best quality of rag-paper, such as is used by the best weekly papers. Paper that has wood or straw in it leaves a linty deposit on the glass. Divide a newspaper in two, fold up one-half into a small square, wet it in cold water, and rub the looking-glass with it. Wet half of the paper, then dry it with the other half. Fly-specks and all other marks will disappear as if by magic.

TO SCOUR MIRRORS.—Make a paste of whiting and water. Smear the surface with it. Let it dry on the glass, and then rub it off with tissue-paper, or with newspaper that is rather soft. Do not bear too heavy, as the particles of grit may scratch the surface.

TO WASH MIRRORS.—It is easy to remove finger-marks and such stains from looking-glasses by rubbing them thoroughly with a soft rag wet with alcohol.

SILVERING A MIRROR.—Here is the way to remedy a scratch that appears on the back of a mirror: Scrape away the mercury to the width of a quarter of an inch from either side of it, and wipe the place with a piece of clean rag wet with alcohol. Take a broken piece of mirror and mark out a piece of silvering larger than the place on the mirror needing repairs. Place a small drop of mercury on the center of that silvering, allowing it to remain a few moments. Clean away the silver from around the patch, and slip it from the broken glass to the place to be mended, pressing it into place with a small piece of cotton-batting.

TO CLEAN MICA

SMOKY MICA.—The beauty of a stove is often marred by dirty mica. To clean it, wet a rag in lemon-juice, and rub the mica with it.

CLEANING MICA.—If the stove with which you heat your best room has mica in it, you will want it to look nice. So, when it becomes dirty, take one tablespoonful of salt and two tablespoonfuls of vinegar, and mix them well. Dip a rag into the mixture, and with it wash the mica.

TO CLEAN IVORY

DISCOLORED IVORY.—When from any ordinary cause ivory becomes discolored, its whiteness may be restored by soaking it in water, and then while wet shutting it up closely in glass, a glass case or jar, and exposing it so inclosed to the action of the sun. When dry, wet it again, and replace it in the glass for another exposure. This has the tendency to bleach it. You may have to repeat that process several times before succeeding.

BLEACHING IVORY.—Knife-handles and other objects of use and ornament made of ivory, may be cleaned when discolored. Take as much prepared chalk as you will need at one time. Take equal parts of *aqua ammonia* and olive-oil. Make into a paste, and rub it on the ivory. When the paste has become quite dry, rub it off. If the article is not wholly free from stain, make a second application.

TO WASH GLASSWARE

CLEANING CUT-GLASS.—Make a warm suds with some nice white soap, and wash the cut-glass in that. Then take clear, warm water, adding to it enough *aqua ammonia* to be just perceptible, and with that rinse the glass. Dry it carefully with a soft rag, and take such a brush as a jeweler uses in his work, and with it go over the glass, giving it a polish, taking care to go into every crevice and mark to remove the stains.

GLASS IN HOT WATER.—When washing glassware, do not put it into hot water bottom first, as it is almost sure to crack from the sudden expansion. Lay the glass in sidewise or edgewise, so that it may heat gradually. Even the most delicate glass can be safely washed in hot water in this way.

WIPING GLASS.—Ordinary tableware is not hurt by being put in hot water, if you fill the articles with the water as soon as they touch it. Shake the glasses around in the water, adding soap enough to make a good suds. Dry the ware as soon as you lift it from the water, as draining leaves it dingy and streaky.

GLASS IN COLD WATER.—For those who are afraid of hot water for the glasses, or who would not be careful enough with it, the following advice is given: Wash the glass in cold water, a process that gives it a clearer look than if washed in hot or warm water, and is also safer.

CUT JEWELS.—Cut jewels should never be wiped after washing. Take castile soap-suds and an old toothbrush, or a jeweler's brush, and wash the jewels carefully. Rinse them in clear, cold water, then lay them in sawdust, shaking them about in it. Have the sawdust fine; boxwood sawdust is the best.

CUPS AND SAUCERS.—After cups and saucers have been used for some time, they become stained with ugly yellow stains. To remove these, take coal ashes, and with them rub the stains thoroughly.

TO CLEAN BOTTLES

CLEANING WITH EGGSHELLS.—You may be forced to use a bottle that is stained, or has become dirty inside. Of course, it must first be cleaned. Take crushed eggshell, and put a tablespoonful into the bottle, half fill it with water, cork, or hold your hand over the top, and shake well. That will clean it quickly.

CLEANING WITH SHOT.—One of the best things to clean bottles with is shot. It will remove deposits of dirt that are found in the bottom. Get common-sized shot, put a handful into the bottle, half fill it with water, and shake it well. Replenish the water when it becomes dirty, continuing this until the adhering deposit is removed.

CLEANING WITH LYE.—Stone jars, glass cans, and bottles that have become dirty, may be easily cleaned, if you desire to use them again. Take any kind of good lye, and wash the article with it until clean.

OLD CROCKS.—Old lard and butter jars, and meat crocks which have stood for a long time and become stale, may be made perfectly sweet and fresh by filling them with hot lime-water, and leaving it in them until cool.

TO PURIFY JARS.—Take strong, hot soda-water, while it is hot, and fill the jar, letting it remain and soak until clean.

GLASS VESSELS.—Glass vessels may be purified of bad smells with charcoal. Scour off the thick deposits of dirt with sand, and take charcoal to scour with afterward.

TO CLEAN LAMP-CHIMNEYS

USE A SPONGE.—The best thing with which to clean a lamp-chimney is a sponge. Much of the ordinary bother of washing lamp-chimneys on the inside can be avoided by using this.

USE SODA.—The smoke from a lamp leaves a deposit on the chimney that is hard to remove. Make a strong solution of common baking-soda and warm water, and wash the chimney with it.

CLEANING WITH SALT.—In order to remove the gummy black that often gathers on a lamp-chimney, put dry salt on a dry rag, and rub the glass with it.

GLASS GLOBES.—When a lamp-glass is partly ground or has rough ornamentation, it is sometimes almost impossible to cleanse the intricate parts with soap and water. Place such globes in a kettle of cold water in which has been dissolved washing-soda, one tablespoonful to a gallon of water. Bring the water nearly to a boil, and after the globes have cooled in it, remove them, and scrub in warm water, to which has been added a teaspoonful of *aqua ammonia* for every pint of water. Drain the globes; do not wipe them. When dry they will look new.

POLISHING GLOBES.—Save the small paper bags of soft paper that come from your grocer. When the lamp-globe needs cleaning, crumple and soften one of them in your hand, then straighten it out, put your hand in it, and push the bag with the hand in it into the chimney, then polish with it. To make it easier cleaning, hold the bag over the top of the globe, and into the other end breathe heavily several times. The bag keeps the moist air in the chimney as you breathe into it.

SMOKE-STAINED GLASSES.—Wash smoke-stained lamp-chimneys in warm soap suds, and while they are yet wet rub them with vinegar until they are clean.

TO CLEAN MARBLE

SALT ON MARBLE.—A plain and easy way to remove ordinary dirt from marble without injury to the surface is as follows: Take common table salt that is quite dry, and with a rag rub it on the article until clean.

TO CLEAN MARBLE.—Here is a way to clean marble that has commended itself to many. Take two tablespoonfuls of baking-soda, one tablespoonful of pumice stone, and one tablespoonful of precipitated chalk, and make these into a paste with water. Rub the preparation on the marble, then wash the marble with soap and water.

RENEWING MARBLE.—After using the following, stained marble will look clean and white as new. Take one pound each of washing-soda, softsoap, and whiting, put into a suitable vessel and place upon the stove, letting them simmer together for several hours. Give the mixture an occasional stirring. Apply it hot to the surface of the marble, and let it remain for one week. Then wash off with hot water and a scrubbing-brush.

TO BRIGHTEN MARBLE.—To whiten a dirty piece of marble, take whiting, or a good quality of common clay, and make into a thin paste with benzole. Then lay the mixture on the marble, and let it remain a few hours. Remove, and wash the marble with soap and water. If one application does not accomplish the desired effect, make another of the mixture. letting it remain on the marble longer.

TO THOROUGHLY WHITEN MARBLE.—When marble becomes discolored, or in any way dirty, it may be easily cleaned. Take a saturated solution of water and concentrated lye. Take as much unslacked lime as needed, and with lye make the lime into a thin paste. Then put the paste upon the marble. Let it remain twenty-four hours, and scrape it off. Then clean the stone with warm water and soap. Should the stone be stained and extra dirty, you may have to repeat it. After this application the marble looks new.

REMOVING STAINS FROM MARBLE.—Marble basins and other marble-lined articles are sometimes neglected, as, for instance, when the house is closed and every one is away. At such times ugly yellow stains may appear on marble that is exposed to water. Should everything commonly used fail to remove such a stain, then you will have to resort to the use of muriatic acid. Shut the water off from the basin, and dry the marble well. Tie a rag to the end of a small stick, dip it into the acid, and with it touch the stain, and immediately the spot will disappear. Put water into the basin at once upon the disappearance of the stain, and then scrub the basin with soap and water. When applying the acid be careful not to get it on the metal about the basin, as it will destroy the plating. Do not get it on the hands, nor drop it on your shoes, nor get it on your clothing, as it will destroy them.

A MIXTURE TO CLEAN MARBLE.—Take one teaspoonful of powdered bluing, two teaspoonfuls of whiting, and one pint of softsoap. Put them in a tin cup, and place it upon the stove, allowing it to come to a boil. While the mixture is still hot apply it with a soft, clean rag to the marble. Let it remain until dry, and then wash off. If the marble is extra stained, put oxalic acid into the rinsing-water. Dry the stone with a piece of soft flannel.

IRON RUST ON MARBLE.—How often a tin vessel with water in it is placed upon marble, and allowed to remain until it leaves a stain; or a nail, a screw, or something with iron in it, is left upon the washstand, and, having water splashed upon it,

causes a stain.   To remove such iron rust, wash it carefully
with nitric acid.   Put one drop of acid in twenty drops of water.
Wash the marble afterward with *aqua ammonia.*

TO CLEAN WINDOWS

REMOVING PAINT SPOTS.—When washing windows of
a new house, or one that has been newly painted, you are apt to
find small paint spots that will not come off with soap and water.
You will also often find specks of hardened plaster on the window.   To remove these, rub against them a copper cent, or
apply hot, sharp vinegar.

POLISHING WINDOWS.—After washing the windows in
the usual way with soap and water, and you come to dry them,
the best thing to use for that purpose is a chamois skin.   It
polishes nicely.

WASHING WINDOWS.—If you have only little time for
the windows, do not wash them with soap, as you will have to
rinse much to get it off.   A few drops of *aqua ammonia* in clear
water will remove all spots which do not come off with clear
water.

WINDOW CORNERS.—Wash the windows with a sponge.
It is best not to wash them while the sun is shining on the
glass, as it is apt to dry the dirty water on the pane, and so leave
streaks.   A piece of pointed whalebone, or of pinewood, is just
the thing to use in cleaning out the corners of the sash.   When
you have washed the windows, polish them with tissue-paper.

COAL-OIL IN POLISHING WINDOWS.—With this
method, when the windows are dried and rubbed with a soft
cloth, they will take a polish like fine china.   Use cold water.
Put one teaspoonful of coal-oil to one quart of water.

CLEANING WITH WINGS.—Manage to save and cure the wings of fowls, such as turkeys, geese, and chickens. Save those with the feathers on, as they are good to use in washing and cleaning windows, for they leave no dust nor lint as a cloth does.

SODA ON WINDOWS.—Dissolve a little washing-soda in the water you are to use in cleaning the windows that are smoky and dirty. Do not let the water stand on the paint of the sash. Wash one pane at a time, using a flannel, and drying with a towel. Polish with a good quality of newspaper.

KEROSENE ON GLASS.—Here is a way to take dirt off of a window pane quickly and neatly, much better than with soap and water. Wet a cloth and then wring it somewhat dry. Now put a tablespoonful of kerosene oil on it, and rub the glass. Dry, and polish with paper.

WIPING WINDOWS.—If hurried, and, therefore, unable to devote the usual time, or use the ordinary method in cleaning the windows, you may find help in the following: Take a chamois skin, wet it, then wring it so as it will be only damp. Put one tablespoonful of *aqua ammonia* on it, and wipe.

TEA ON WINDOWS.—Soap is hard to get off of glass, and should be little used on windows. To get specks off glass, wash them with warm tea. To polish them, make a paste of tea and whiting; smear on the glass with a rag and polish with it. Then rub the glass with a nice close piece of flannel.

KEEPING FLIES AWAY.—After cleaning the windows it is very annoying to have flies dirty them immediately. To keep flies off, dampen a rag with kerosene oil and rub it on the glass. The disagreeable odor soon evaporates from the room, and you are at rest from the flies on the windows.

VIII—TEMPERING GLASS

TABLE GLASS

TO SEASON GLASS.—To season glass and chinaware to sudden changes of temperature, so that it will remain sound after exposure to sudden heat and cold, place the articles in cold water, which must gradually be brought to the boiling point, and then allowed to cool very slowly, taking several hours to do so.

TO PREVENT BREAKING.—Hot preserves, hot jellies, and such things, do not injure the glass they are put in if the following is observed : Put a spoon in a glass in which you are about to put hot water, or any hot substance, and it prevents cracking the glass, because the metal quickly absorbs a large part of the heat.

SUDDEN HEATING.—Probably more articles of glass are daily broken by being suddenly heated than by blows, or other acts of carelessness. Glass is a very poor conductor of heat, and when hot water is poured suddenly into a tumbler or goblet, it is almost certain to break, unless the glass is quite warm. Tepid water should be used first, or a little cold water be poured into the glass on which the hot water may be poured.

STONEWARE

TEMPERING POTTERY.—Proceed as in the case with glassware described in the paragraph above, headed "To Season Glass." Remember that when potter's ware is boiled for the purpose of hardening it, a handful or more, according to the quantity of water used, of bran, should be thrown into the water. This is done to give any destructive element something to work on, and so result in neutralizing it. In this way the glazing will never be injured by acids, or salt, or any combination of elements.

LAMP-CHIMNEYS

TO ANNEAL GLASS.—To keep lamp glass, or any other kind of glass, from breaking from sudden heat, put the required amount of cold water in a suitable vessel, and add enough salt to make it quite salty. Do not fill the vessel with water, but have only enough to cover the chimney or fruit dish, or whatever glass it may be. Wrap the glass in a piece of muslin, having the wrapping thick about the article. Put the article in the water, and bring the water to a strong boil. Then take the vessel from the fire, and let the water cool, leaving the glass in the water to cool with it. When it has become perfectly cold, the glass may be removed from the water, and used. By repeating this operation several times, the glass will become thoroughly toughened, and there need be no fear of cracking it by the ordinary fluctuations of heat.

KEEPING CHIMNEYS.—A cold draft upon a heated lamp-chimney will often break it. Many times to raise the wick too high, causing a large flame and much heat, is to make the chimney fly to pieces. It is advisable to place the lamp-chimneys into the tea kettle in the morning before you build the fire, and let them stay there until the next morning, having boiled and cooled, as the kettle has been refilled all day. In the morning, while the water is cool, remove the chimneys.

IX—LAMPS

TO MEND LAMPS

FASTENING LAMP TOPS.—When the brass ring to which the burner is screwed gets loose, mend it in this way: Take it off the lamp, clean out the hard paste and the oil that adheres to it, wiping it clean and dry. Then take a tablespoonful of plaster of Paris, and with water make it into a paste thin enough to run into the crevices. Where you dug out the old plaster refill with the new, heaping it up. Turn it over the neck of the lamp into position, and press it down. Let it remain so to harden. After twelve hours it is ready for use.

FITTING THE BRASS.—Do not throw away the old lamp, fix the top back, and it will do as good as new. Powder some alum, with it fill the hollow part of the brass to which the burner fastens, and place it on the stove to melt. When the alum is melted, place the brass immediately on the lamp. When the alum is cold, the lamp is ready for use.

TO RENEW LAMPS

THE BURNER.—When the burner gets old, and every crevice is covered with gum, making the wick hard to turn up or down, it should be cleaned. For that purpose take enough borax to make a strong solution with water, using enough to boil the burner. Let it boil until the dirt loosens, then rinse it well in clear water and dry quickly.

CLEAN THE BURNER.—Old lamp-burners should be boiled often in water made strong with baking-soda. Let them boil for one hour and polish them.

FIXING THE BURNER.—The little apertures through which the air gets into the bowl of the lamp, so aiding it to burn, often become stopped with dust from the sweeping. This makes the light poor, and it should be remedied. Put as much concentrated lye in one pint of water as it will dissolve. Into this solution place the burner, letting it remain a few minutes at least, until you see the dirt beginning to dissolve. Then rinse it thoroughly in clear water and wipe dry.

CLEANING THE LAMP.—There are many ways of making the brass about a lamp look nice. Take a woolen rag that has been dipped in gasoline, and rub the brass vigorously with it.

RENEWING THE BRASS.—These days most houses have gas fixtures, electric lights, brass, or old lamps, and many of them have become badly worn, showing ugly marks. These may be made to look like new. The following is an easy and simple method: Take a bottle of the gold paint sold at drug stores, and with a small brush go over them with it.

LAMP WICKS

GOOD WICKS.—To be sure of a good light wicks must be changed often, for they soon become clogged and do not permit the free passage of the oil. Do not throw the wicks away, unless they are too short to use again, but treat them in the following way: Take the wicks, new or old, and soak them in vinegar for twenty-four hours before placing them in the lamps, and you will be sure of a clear flame. Let the wicks dry before using them.

CARE OF WICKS.—Felt wicks are regarded by many as the best, but of whatever kind they are, they need to be cared for properly. As a quick, but not the best method, you may scrape off the charred part of the wick. Lamp wicks give a better light when cut squarely across, and so removing the burnt part. There are scissors made especially for the purpose of trimming lamp wicks, which save trouble in looking for scissors, and they are clean to work with.

IMPROVING THE LIGHT.—A clear light may be obtained by soaking the wick in vinegar. The same result may be accomplished by putting a small piece of camphor in the lamp-bowl with the oil. There is this difference, the camphor has a tendency to make the lamp smoke, while the vinegar has the opposite effect.

CARE OF LAMPS

KEEP THE LAMPS FILLED.—Lamps burned with little oil in them are likely to generate a gas which is liable at any moment to explode. Fill the lamps to within half an inch of the top. If filled quite full, the oil will leak out and cover the lamp. Then, through heat expansion, the oil will run over and grease whatever it touches.

ATTEND TO LAMPS REGULARLY.—Lamps should be attended to every day—trimmed, filled, and rubbed dry with a soft cloth. Once a week they should be thoroughly washed in good warm suds, and properly dried and polished, the chimneys receiving the same attention.

X—TINS AND KETTLES

IRON POTS

TO CLEAN OLD POTS.—The best way to clean the inside of old pots and pans is to fill them with water in which a few ounces of washing-soda has been dissolved, and set them on the fire. Let the water boil until the inside of the vessel looks clean.

TO SCOUR IRONWARE.—Iron vessels should be washed and well cared for as soon as possible after using them. Take finely-sifted coal-ashes and a good rag; with these scour the kettles well, and the next time you use them they will be ready without delay.

TO PREPARE NEW KETTLES.—There are so many small particles of iron on the surface of a new kettle that they would blacken anything cooked in it. It would also taste of iron. To prevent this, take as much hay or grass as you can grasp in one hand and boil it for five hours in the kettle. Then scour with brick-dust and soda mixed equal parts. Ashes will do, or sand. Put clear water in the kettle and let it boil for an hour. Then it may be used without danger from the loose iron.

ENCRUSTED POTS.—Do not allow the outside of pots to become coated with thick scales of burnt grease, smoke, dishwater. Have a rag used only for wiping the pots when done using them. If they become coated in spite of you, place them on hot coals for a short time, and burn them well, after which the scales can be scraped off. Then scour them with soap and sand.

TO CLEAN KETTLES. — Half fill the wash-boiler with water; add to it enough concentrated lye to make a strong solution, and put in a piece of soap. Bring the water to a boil; put the pots in it, and allow them to remain one half-hour. Remove them and rinse them in clear water. Then set them on the stove to dry. They are now ready to be used.

NEW TINS

TO PREPARE NEW TINS.—You can not be sure what has been on the tin that is harmful. New tin is apt to give a tin-taste to anything that is cooked in it. To avoid this, pour hot water in it, and add soda or *aqua ammonia*, a tablespoonful of ammonia to each quart of water, and the same of soda. Let it remain on the stove for a while, and then remove and scour.

TO CLEAN NEW TINS. — Scalding-hot water kills any poisonous germs. Pour scalding water into your tins, letting it remain until cold. Then scour them thoroughly with baking-soda. Wash with soap and water, being careful to clean out all the corners and crevices of the tin.

THE TEAKETTLE

CLEANING THE KETTLE. — The teakettle is often neglected until it becomes black with smoke and anything that may spatter on it. To brighten it, saturate a woolen rag with kerosene oil and rub the kettle with that.

KETTLES INCRUSTING.—If the kettle is inclined to become incrusted inside with any deposit from the water, it may be remedied in the following manner: Put an oyster shell or a piece of marble in the kettle. That will attract the particles to itself.

MENDING TINS

METHOD FOR MENDING.—Take an ounce bottle, put into it enough muriatic acid to make it half full; then drop in little pieces of zinc, a few at a time, until the acid stops boiling and will not dissolve more. Add to that sal-ammoniac, the size of a pea, and fill the bottle with water. When using, dip into it a feather or a little stick, and with this wet the place to be mended. Then take a piece of zinc or lead, wet it with the preparation, and put it over the place to be mended. Hold a lamp flame under it, which melts the zinc or lead, and causes it to stick.

METAL FOR PATCHING.—At almost any novelty store you can get a small flat piece of metal made for the purpose of mending tins. Directions are given with it. There is also a small coil of lead sold at the same stores that is used by holding a lighted match to the broken place, to which the lead is touched.

MENDING IRON POTS

PASTE FOR POTS.—For almost any ordinary fractures, apply the following to the fracture, and the vessel will be found nearly as sound as when new: Mix finely-sifted lime with some white of an egg until a thin paste is formed, then add some iron filings.

RIVET THE POT.—If the old iron boiler, or any pot, should have a small hole in it, that may be fixed with great ease and niceness. Put a copper rivet, or a Swedish iron rivet, into the aperture, and rest the rivet on something solid, so as to hammer it well. Then hammer it down tight. Be careful not to hit the kettle and break it.

CLEANING TINS

MILK-CANS.—The following will leave your milk-cans sweeter, and clean them quicker, than any other method: Put borax into the water until it is quite strong, and with that wash out the cans.

SCOURING MATERIAL.—Take marble-dust, red sand, bath-brick, pumice-stone, or white sand. Any of those are good for polishing tins. Now put on the polishing cloth soap-suds, *aqua ammonia*, or kerosene oil, any one that is convenient, and dip the cloth in the material you are using, and with it scour the tin until it is bright.

SALT ON TIN.—Rub salt on the inside of the coffee-pot when washing it, and it will remove the coffee and egg adhering to the tin very quickly. Be careful to rinse the pot thoroughly before using it again.

TO POLISH TIN.—To make tinware look bright and new, giving it a splendid polish, use whiting. Take a woolen cloth, wet it with kerosene oil, then dip it into the whiting, and rub the tin with that until it shines.

TEA AND COFFEE-POT.—When dark stains adhere to the sides and spout of the tea or coffee-pot, it is time some measures were taken to remove them. To brighten the inside, fill the pot with water, and add a small piece of soap. Now let the pot boil for about one hour. The soap removes the gum and stain.

TO WASH GREASY TINS.—Pour sufficient hot water into the greasy tin or pot, and then add a few drops of *aqua ammonia*.

WHEN TO WASH PANS.—Never allow the pans to stand with the scraps of food drying on them, for this doubles the work of cleaning them. When you are through using them, pour water into them at once, adding some cleansing agent, and the work is half done.

TO PREVENT TINS RUSTING.—Thus treated, any tinware may be used in water constantly, and will remain bright and free from rust indefinitely. Rub lard over every part of the tin, and then put it in a hot oven and heat it thoroughly, letting the lard strike in.

TO WASH TINS.—The work of washing greasy pots and tins may be reduced to a small task by the use of washing-soda. As soon as the gravy has been poured from the roasting-pan, fill it with water and sift washing-soda into it, and set it on the stove. When the dishes are washed, the pan is ready, the grease all dissolved, and may be washed as easy as a plate; so with the greasy kettle, and the like.

XI—POLISHING METALS

POLISHING KNIVES

TO TAKE OFF RUST.—By laying away, after being used, knives will become rusty, or spotted with rust. To remove this, take a flannel rag, dip it in kerosene oil, and rub the rust vigorously. It dissolves and removes it.

TO REMOVE STAINS FROM KNIVES.—The following is one of the best and simplest ways of removing any discoloration from the table-knives. One good feature of it is that the material is always at hand: Take wood ashes, pick out the largest portions of unburnt matter, so as to have the ashes as fine as possible, and with a woolen rag rub the ashes on the wet knife-blades.

TO CLEAN KNIVES.—When your best knives and forks have become stained, or even before that, when they are simply dull, they may be cleaned in this way: Scrape some bath-brick into dust and rub the knives.

A GOOD CLEANER.—This is an excellent way to remove stains and spots from steel knives and forks, or other metals: Take a piece of chamois skin or soft flannel, dip it into kerosene oil or benzine, whichever you happen to have, and rub the article. After you have rubbed with that, then dip the chamois skin into fine emery powder, and polish the article by vigorous rubbing, continuing to apply until nicely polished.

A QUICK POLISH.—For an easy and quick polish bath-brick is the best; but, if you use the ordinary brick, make it as fine as possible. To one tablespoonful of brick-dust, add one-half a teaspoonful of baking-soda, mix well, and with that scour the metal.

ORDINARY CLEANING.—This should be done at least once a day in the ordinary routine of cleaning. Have a soft flannel, moisten it in water, rub it on the kitchen soap, then dip it into the baking-soda. Now polish the knives with that.

A CLEANING MIXTURE.—There is nothing better than this for removing spots: Take one ounce of baking-soda, one ounce of pumice stone, or a nice quality of white sand, and one ounce of wood-ashes dust, and mix them together. When using, apply it with a piece of raw Irish potato.

TO CLEAN RUSTY INSTRUMENTS.—When knives, instruments, or any kinds of metals are subjected to the following treatment they will soon take on a neat silvery whiteness. Fill a suitable vessel with a saturated solution of chloride of tin in distilled water. Immerse the rusted instruments in that, and let them remain over night. The next morning rinse them in water running from the hydrant, or any running water. Rub them dry with a chamois skin until they are bright.

A RAZOR STROP PASTE.—This emery is better for polishing and sharpening than that prepared at emery mills. Take the coarse kind of emery, and pound it thoroughly in a mortar. Then put it into a large jug, and fill up with water, stirring it well. When the large particles have sunk, pour off the water with the fine particles in it into a shallow pan, and let the water evaporate. Then you have a nice quality of emery. When it is dry, take what you wish of it, and mix it thoroughly with mutton or other tallow. Add enough beeswax to give it the proper consistency, making it into a paste, and apply by rubbing it into the leather strap.

TO CLEAN NICKEL

RUBBING NICKEL.—Here is a simple and good preparation for rubbing nickel when only slightly dirty. Take as much jeweler's rouge as is needed, and mix with it just enough lard, or vaseline, to make it into a paste. Mix these ingredients thoroughly, and it will make a nice-looking preparation. Apply it with a flannel rag, or a piece of chamois skin, rubbing it well on the article.

NICKEL ON STOVES.—It is desirable that the nickel on stoves should look nice and clean, being so much in view. Take the amount of baking-soda you wish to use, and add enough *aqua ammonia* to it to make a thin paste. Apply with a rag, and then rub the article with a woolen cloth until it is bright.

A PASTE FOR NICKEL.—Take equal parts of *aqua ammonia* and alcohol, add to these enough whiting to make a thin paste, and apply to the nickel with a piece of chamois skin, let it remain on until dry. Then polish with a clean, dry piece of chamois skin until clean and bright.

TO BRIGHTEN NICKEL.—Very often nickel plate does not need cleaning, only rubbing off. Put dry flour on a woolen rag, and polish the nickel with that.

TO WASH NICKEL PLATE.—Scour the nickel-plated article with powdered borax and a damp rag. When that is done, rinse the article with hot water and a suspicion of soap, rinse with clear hot water, and rub the article dry with a clean, dry cloth.

BADLY STAINED NICKEL.—When you wish to clean a piece of nickel plate, or an article that is portable and nickel-plated, and you have not some recommended ingredient in easy reach, or do not wish to undertake it for fear of making a bad job, you will find the following to your notion : Make a strong solution of alum and water, put the article into that, and let it boil until you see it is getting clean. Dry it, and apply any of the above pastes you wish.

A CLEANING POWDER.—Take the required amount of whiting, and make it into a paste with soap foam. Mix until smooth, having it thick enough to make into small cakes. Let these dry. When using, scrape some powder from a cake on to the article to be cleaned, or simply rub a damp cloth on a cake, as the case may require. Then rub the article with the damp cloth. The soap removes the grease and dirt, while the whiting polishes. After rubbing, take a dry cloth and polish.

ACID ON NICKEL.—Here is a good preparation of sulphuric acid and alcohol, to remove stains from nickel when very much discolored. Take fifty tablespoonfuls of alcohol, and add to them one tablespoonful of sulphuric acid. Let the nickel-plated article, or a piece of nickel, lie in that solution for five seconds (the yellowest article will be restored to brightness if soaked for fifteen seconds). Then wash with clear water, and rinse with alcohol. Rub dry with a linen cloth.

TO CLEAN ZINC

STOVE ZINC.—Clean stove zinc as follows: Take a flannel rag and saturate it with kerosene oil, and rub the zinc until clean and bright.

TO WASH ZINC.—Put softsoap on it, spreading it around with a rag. Then let it remain two or three minutes, and wash it off. Or, try two ounces of alum in one quart of vinegar, applying it hot. Wipe at once with a dry rag.

TO CLEAN SILVERWARE

POLISHING LIQUID.—There is nothing better for cleaning plain or frosted gold and silverware than the following: Take one tablespoonful of whiting, or more if needed; put into a bottle and pour onto it equal parts of alcohol and *aqua ammonia* until the mixture becomes liquid. When using, daub the article with it, and polish with a flannel. When you want an extra nice polish, it is not well to put soap on silverware. Remember that when you have new ware that you would have retain its luster. Soap-suds make such ware look dead like tin or pewter. Do this instead: Wet a flannel cloth in kerosene oil; dip it in dry whiting, and rub the plated ware, letting it dry on the article. Then take an old, soft newspaper and polish.

A GOOD POLISHING POWDER. — To polish silver or gold, and give the article a good bright new look, is desirable. To do that something is needed to cut off the grease and finger-marks. Take equal parts of bicarbonate of ammonia and whiting. The ammonia removes the dirt, and the whiting polishes. Apply with a rag or chamois skin. Considerable rubbing is required.

ANOTHER POLISHING MATERIAL.—As good a thing as any to brighten gold, silver, nickel, and brass is this. The cream of tartar is acid enough to remove any greasy adherence; the liquid adds to the ease of applying. Venetian red adds to the friction in polishing. If you wish a powder, take equal parts of cream of tartar and Venetian red; mix them well. If you wish a liquid, add any one of these, alcohol, naphtha, benzine, gasoline, enough to make it the consistency you wish. Smear that on the article, then polish with a brush or flannel cloth.

A GOOD SILVER POLISH.—Here is a very good and common powder used in brightening silverware in every-day use. Should you wish a liquid, add enough *aqua ammonia* to make it such. When applying it, let it dry on the article, then polish with tissue-paper. Use the powder in the usual way by rubbing it well. Venetian red, one-half pound; Spanish whiting, one pound. Mix well.

A HANDY POWDER.—Should you not have any of the usual preparations for cleaning silverware, then try this, and you will be pleased. It will make a dingy article look new.

Take cream of tartar; use it dry. Rub it on the article with the bare hand, or with a chamois skin, if you have it. Rub until the article is bright, which will be very soon. Then rub the article with a cloth until free from the cream of tartar. It being a powder, causes friction when rubbed, and not being gritty does not scratch; also, being slightly acid it removes any grease from the article polished.

ANOTHER SILVER POLISH.—No matter what kind of stain is present—egg, mustard, bean, spinach, or any other— which you wish to remove, and at the same time brighten the silverware, you can do this as follows: Take a cheap, stiff toothbrush, dip in alcohol, then in powdered borax, and rub the stain with it.

TO REMOVE INK FROM SILVER.—Take chloride of lime, and make it into a paste with water. Then rub it well into the stain and it will disappear. Wash the article in scalding water, and dry it as usual.

TO REMOVE EGG STAIN FROM SILVER.—Egg makes a dark ugly stain on silver—silver spoons, for instance. This stain is easily removed. Take as much table-salt as required, and moisten it with water; then rub it on the stain with a piece of chamois.

TO REMOVE MEDICINE STAINS FROM SILVER.— A spoon is often used in administering medicine when care can not be taken of it, and it becomes stained. In such a case use sulphuric acid. Pour the acid into a saucer, then dip the stained part into it, letting it remain for a second. If the stain has not disappeared, repeat the process. When the stain has gone, wash the article in very hot water, and polish it.

TO WASH SILVER.—With a piece of fine soap make a good hot suds, and wash the silver in that. Put the silver in a clean vessel, and pour over it boiling-hot water, being careful that the water boils before using it. Rub the article dry with a clean, soft cloth.

PUTTING SILVER AWAY.—Silverware may be kept bright, when not in use, by putting it away in unbleached cotton-flannel bags. Put a piece of camphor-gum in each bag. The bleached cotton is not best, as the sulphur used in bleaching is likely to turn the silver dark.

CARE OF SILVER.—To keep silverware from discoloration put it in a case as nearly air-tight as possible, then put into the case a lump of camphor. A small case for spoons may be made of chamois skin. Rub the skin on the outside with wax to help make it air-tight.

SETTING AWAY SILVER.—It is not easy to keep unused silverware from getting discolored. Many ways are tried and recommended. One of the best ways is to wrap it in blue tissue-paper, wrapping carefully to exclude air.

A COVERING FOR SILVER.—Anything that attracts moisture should not be used to cover silverware, as moisture makes the ware tarnish. Some housekeepers use flannel cloth. Articles of silver plate, which are not in daily use, should be put away in green baize, either carefully wrapped or made into bags of sufficient size and shape.

TO CLEAN JEWELRY

GOLD JEWELRY.—It is not difficult to renew the brightness of jewelry when only ordinarily dirty. Make a lather of plain yellow soap and warm water, and wash the articles in it. Dry by pressing in your hands between two cloths. When thoroughly dry, take a common cheap toothbrush, dip it in dry whiting, and brush the articles. At last polish them with a soft piece of leather, such as chamois skin.

ANOTHER COMMON METHOD.—Take a chamois skin, or a piece of flannel cloth, lay some prepared chalk on it, then put the ornament in it, and fold the material over. Rub it well. Then take the ornament into your fingers, and rub it into the chalk, which soon cleanses.

LAYING AWAY JEWELRY.—When not in constant use, jewelry is apt to become tarnished. All gold and silver ornaments may be kept bright by putting them in a card or wooden box, and covering them carefully with boxwood sawdust. You can get this at any jewelry store. Boxwood sawdust is what jewelers use to dry their ornaments after they have been dipped in benzine, or washed. You will find it excellent for drying your ornaments. Put the article in the sawdust, cover the box, and shake it. When no dust sticks to the article, it is dry.

TO CLEAN JAPANNED WARE

TO WASH JAPANNED WARE.—Here are good general directions for washing japanned ware. Put a little warm water in a pan, shake the soap in it until a nice suds is formed, and with that wash the article until clean.

TO POLISH TRAYS.—To give a new look to the tray, polish it now and then, being careful not to scratch the varnish. You can accomplish the purpose with a little powdered whiting or dry flour placed on the tray. Rub gently with a soft cloth, to get the flour off.

TO CLEAN BRONZE

A GOOD METHOD.—When an article of bronze needs cleaning, the following method will be found good. Pour sweet-oil on a flannel cloth, and rub it on the bronze thoroughly, thus removing stain and dirt. After that polish the articles with a chamois skin. It should be mentioned in this connection that the use of sweet-oil as above, will also clean britannia ware, which should afterward be washed in warm soap-suds.

TO WASH BRONZE.—When an article is of genuine bronze metal, and not simply varnished to look brown, it may be cleaned in the following manner: Immerse it in boiling water, have a good soap-suds ready, into which dip a flannel cloth, and with it clean the article, rubbing it dry with a chamois skin. A bronze urn should be filled with boiling water, to thoroughly heat it before the exterior is cleaned as described above.

TO CLEAN BRASS

BRASS KETTLES.—This is as good for other articles of brass as for kettles, but care must be exercised with kettles, lest some one should be poisoned with the verdigris. Dissolve a rounded tablespoonful of salt in a teacupful of vinegar, put it on the stove, and bring to a steaming heat. With this rub the brass thoroughly, then wash it out, and scour the brass with wood ashes sifted fine. When washed, it is ready for use.

KITCHEN UTENSILS.—Among the best things known to brighten the copper on the coffee-pot, tea-kettle, or any other kitchen utensil, is the following: Have a saucer of buttermilk, add a teaspoonful of salt, and dissolve it. Dip a cloth into that, and rub the vessel, being brisk and thorough. Apply that until you get the desired polish.

TO SCOUR COPPER VESSELS.—It is not often necessary to scour a coffee-kettle in order to make it pure from poison. Your purpose may be simply to brighten the copper. Such being the case, here is a simple method : Take two tablespoonfuls of bath-brick dust, and one tablespoonful of baking-soda, and mix them. Dampen a cloth in gasoline or coal-oil, whichever is at hand, dip it into the mixture, and polish with that, rubbing thoroughly.

TO REMOVE VERDIGRIS.—Verdigris is a poison, and care must be taken that it does not get into a sore, if you should have such on your hands. It would be well to always wear a pair of old gloves while cleaning the vessel. Here is a good cleanser: Take the juice of one lemon, add to it one teaspoonful of salt, such as is used on the table, mix well, and apply with a soft flannel, rubbing well. Rinse, and rub the kettle well with a chamois skin or clean cloth until quite clean.

TO BRIGHTEN BRASS.—There are many ways of cleaning and brightening brass. Here is one of the best: Take putty powder, add to it enough sweet-oil to make a thin paste, and mix them well. With this rub the brass or copper until all foreign matter is loosened. Then wash the article with soap and water, and rub with a clean cloth.

TO POLISH BRASS.—All corrosions and stains should be removed from brass cooking vessels. People who do most of their cooking and serving in brass vessels, clean them with earth mixed with some natural acid, such as lemon juice or orange juice. A good preparation would be lemon or orange juice, this thickened into a paste with whiting. If a good powder be preferred, take equal parts of citric acid and Spanish whiting, and mix them well. Apply with a chamois skin or a good flannel rag. Such mild acids will not injure the hands or the article cleansed.

A GOOD BRASS CLEANER.—This will clean the dirtiest brass or copper quickly: Take one ounce of powdered bichromate of potash, two ounces of sulphuric acid, and two ounces of pure water, and mix them thoroughly. Apply to a vessel by pouring some of the mixture into it, and then rub it well in with a mop on a stick. On other articles, wet the mop with the liquid and apply, and rub thoroughly. Finally wash the article with warm water and soap.

TO CLEAN COPPER BOILERS.—The copper boiler looks really ornamental when brightly polished, but, being conspicuous, a little dinginess is soon seen, and then it becomes an eyesore. To scour the boiler, take as much oxalic acid as is needed for the occasion, dissolve it in enough water to make a saturated solution. Rub the boiler with this, and then scour with pumice stone and olive oil. To save such labor, it is suggested that the boiler be painted a color to match that of the kitchen.

TO CLEAN OLD BRASS.—One of the best methods for cleaning old brass is to use strong ammonia on it. With that method, after weeks of standing, there will be no sign of discoloration or dimness on the article. During the process of cleaning, the vapor from the *aqua ammonia* may turn the brass a dark bronze-like color, but the application of the liquid ammonia will remove this at once. Pour the *aqua ammonia* onto the brass, take the scrubbing brush and give it a thorough scrubbing. In a few minutes after such work the brass will become as clear, bright, shining, as new metal. Rinse the article in clear water and wipe it dry.

TO PREVENT TARNISH ON BRASS.—Brass finish on beds, chairs, and other like things may be kept from tarnishing by the method here given. Brighten the brass first, then heat it a little before applying the mixture : One ounce of shellac, one-fourth of a pint of methylic alcohol, mixed in a bottle. Let it stand a few hours. Then pour off the liquid as you need it, and apply that with a camel's-hair brush as smoothly as you can.

A GOOD CLEANING MIXTURE.—Here is a good mixture for general use on metals of various kinds; with it a beautiful and durable polish will be obtained. The article to be cleansed should first be washed with hot water to remove any grease. Then rub the metal with the mixture. Take rotten-stone, which is a mineral, called also " Tripoli," from the country from which it was formerly brought. Have as much of it as you will need for the time being. Take equal parts of softsoap and oil of turpentine; mix them, and with them make the rottenstone into a paste of the consistency of putty. When ready, thin it with water, so thin as to be easily smeared, and polish well with the mixture. Then rub the mixture off briskly with a dry clean rag or chamois skin.

THE STOVE

HEATING.—The care of a new stove and new cast-ironware, is a good thing to know. It is a decided disappointment to have the cast-iron stove spoiled the first time it is used, and yet it has been done many a time by injudicious heating. The first time apply the heat to the stove and ironware very gradually, else they may snap or warp, and so be ruined.

TO POLISH STOVES.—The cooking-stove is kept bright and nice by thoroughly blackening it once a week, and then by daily brushing. Also rub the nickel-plating with an old woolen cloth. An easier, more brilliant, more durable polish for the stove may be obtained by this method: Having the required amount of blacking, add to it one tablespoonful of vinegar, one-half teaspoonful of sugar, and a shaving of soap half the size of your little finger. Mix these thoroughly. See that the soap dissolves. Now, mix it with enough of the coffee that was left from the last meal to reduce the paste to the consistency required. It is ready for use when properly thinned. The vinegar prevents the dust from flying, and also makes the stove brighter.

A GOOD STOVE-POLISH.—A little soap, such as is used in the kitchen, eases wonderfully the labor of cleaning the stove. The work will be done quickly, and will last much longer than without the soap. Rub a flannel cloth on the soap, then dip it into ordinary stove-blacking that has been powdered, and apply it to the stove, smearing it on evenly and thoroughly. Do the polishing and finishing with a dry cloth.

ANOTHER GOOD POLISH.—This makes a brilliant polish, altho when the stove is heated very hot it does not last long. The stove should be cold when this is used. Have as much powdered blacking as is needed. When ready to use, mix with gasoline. Make the liquid quite thin, as it then spreads well and even. Rub the blacking as you apply it, for the gasoline evaporates very fast, and may dry before you can spread it. The work of rubbing is slight.

TO POLISH WITH PAPER.—Rub your stove with a newspaper instead of with a brush. Save the big paper-bags that you get your groceries in, and use them for polishing the stove. Put your hand half way into one, then ball the other half into the hand. After you have put the blacking on the stove, do the polishing with the paper-bag. When you are done, the hand is clean, and you can burn the bag, so getting it out of the way.

A POLISHING-GLOVE.—To keep the stove looking bright, it should be rubbed every day. A good time for that is just after kindling the fire, before it begins to burn well, and here is a good aid to the work: Get a buckskin mitten, and sew on the band of it several thicknesses of old flannel, or, what is better, a piece of sheepskin, with the wool on, as a polisher.

A STOVE LUSTER.—Stove-polish, when mixed with oil of turpentine, and applied in the usual manner, is blacker, more glossy, and more durable than when mixed with any other liquid. The turpentine prevents rust, and makes an old, rusty stove look as well as new.

TO PREVENT RUST

TO PREVENT STOVES FROM RUSTING.—It is quite difficult to keep the stoves from rusting when they are put away in the spring, unless something is done to keep the rust off. As a good, simple preventive kerosene oil should be used. Dampen a woolen rag with the oil, and then rub the stove well with it.

A BLACK VARNISH.—When it comes time to put away the stoves for the summer, it would be well to give them a coat of black varnish, which will prevent them getting rusted while they are not in use. At a good house-furnishing hardware store get a pint of asphaltum, and, should it be necessary, thin it to the proper consistency with spirits of turpentine. Apply with a paint-brush to the stoves, stovepipe, grates, etc. The iron work about the fireplace is made to look like new by giving it a coat of asphaltum. Indeed, any part about the hearth is improved by its application.

TO KEEP OFF RUST.—Stoves, piping, grates, brass, copper, steel may be kept from rusting when put away, even where it is damp. As a good means use lard and common resin, three tablespoonfuls of lard and one tablespoonful of resin, melted together. While it is melted, apply a very thin coat of it to the articles to be kept.

TO KEEP KNIVES POLISHED.—Many housekeepers have steel table-knives. These are difficult to keep clean from rust, especially if they are used only occasionally, and then laid away for some time before using again. If you would keep such polished steel from rusting after it has been cleaned, and when not in use, you should oil it. Pour sweet-oil on a flannel cloth, not using much oil, just enough to dampen the cloth. Then wipe the articles with that, going over them so as to evenly and slightly oil them. Then lay them away without removing that slight coating of oil.

CARE OF KNIVES.—Here is the way to keep your good set of knives and forks in a good state of preservation, to be used when company comes or on some special occasion. Get a sheet of cotton-batting of common size, or more if needed, and wrap the knives and forks in that. Roll a fold around one knife, then place another on that and wrap that, continuing the process until all are wrapped. Put the bundle in a drawer out of the way of dampness.

A VARNISH TO PREVENT RUST.—Polished iron and steel, that must be laid away, should be so protected that rust can not injure it. Anything that will resist chemical action and can be easily used, will answer the purpose. Paraffine will do this. Melt two ounces of paraffine to a liquid. Have a paint-brush used for this purpose only. Put a slight coat of the melted paraffine on the part to be kept from rust, then lay them away carefully.

SODA PREVENTS RUST.—Steel knives have been found so troublesome that silver-plated ones, which are not nearly so good for cutting, have almost displaced them in the home. And yet every one would rather have a good steel knife, for it cuts better. Those who have steel knives are glad to find that they can be kept from rusting, if they are dipped in a strong solution of baking-soda. Take four tablespoonfuls of soda and one tablespoonful of water. Put the steel into the soda after cleaning it. Work it in the soda, and then take a dry cloth and wipe it dry. Then roll it in a flannel, and keep in a dry place.

TO PREVENT RUST ON PENS.—Steel pens are a source of annoyance. Most inks have acid in them, and this acts on the pen, causing it to rust in a short time. To lessen the rust, and continue the usefulness of a pen, put a new nail into the bottle of ink. The acid will take effect on the nail, and not rust out the pen.

XII—FURNITURE

TO REMOVE STAINS FROM FURNITURE

TO REMOVE WHITE SPOTS.—When the dining-table, window-sill, or any piece of varnished wood becomes discolored and turns white, it may be restored easily. Sprinkle baking-soda on the spot, applying enough to hide the discoloration. Then heat the kitchen shovel, or a flat-iron, or a stove-lid. You must judge of the heat. You do not want to blister the varnish, but to remove the white spot. Hold the heated article close over the spot, but not near enough to burn. When you think the heat has been applied long enough, take it away, and brush off the soda. Usually the spot will be gone. If one application has not removed the stain, apply to it more soda, and another application of the heated article.

TO RESTORE VARNISH.—White spots appear on varnished furniture suddenly. They are disfiguring to the furniture, and it is often a puzzle how to get them out. A good way is to first rub the spot with kerosene oil, which removes any grease or other objectionable substance. You apply the oil with a flannel cloth, then put a few drops of cologne water on the spot; the alcohol in it dissolves the varnish and removes the stain.

DISCOLORED VARNISH.—Varnish on the table, sewing-machine, and other places is often turned white by a hot plate, hot water, or some such cause. It may be easily restored. Mix equal parts of linseed-oil and alcohol, and with this rub the spot until it disappears.

145

WHITE SPOTS ON FURNITURE.—A good chair may be spoiled by having the varnish turn white from steam, or steam heat, or water. Take spirits of camphor and rub the white spots with it.

TO REMOVE MARKS FROM FURNITURE.—In spite of all care, ink marks will get on the writing-table or desk. If the stain is on the wood, it may be taken off with little trouble. This applies to any piece of furniture stained with ink. Make a saturated solution of oxalic acid, wet the cloth with the solution, and rub the stains, letting the acid remain on the spots a few minutes. Then rub them with a cloth wet in warm water.

TO REMOVE SCRATCHES FROM VARNISH.—Furniture requires care to keep it nice when children are around, or when it is moved often, for under such circumstances the varnish is apt to become scratched. When varnish is blistered by heat the effect is to leave a mark as of powdered varnish. It is easy to remove such scratches or marks. Have camphor made with alcohol, dip a sponge or cloth in it, and rub the mark well. The alcohol dissolves the varnish and so removes the scratch.

TO REMOVE INK STAINS FROM FURNITURE.—If any piece of furniture is stained with ink, use this to remove it: Add to a teaspoonful of water six drops of niter, and apply to the stain with a feather. When the ink disappears rub the spot with a wet cloth, as the niter will leave a white spot if you do not remove it. If the ink does not disappear at once, make the mixture stronger, and try again.

FURNITURE POLISH

A FURNITURE RUB.—The neatness and cleanness of the furniture always has much to do with the good appearance of a room. It is no little care to keep the different articles of furniture found in a home in the proper condition, yet that labor may be lightened by some such simple means as the following. This makes the furniture look like new: Take equal parts of alcohol, linseed-oil, and vinegar, and mix them well. Rub on well with one cloth, and dry it off by rubbing with another cloth.

A FURNITURE POLISH.—Those who take a pride in having their furniture look bright and new, often expend much care and work without attaining the best results. To employ a good polish in such work is only a matter of common wisdom, as it lightens the work and heightens the effect. This polish has been tried during many years with uniformly good results. Eight ounces of linseed-oil, one-half pint of vinegar, one-half ounce of alcohol, one-half ounce of butter of antimony, and one-half ounce of muriatic acid. Mix well together, and apply with a rag. Rub the furniture clean, taking off fly-specks, and other marks, then rub it dry with another clean cloth, until the effect is satisfactory.

A MAHOGANY POLISH.—The reddish-brown color of this wood is very pretty, and, being a hard wood, mahogany is capable of a high polish, and also a very beautiful one. Take one ounce of beeswax, and two ounces of olive-oil. Melt the wax, add the oil, and stir until cool. Rub it on with a cloth.

A SPLENDID POLISH.—There is no better finish for a good piece of wood than a polish. Take half pint of alcohol, half an ounce of resin, half an ounce of gum-shellac, and a few drops of aniline brown, enough to give the desired color. Mix these and let them stand over night, and add three-fourths of a pint of raw linseed-oil, and half a pint of spirits of turpentine. Shake well before using. Apply with a cotton cloth, and rub with a clean cotton cloth.

A SIMPLE RESTORER.—One of the simplest preparations for restoring dull and scratched furniture, is a mixture of turpentine and linseed-oil. It revives the color of the wood, gives a nice gloss, and covers the scratches as well as anything except a thorough scraping and refinishing. It is very easy to use. Take three ounces of linseed-oil, and one ounce of spirits of turpentine, and mix well. Rub it on with one cloth, then rub it in, and dry with another.

TO POLISH A TABLE.—Your dining-room table may be kept in beautiful condition with very little attention. Nothing is of such satisfaction to a housekeeper as a good, natural-wood table, and this is the way to keep it in splendid order: Take one ounce of olive-oil, and one ounce of spirits of turpentine, and mix them well. Rub the table with this mixture once a week, with a flannel.

A SIMPLE POLISH.—Should you wish to renew the old bed, bureau, washstand, or table and chairs, it can be easily done, and you can do the task as well as anybody. Here is a good, simple polish: Two ounces of olive-oil, two ounces of vinegar, and one teaspoonful of gum arabic. Dissolve the gum arabic in the vinegar, and mix them all together. Apply with one cloth, then rub dry, and polish with another.

A FURNITURE LUSTER.—This mixture brings out the original color of the wood, adding a luster equal to that of varnish. When it fades, take a fine piece of cork, and rub over it, and you will bring out the rich color again. Take two ounces of beeswax, put it into a vessel over a moderate fire, and let it melt. Take from the fire, and add four ounces of spirits of turpentine, stirring the mixture until cool. Apply it with cotton flannel, and polish with a clean cloth.

ANOTHER GOOD POLISH.—This is especially good on dining-room tables, as anything hot will not affect it. If the table has been varnished, it would be well to take it off before applying the polish, as then you would get the best effects. If the varnish is French polish, it would have to come off before applying this polish. Half an ounce of gum arabic, dissolved in four tablespoonfuls of vinegar; one pint of raw linseed-oil, and one ounce of spirits of turpentine. Mix them well. For the first week, apply it at night, and let it stand until morning. Then rub it with linen cloths. Apply it many times for the desired effect.

TO CLEAN FURNITURE

FINGER-MARKS.—A nice chair or a parlor table may be very much disfigured by dirty finger-marks. Do not use soap and water to remove them. A little olive-oil will remedy the matter in short order. Put a few drops of olive-oil on a flannel cloth, and rub it over the marks. This leaves the furniture clean and glossy.

TO CLEAN FURNITURE.—Furniture that has not been varnished may be beautifully cleaned by an application of kerosene oil. It will bring out the natural color, and show the grain. The odor will soon evaporate. Moisten a cloth with the oil, and with it rub the article.

TO WASH FURNITURE.—Furniture may get in thát condition, from moisture and dust, when it may be much improved by being washed with clear water that has been heated until only tepid. Apply this with a soft cloth. Be very particular to wipe the article dry at once. Polish with a dry cloth; a chamois skin is better.

USING POLISHES.—The mistake people make in using all kinds of polishes, oils, or anything of the sort for furniture, is that they act on the principle that if a little does good, a larger amount will do better. So they cover the surface, fill the cracks, and besmear inside and outside of any article they may have to put in order. Do not put polish or oil directly on the furniture. Put it on a cloth, and then never in sufficient quantity to have it run down upon the surface of the wood. This work is not without fatigue. It means hard, patient labor. Apply a little oil, or polish, and do a large amount of rubbing. Fine wood cabinets should be wiped out with a soft cloth, and the corners should be brushed with a small hair whisk. If the surface has been polished, and has grown dull from use and exposure, it may be brightened by going over it with a flannel that has been moistened with linseed-oil. Surfaces that have been varnished are more difficult to deal with, as they are apt to become sticky and rough by the use of many preparations on the market. The simple application of linseed-oil, as advised above, and then a good rubbing, is sufficient for them.

TO CLEAN A SEWING-MACHINE.—After much use a sewing-machine becomes gummy and sticky, with an accumulation of oil and dust. It is certainly not an object of beauty when thus neglected, but it may easily be made as bright and clean as new, and without much trouble. Wet a flannel rag with coal-oil, and apply it to the oily dirt. If it is very much caked, put a few drops of coal-oil on it, and let it stand an hour or two, then apply the rag, and it will soon come off.

TO RENEW FURNITURE.—Plush-covered and hair-covered furniture will become worn, and look shabby. The back of a rocking-chair, where the head rests, soon becomes dirty with grease. There is one good way of remedying this. Put on a new cover. The most serviceable material is the striped linen sold for the purpose. Cut exact paper patterns of each piece of furniture, fitting the seats before cutting the linen covers. Baste the pieces together, and fit them before stitching. Turn the seams on the right side, and bind with braid, so avoiding unsightly edges. You can easily do this yourself.

THE PIANO

PIANO KEYS.—When the ivory keys on the piano begin to turn yellow, wet a cotton-flannel cloth with cologne-water, and with it wash them carefully and repeatedly. On bright, sunny days open the piano, and that will aid in keeping the keys from turning yellow.

TO BLEACH IVORY KEYS.—By constant contact with the fingers the piano and organ keys absorb grease and perspiration from the hand, and that is what turns them yellow. With the proper care that ugly stain ought to be removed, with the cause that produces it. Make a saturated solution of potash (you get it at a drug store) and enough whiting to answer your purpose. Mix the whiting into a paste with the solution of potash. Have it thick as putty. Put it on the keys, and let it remain over night. In the morning remove it. Polish the keys with prepared chalk.

STAINS ON IVORY.—You may have to persist in the application of any method in order to remove old stains from ivory. Some innocent acid laid upon ivory that has become yellow, will restore it to its former freshness. If the stain is not removed at first, make another application, and repeat it until the whiteness is restored to the ivory. Take as much coarse sawdust as is needed, and thoroughly saturate it with lime juice (lemon juice may be used if the limes are not to be had). Lay the sawdust on the keys, and let it remain all night. Remove it in the morning, and, if the case needs it, add fresh lime juice. Polish the ivory with whiting, rubbing with a chamois skin, or piece of cotton flannel.

A GOOD BLEACH.—Whatever the cause of discoloration in the piano keys, it may be removed, no matter how old the stains are. Make a saturated solution of oxalic acid and water. Saturate a sufficient piece, or pieces, of cotton flannel, with the acid, and lay the cotton flannel on the keys. Watch it, and when the stains disappear, remove it. If needed, wet the cotton in the acid again, and make another application. This is a great bleacher, and care must be taken to keep it from touching anything from which you do not wish the color removed. If by accident it should discolor something, refer to chapter entitled "Removing Stains," for a method to remove it.

ANOTHER WAY TO CLEAN PIANO KEYS.—Whether the keys of the piano or organ are discolored or not, it is a good practise to keep them clean, as that will aid in preventing them getting stained. Dampen a soft piece of muslin with alcohol, and with it rub the keys. Do this as often as needed; it can do no harm to the keys.

CARE OF THE PIANO.—The piano should not be neglected. A little neglect in that part of the furniture may be costly. Moisture is the greatest enemy to the piano, and it can not be too carefully guarded against. Put it in a dry room, or in damp weather make a fire where it is kept. It is best not to place the piano close against the wall of a room. A piano should stand two or three inches out from a wall, so that it can get plenty of air. From one to two hours exercise a day will keep a piano at its best condition. When you dust it use an old silk handkerchief, as it is not likely to scratch the varnish.

WICKERWARE

TO CLEAN WILLOW FURNITURE.—Wickerware is pretty, and the wicker chair is easy and cool, but it soon gets soiled, and looks old and shabby. When the willow or wicker chair, and any other willowware, becomes soiled, it may be cleaned with salt and water. Take as much water as will go over the article to be cleansed, then add enough salt to it to make a strong brine. Apply this to the article with a brush, such as you scrub with. Scrub it well, then dry it, and place it in the shade.

TO TIGHTEN CANE SEATS.—It is easy to tighten the cane seats of chairs. Turn the chair upside down, having ready enough hot water. Take the scrubbing-brush, and with the hot water, wash the cane until it becomes thoroughly saturated. If it should need cleaning, soap will not hurt the cane. Let it dry in the shade out in the air, and it will become tight and firm as when it was new.

TO BLEACH WILLOW CHAIRS.—You can easily restore your willow chairs to their original beauty, if they have become discolored. Get two ounces of chlorine, a powerful bleaching agent, from the drug store. Put this in one quart of water, and with it wash the chair, or other willowware you wish to bleach. If the chairs are dirty, they could be washed with warm water to which has been added *aqua ammonia*, or salt, if the latter is more convenient than the ammonia. Use the scrubbing-brush in this cleaning process. When through with the bleaching and cleaning, rinse the article with clear, cold water, and dry in the shade.

TO REPAIR FURNITURE

TO REMOVE SCRATCHES.—You can fill the scratches on furniture and woodwork, and then the article will look fresh and new. Take an ounce of beeswax and melt. Add enough spirits of turpentine to reduce it to the consistency of molasses, and apply it with a flannel cloth. Then take a clean flannel cloth, and rub the article briskly until dry.

TO REMOVE BRUISES FROM FURNITURE.—Heat and moisture combined will raise the bruises or dents that have been made in a piece of furniture by a blow, when the fiber of the wood has not been fractured. Wet a cloth in warm water and lay several thicknesses of it upon the bruise. Then place upon or hold near the cloth a warm iron. See that it is not too hot. A few applications of this kind will swell the wood to its natural position and condition. If by that process the varnish is turned white, and there is no doubt that it will be, rub the spot with any preparation commended in this chapter.

BUREAU DRAWS.—What an annoyance it is to have the bureau draws catch and hitch when they are opened! That may all be easily avoided. Take a piece of any soap and rub it on those parts of the bureau draw that fit too tightly. Put the soap also on the under part of the drawer where it slides. Then it will not squeak.

CREAKING BEDSTEADS.—A good bed is one of the essentials to health and happiness, but both are diminished by sleeping on a bedstead that squeaks and snaps when the occupant changes position. There is nothing easier of accomplishment than the stopping of that noise, if the trouble is with the slats. Take the offending slat or slats out, and wrap the ends with any kind of paper, or a cloth, and then replace them, fitting them tightly into the proper notch.

XIII—PICTURES AND FRAMES

TO RESTORE FRAMES

TO REMOVE FLY-SPOTS.—Sometimes a gilt picture-frame is as good as new in the gilding, yet it is unsightly because of the fly-spots upon it, which make it look old. Here is the approved way to remove these spots: Get a soft brush, like a camel's-hair pencil, dip it into alcohol, and apply it to the spots. This softens them. Now take a soft cloth, and rub the frame lightly until the spots are removed.

TO CLEAN GILT.—When gilt frames, or molding, become dirty from dust, or flies, they cease to be objects of beauty. If the gilt is worn it may be restored. Take the white of an egg, beat it with a fork until it is broken, then dip a soft cloth into it, and gently wipe the spots and dirt from the gilt. A large camel's-hair brush will answer for the cloth.

TO KEEP FLIES AWAY.—Flies may be kept away from gilt frames in this way. Early in the spring, about the time the flies begin to appear, or at any time you choose when flies are about, use this simple method: Boil any number of onions you wish; take the water in which they have been boiled, and gently wash the frames with it. A soft brush is best.

TO RENEW GILT FRAMES.—Should a gilt frame be very much discolored, there is only one proper way to restore it, and that is to regild it. If the matter is not worth that trouble and expense, the use of a little bronze powder may answer the purpose. Take care to select the best quality of powder and the exact color you wish. There is a special liquid that goes with the powder. In mixing it yourself you know what you have. Brush that mixture over the frame or molding. It will look well for some time, and have the effect obtained by regilding. Use a camel's-hair brush in applying it.

TO RESTORE GILT FRAMES.—When a picture-frame that has been covered with gold leaf becomes defaced by insects, or looks rusty, the spots may be removed in the following simple way: Dip a camel's-hair brush in alcohol and apply it to the spots, brushing over them gently until removed. Sometimes these frames have to be cleansed of dust and that soiling, which is caused by humid weather following a dusty season. Do this with a soft sponge moistened with alcohol, the sponge not too wet. It must also be lightly used on the gilt as you brush off the stains.

TO CLEAN GILT.—Dull gilding may be treated in this way: First it should be carefully dusted, then take a saturated solution of concentrated lye and water, not too strong, and into this dip a piece of clean flannel. With that clean the gilt; do not let the lye stand on the gilt, but quickly wipe it dry with a piece of soft linen. If any of the coating has come off the frame, exposing the wood, the spots may be perfectly hid by being painted over with gold-paint, which may be obtained at any drug store or novelty shop. Should you wish to replace the stucco, moisten the spot with glue, and lay on it the required amount of putty. Let it harden, then touch it with the gold-paint.

TO RETOUCH GILT FRAMES.—If the frame is rubbed or chipped, and you wish to restore the gilt, take isinglass, which is a form of gelatine (get it at the drug store), dissolve it in wood-alcohol, and with that dampen the chipped place.

Watch it, and just before it dries lay gold-leaf upon it, and press the gold gently with a soft clean cloth. Let this stand until it is dry, and then secure a burnisher, such as a shoemaker uses, and polish the gold. If you do not care to remedy the break in that way, it can be done with effect equal to regilding by using liquid gold-paint, which can be secured at any drug store or first-class paint store.

REGILDING.—Should the gilt molding be only slightly tarnished from moisture and dust, make a weak solution of salts of tartar in water, and apply it to the frame with a piece of cotton batting, brushing over it lightly; then rinse well with cold water. If the picture molding is so badly defaced as to need regilding, it may be done in the following manner: Rub the molding with sandpaper, dusting off any particles that may be left upon the frame from the sandpaper, and apply one coat of shellac-varnish. When that is dry, apply one coat of Japanese gold-size, which you can make yourself by dissolving isinglass, as described in "Retouching Gilt Frames," given above. Before the size has quite dried apply gold-leaf. Ball a piece of cotton batting in your hand, lay a piece of gold-leaf upon it, and so lay it upon the frame, pressing the leaf slightly to make it stick to the size. Make each application of leaf overlap the adjoining one. When dry enough, go over the frame, gold-leaf and all, with a coat of shellac-varnish, as this will protect the new gilt from damage through vapors and dirt.

TO PROTECT GILT FRAMES.—It is almost impossible to keep the gilt frame from getting dirty. Somehow, in spite of the greatest diligence, they become soiled. They may be so protected as to cause little trouble from dust, by giving them a coat of white varnish, when the frames are new. Then if fly-specks or dust get on them, they may be washed off with weak suds and tepid water.

BLACK WALNUT FRAMES.—Natural-wood frames are very pretty, and may be kept clean and new looking with a little care. Walnut frames are perhaps prettier than others in natural wood, and are more used than any of the others. When the walnut frame becomes dull and rusty looking, it may be renewed by dusting off the dirt. Then dampen a woolen rag with linseed-oil and rub carefully over it. Should it be varnished, and that has been chipped, go over it with sandpaper, smoothing down the rough places. Have a fine quality of sandpaper, so as not to scratch too deep. Dust the frame, and apply a coat of shellac-varnish to it. It will then appear as good as new.

CLEANING PICTURES

TO CLEAN CHROMOS.—If showing the effects of damp and dust, which cause the chromo to look dim and dirty, some simple remedy like the following will in most cases clean it, and bring out the original beauty. Slightly dampen a linen cloth (be careful not to get it too wet), and with that go over the picture, bearing on only gently. If the varnish has become defaced, it may be renewed by a coat of quick-drying varnish, usually known as "mastic varnish."

ANOTHER WAY TO CLEAN CHROMOS.—As chromos are usually printed upon paper, care must be exercised in wetting them. Make a towel slightly moist, and lay it upon the face of the picture until the dirt is completely loosened. Then remove the towel, and carefully rub the dirt with a moist linen cloth. If the dirt still adheres, replace the towel. Repeat this process until the dirt is off. Then moisten a cloth with linseed-oil and rub the picture with it, and it will look like new.

TO PRESERVE A CANVAS.—With age a canvas becomes dry and loses its strength, when it is easily broken or punctured. Such canvases should be strengthened that they may remain intact for years. A new canvas should be so treated as to prevent early decay. Give the back of the canvas two thick coats of white lead, or any preparation that has tenacity and strength.

TO CLEAN OIL-PAINTINGS.—An oil-painting should be treated with great care. A painting in oil has a coat of white varnish applied, which makes it easier to clean when dirty. If the painting is disfigured with fly specks and dust, it may be cleansed by washing. Take as much sweet milk as is needed, and make it lukewarm by adding warm water. With a sponge dipped into this wash off the dirt, going over the canvas carefully and lightly. The milk is the most delicate kind of oil, and not only softens and loosens the dirt, but adds a finish as if oiled in the ordinary way. Dry the canvas.

ANOTHER WAY TO CLEAN OIL-PAINTINGS.—It requires great care to clean oil-paintings. It is difficult to remove such accumulations as smoke, grime, and such stains. There is one process known, however, that does not require the utmost caution in its use to keep from doing some little harm to the picture. Soap should not be used, as it mixes with the oil in paint, and is apt to make the colors fade. The best way is to wash the painting gently with clear water, using a soft cloth, and then, after it has dried, to rub it with a clean cloth moistened with fresh olive-oil. The oil will remove some accumulations from the picture that the water has softened, and it contains nothing to fade the colors.

TO TRANSFER PICTURES

HOW TO TRANSFER.—Colored or plain engravings, photographs, water colors, oil colors, crayons, steel plates, newspaper cuts, mezzotints, pencil writing, showcards, labels can be transferred to glass in the following manner: Take glass of the size and shape you desire. Have it perfectly clear; window-glass will answer. Clean it thoroughly and then varnish, taking care to have the varnish perfectly smooth. Place it to dry where it will be perfectly free from dust, and let it stand over night. Take your engraving and lay it in water until it is wet through. It may have to lay in water ten or fifteen minutes.

Treat a photograph in the same way until the picture leaves the card. Then lay it upon a newspaper, face downward, so that the moisture may dry from the surface, and still keep the other side damp. Varnish the glass the second time at once. Then, before it dries, place your engraving, face downward, on the varnished side of the glass, pressing it down firmly, so as to exclude every particle of air. Then rub the paper from the back until it is of uniform thickness, making it so thin that you can see through it. Put a coat of varnish over it, and let it dry, and then it may stand. The picture so transferred may be put in a frame or mounted as desired. This process refers only to such pictures as are upon paper or card ; canvases are not included. Be careful that the varnish you use is a quick-drying, white kind, as a yellow varnish would show and spoil the effect of the picture.

TO MAKE PICTURE-FRAMES

A PLUSH PICTURE-FRAME.—This will form a pretty frame, and it does not require any great skill to make it. At any carpenter-shop you can find plain molding. Choose whatever shape or pattern that suits you. You can use your own skill or have a carpenter make the molding into any desired shape frame. Smear the sides and front of the frame with glue. Take whatever color of plush you wish, and cut it into strips the shape of the frame. Then fit it on the frame before it is glued. Lay those strips down on the half-dried glue, where it will stick, pressing them down evenly over the molding. Let the frame stand until dry before handling much.

A RIBBON FRAME.—Framed photographs are a very attractive decoration. These frames are very appropriate for the children's photographs. Have a piece of clear window-glass cut the size of the picture. Select any pretty ribbon you prefer that is three-quarters of an inch wide; bind around the edge of the glass, and secure it by a few stitches at the corners, concealing the joinings with bows. These may be made into panels, if desired. The picture is put in place by slipping under the ribbon at the back of the frame.

CANVAS FRAMES.—Picture-frames of various shapes may be easily made at little expense. Cut heavy pasteboard into any size and shape desired, and fit gray canvas over it. Then daub the frame with glue, and when it is nearly dry, put the canvas on the frame, pressing it down so as to make it stick. When it is dry, any favorite flower may be painted upon the surface, or, if preferred, the flowers may be worked upon the canvas before it is stretched upon the frame.

A GILT FRAME.—An attractive and inexpensive frame is not difficult to make. Have a carpenter join a piece of pine molding, or plain pine, into any shaped frame desired, and cover the front and sides with a coat of varnish. When the varnish is dry, give the frame a coat or two of gold-paint. Should you prefer, while the varnish is still wet, sprinkle it heavy with sand, rice, or oatmeal, then, when thoroughly dry, give the surface a coat of gold or silver-paint. Put on as many coats of gold or silver as seem necessary to make the effect perfect. Let the frame become thoroughly dry before handling.

ORNAMENTS ON FRAMES.—Ornaments on gilt frames may be done with the proper paste — one that can be pressed into any form required. The following will answer perfectly: Boil together in a kettle two pounds of resin, one pint of linseed-oil, and one gill of Venice turpentine, which is a kind that has a tendency to solidify. Dissolve one pound of glue in one gallon of water, and mix it with the above ingredients. Continue to boil and stir together until the water has evaporated from the other ingredients, and then take from the fire, and add finely pulverized whiting, until the mass is brought to the consistency of soft putty. This composition is hard when cold, but when warmed it can be molded into any shape.

TO FRAME CUTS.—Newspapers often contain admirable pictures of great persons in whom we are interested enough to desire having their picture. Clip out those cuts, and mount them on a photographer's card. Then glue to the mounted picture a frame made of canvas, as above described. Ribbon tied around the edges, with bows at the corners, looks pretty.

HANGING PICTURES

THE POSITION OF THE PICTURE.—Pictures should not be hung so as to make it necessary to mount upon something in order to view them. Hang your picture so that its center will be about five feet and one-half from the floor, on a level with the line of vision of a person of average height.

A GOOD EFFECT.—Hang a picture so as to give a symmetrical effect, and make the walls look finished. Then never hang a picture from one nail. Aside from the matter of mere safety, it is better to use two nails. Let the cord stretch across them, so as to come down squarely to the corners of the frame. That gives the impression of carefulness and completeness.

PICTURES IN GENERAL.—In furnishing your house, pictures for adorning the walls should not be forgotten. A great variety of beautiful engravings and etchings are within the reach of all, and the matter of framing them is only a trifle of expense. It seems strangely neglectful that so many homes are without pictures, except of an inferior kind, on the order of the poorest sort of chromo that has no special form or color in it, but is simply a mass of colors and shapes thrown together.

ARRANGING PICTURES.—The primary purpose in hanging pictures is to ornament the walls. So, when hanging water-color paintings, engravings, and photographs, that object should be kept in view. Remember that it is not necessary for good effect that they should be placed close together. It is thought by those who claim to have taste in such matters, that it is better to separate the pictures by such small objects as wooden brackets, or a fixed hanging as a sconce. The brackets should support statuettes. A very pretty method is to divide the wall space with various sizes of right-angled panels, by means of flat moldings, then fill each space with a picture that is of the proper size and shape. The effect is very striking and artistic. This is especially adapted to etchings and engravings, but may be used for any kind of picture. A stenciled ornament may be used instead of the molding, in making the panels, if desired.

XIV—CARPETS

CARPETS IN GENERAL

TO MAKE CARPETS LAST.—It should be a matter of pride in housekeeping to exercise ingenuity in the management of carpets in order to make them last well. Here is a good method. When a carpet begins to show wear, rip out the seams and change the strips about, putting the least worn strips where the most worn ones are. This makes the carpet last twice as long as it otherwise would.

A CHEAP CARPET.—There are rooms on which a housekeeper does not want to put a good carpet. Yet, if a good cheap one was easily obtained, there would be no hesitation in putting it down. Here is a carpet that will not cost much, and yet it will look well. Place upon the floor the carpet-paper commonly used. Take stout cotton-jean, or any other kind of goods, sew the strips together the length wanted, and tack down to the floor. It may be dyed any color before being sewed. Such a carpet will last during the summer, and look well.

SELECTING CARPETS.—It is never wise to select a carpet the pattern of which is of extra large roses or any other actual flower. You would find that such a carpet could not be made to harmonize with anything in the room. The pattern and colors of a carpet should be selected to harmonize with the room, and, as far as possible, to be in harmony with the colors adopted for the room. Guard against having a dark carpet and dark walls in a room that is deficient in light. Only rooms open to the outside light will permit gloomy tones in decora-

164

tion. In a community where the air is laden with smoke, light-colored carpets should always be selected, as the smoke soon deepens the tone, and it does not seem too light, as at first, and yet it is light enough to look pretty and bright and clean.

CARE OF CARPETS.—Carpets on the floors look nice, are comfortable, and almost a necessity. Yet how often one is nearly choked, when walking on some carpets, so full of must, dust, and bad odor are they. Beware of a dusty, musty carpet. Better have a sweet, pure room and a bare floor, than such a carpet.

DUSTING CARPETS

TO BEAT A CARPET.—A heavy, closely-woven carpet should be beaten on the wrong side first. Do this as thoroughly as possible. Then beat gently on the right side. A bunch of heavy switches, such as hickory, is the best instrument to beat with, as there is danger of punching holes in the carpet if a stick is used. Of course, it is understood that the carpet is thrown over a clothes-line when the dust is being beaten out.

TO DUST RUGS.—Rugs are pretty, and when properly laid, add much to the comfortable appearance of the room. Yet they require to be cared for in order to keep them nice and attractive. But remember, in cleaning the rugs, they should be handled by the middle when shaken; if they are caught by the ends they soon tear out and begin to unravel.

SHAKE YOUR CARPETS OFTEN.—To handle carpets is not so much trouble as it seems. Those whose business it is make quick work of cleaning and putting them down. Carpets should be shaken often; the oftener they are shaken, the longer they wear, as the dirt that collects under them grinds out the thread quickly.

SWEEPING CARPETS

USING TEA-LEAVES.—In sweeping light-colored carpet, remember not to use tea-leaves on it, as they will surely leave a stain. If the carpet is of dark color or yellow tints, damp tea-leaves scattered over it before sweeping will improve the colors, and give it a fresh, clean look. In any case do not let them stand long on the carpet.

TO MOP THE CARPET.—The cleaner the carpets can be gotten the better. One thorough cleaning makes cleaning less frequent and easier, and then it is satisfactory when it is done. Not every housekeeper likes to add to that kind of work, yet it is shown to be the best method to be thoroughgoing. After the carpets have been carefully and thoroughly swept, take a flannel mop that is slightly damp, and with it wipe them well. This will remove all lint and dust, and brighten the colors.

SALT ON CARPET.—It is known that some small, loose substance thrown upon the carpets before sweeping adds greatly to the ease of gathering up the dust, and also of keeping the dust from rising. If the carpets are sprinkled quite liberally with salt before the sweeping begins, it will be found that not very much dust will arise, and that the carpets will be decidedly brightened. The salt does no harm.

WHEN SWEEPING THE STAIRS.—To keep the stairs clean is a troublesome task, and yet it is important, as they are open to the gaze of strangers, in the way many houses are built in these times. The common broom is too unwieldly in such close quarters. The stairs, and the carpet on the stairs, should be swept with a short-handled brush, or a good whisk, at the same time holding a dust-pan at each step to catch the dirt. The corners are difficult to reach, and when the best effort has been made, they still look dusty. Tack into each corner a triangular block of some ornamental wood. The blocks need only be large enough to fill the corner an inch or two, or not that much, if preferred.

GRASS IN SWEEPING.—Should the carpet be light-colored, and likely to be stained by tea-leaves during the summer and fall months, take the freshly-cut grass from the lawn and scatter it over the carpet when about to sweep. In sweeping it prevents dust from rising, and helps to take up the dirt. Grass is better than tea-leaves or salt as an aid in sweeping.

PAPER IN SWEEPING.—For sweeping a carpet neatly there is nothing better than scraps of paper. Take one page of newspaper at a time, dip it into hot water, and squeeze it until it does not drip. Then tear it into pieces about the size of one's hand, and throw them about over the carpet quite thickly. As you sweep most of the dust on the carpet will adhere to the paper, and be taken up with it. In sweeping matting, use large pieces of paper and brush them on ahead of the broom as you sweep, so that they may take up any lint and dust that have gathered about over the floor. If the sweeping is done carefully, once going over in that way will be sufficient.

TO CLEAN CARPET

AMMONIA ON CARPETS.—During the winter coal-dust and small particles of ashes make the carpet dull and faded-looking. So it is well every now and then to give the carpet a cleaning, restoring its colors and beauty. Into two quarts of warm water put two ounces of ammonia, and apply it with a clean floorcloth, rubbing it well into the carpet. This will clean and brighten the carpet.

NAPHTHA ON CARPET.—Where there are children the carpets often become spotted with dirt and grease, for it is next to impossible to keep the little ones from throwing crumbs of bread and butter on the floor. Use naphtha to remove such dirt from the carpets. Rub it well into the dirt-spot with a stout flannel cloth, making two applications, if the first does not remove the stain. The naphtha soon evaporates, leaving the spot clean. Do not handle naphtha around a flame of any kind, as it ignites very quickly.

TURPENTINE AND TEA.—Take a cupful of cold tea; add to it one tablespoonful of spirits of turpentine, and put them into two quarts of warm water. Dip a scrubbing-brush or a broom into the mixture, and go over the carpet, giving it a thorough rubbing.

SALT ON MATTING.—Matting can be made to look fresh and clean as new if it is simply soiled. Of course, if it is worn, nothing can restore it. Make a strong solution of salt and warm water, as much as is needed. Dip a cloth into that solution; wring it so as not to have it dripping wet. With that go over one strip at a time, drying the washed part as you go with a clean cloth. Do not get the matting soaking wet.

KEROSENE ON CARPET.—To remove kerosene from carpet, lay blotting-paper or soft brown paper over the spot and press it with a hot iron. Repeat the process with fresh paper until the spot is removed.

TO WIPE CARPET.—In the general cleaning, before taking up a carpet, it should be thoroughly swept, as the dirt is removed more easily while the carpet is down. After it has been thoroughly beaten, wipe the carpet carefully. Take one ounce of ammonia, and put it in one quart of warm water; dip a sponge in that, squeeze it nearly dry, and wipe the carpet with it. This removes what dirt adheres, and brightens the colors of the carpet.

TO BRIGHTEN COLORS.—If you have no ammonia at hand, and you wish to enliven the colors of the carpet, use soda or alum. Make a weak solution in water and rub it on with a small scrubbing-brush, using little at a time, so as not to make the carpet too wet. Then rub it with a clean dry cloth to dry the carpet.

TO REMOVE GREASE FROM CARPET.—Here is a method many old folks use, but it is as good as new: Take the grease out of carpets by covering the spots with powdered French chalk. a quarter of an inch deep. Lay blotting paper over the chalk, and lay on all a hot iron; let it stand until cold. The chalk and paper absorb the heated grease.

A GOOD CARPET CLEANSER.—Thoroughly sweep the dingy carpet and remove what you can of the coarse dirt in an ordinary way. Then wipe it well and carefully with this simple mixture: Take two tablespoonfuls of ox-gall (you can get it at a drug store), and four quarts of lukewarm water. Mix well. Dip a cloth in the mixture, wring it so it will not drip, and with that wipe the carpet.

A GOOD GENERAL CLEANER.—Here is a good general cleaner. It can be used on clothes, good also to wash paints, carpets, and like things. Take one-half a bar of good soap, a tablespoonful each of sal-soda and saltpeter, two quarts of soft water at boiling heat, and put these things into the water, stirring them until dissolved. Let the mixture cool, and then add three ounces of *aqua ommonia*. Bottle for use, and apply as usual.

OX-GALL.—Among the many things used for cleaning and renewing the colors of carpets there is nothing better than ox-gall properly applied. Take a small portion of one strip of the carpet at a time, and clean as directed. One gill of ox-gall should be put into two gallons of cold water when ordinary cleaning is done. If the carpet is very dirty, the mixture may be made stronger. One quart of ox-gall should be added to three quarts of soft cold water. A very dirty spot should be rubbed with pure ox-gall, using a clean flannel or house-cloth, but the weaker mixture may be rubbed into the carpet with a clean brush. It makes a lather, which must be wiped off with clean cold water, then rubbed dry with a dry clean cloth. Do not soak the carpet.

TO CLEAN INGRAIN CARPET.—Should the ingrain carpet get too wet while being cleaned, it will not pull the tacks out as Brussels carpet will, but it is not necessary to saturate either. Have the bare floor thoroughly cleansed, then, after the carpet has been properly beaten and swept, lay it down on the bare floor, spreading it out even. Wash the soiled spots with soap and hot water. Rub the soap on the spots, dip a small-sized scrubbing-brush into the water (do not have the brush too wet), rub the spots well and dry them as soon as scrubbed. With a damp brush and soapy water go all over the carpet. Then take a cloth wrung out of clear water, and wipe over the carpet, getting off all traces of the soap, as the cleaning will look more uniform. Wipe the carpet dry with clean dry cloths. If you prefer, wrap a hot iron in the cloth used.

A GOOD METHOD WITH SOAP.—The success of cleaning carpet depends largely upon the way it is done. As a good general method, here is a suggestion for cleaning without removing the carpet from the floor: Take a piece of soap made from the formula named "Soap For All Purposes." Have a basin of warm water, and take two towels, one wet with the warm water and the other dry. Take one section or strip of carpet at a time, go over it with the damp towel and simply moisten the carpet. Now take the dry soap and rub it all over the damp surface, then, with a wet cloth, rub vigorously over the part that has been soaped. A lather will be made, which must be wiped away with the damp towel. It may take several wipings to remove it well. Finish by wiping with the dry towel, making the carpet as dry as you can in that way. Go over each section of the carpet in this way until it is all clean.

TO SCOUR CARPETS.—After a carpet has been dusted and shaken, it may be necessary to scrub it. Lay it back on a clean floor. Take a basin of warm water, add to it a tablespoonful of kerosene-oil, dip a hair scrubbing-brush into this and go over the carpet. Wipe it as dry as possible.

A GOOD CLEANING MIXTURE.—When everything is ready to commence, use this to clean the carpet, as it will both take out the dirt and brighten the colors. Take two quarts of water, slice into it two pounds of "Soap For All Purposes," add to that one-half pound of washing-soda, and boil until these are completely mixed, making one. When the preparation is luke-warm, add to it half a pint of *aqua ammonia* and half a pint of alcohol. Apply it as directed in "A Good Method" given above.

TO CLEAN RUGS.—Lay the rug face down on a clean bare floor, then take a carpet-beater, such as is described at the end of this chapter, and beat the rug until no dust comes from it and no dirt is left on the floor when you are through the last beat-ing. Take a hair scrubbing-brush, dip it into kerosene oil, and rub it on the face of the rug to brighten it. Hang it outdoors to dry.

TO CLEAN TAPESTRY. — Tapestries hung upon the walls catch the dust. Take gasoline in a shallow tin, dip into it a clean hair scrubbing-brush, and brush over the goods; it will brighten the colors and clean the goods. It will keep off moths as well. Keep away from fire with gasoline.

TO CLEAN OILCLOTH

HOW TO WASH OILCLOTH.—Oilcloth should never be scrubbed; strong soap should not be used on it, nor should hot water be used in cleaning it, as these things dim the colors, and also take off the paint. Wash the oilcloth with a flannel cloth and tepid water, and dry it thoroughly. Then go over it with a rag dipped in skimmed milk and wrung slightly.

TO REMOVE WHITE SPOTS.—Anything hot placed on oilcloth will turn it white. The spot is unsightly, and should be removed. If you have no alcohol at hand, put a few drops of spirits of camphor on the spot, and rub it with a dry cloth. The alcohol in the camphor is the remedy.

TO MAKE OILCLOTH LAST.—When the oilcloth is new, take care to wash it as directed above, and then, before it begins to show signs of wear, give it a good coat of varnish, letting it dry before sweeping. Apply the varnish twice during the year. With a good oilcloth to begin with, such usage will make it last as long again as it would otherwise. Put on a thick, good coat of the varnish.

ANOTHER WAY.—To make oilcloth last, and look well, fit it to the room in which you want it, and then take it to a room not used much, and give it two coats of boiled linseed-oil, using a new paint-brush to apply it. Let one coat dry before applying another. When the oil is dry, add a coat of varnish. When that is dry the oilcloth may be put down on the floor.

LINOLEUM.—Linoleum is better than oilcloth for the kitchen or dining-room floor, as it lasts longer and looks better, and, in the long run, it is cheaper. If you wish to keep it looking fresh and new, take tepid water in a basin, and add to it enough sweet milk to make it of a milky color. Then take a large sponge or soft cloth, dip it into the preparation, and wash the linoleum. Squeeze the sponge quite dry, and with it dry the floor.

KEROSENE ON OILCLOTH.—Some housekeepers keep the oilcloth looking bright and new, but they never put water or soap on it, and it is true that many oilcloths are ruined by too much soap and water, especially hot water. Take a piece of flannel goods, moisten it with kerosene oil, and with that rub the oilcloth thoroughly, making it perfectly clean. You may have to wring the cloth, and dip it in kerosene several times during the process of cleaning. When done with that part of it, take a dry flannel and rub the oilcloth dry. That preserves the freshness and material.

GLAZE AN OILCLOTH.—Glaze the special pieces of oil-cloth, such as the rug under the washstand, the mat under the stove, the strip before the open fireplace. Should you break an egg that does not look fresh, or concerning which you are in doubt about eating, use it for that purpose. Dip a rag in the white, and smear it over the piece of oilcloth. It imparts a nice gloss and pretty finish to the cloth.

TO POLISH OILCLOTH.—This will preserve the oilcloth and give it a beautiful gloss. It will only require dusting for some time after this application: Put two ounces of common glue into a pint of water. Put the vessel containing the glue into a vessel containing some hot water. Put this on the stove, and let it stand until the glue is melted. When it is cold, it should not become thick, but remain in a liquid state. If it should become thick, add water until liquified. First clean the oilcloth, and let it dry thoroughly. Apply the glue by dipping a linen rag into the glue water, and with it rub the oilcloth. Keep off of it until the glue is dry, which should not take long.

KEROSENE AND WATER.—To the housekeeper who does not like to use pure kerosene oil on the oilcloth, we commend the following, as it gives a bright, new look to the cloth: Take four quarts of tepid water, and add to it three tablespoonfuls of kerosene oil. Apply that to the cloth with a piece of soft goods, like cheesecloth, or an old piece of gauze underwear.

BUTTERMILK AS A CLEANSER.—There are many things useful in housekeeping that an ingenious housewife will think about. Among such things is buttermilk, used in washing the oilcloth. Put as much of the milk in a basin as will be needed, and apply it with a soft cloth, rubbing it well on as you go.

CARPET BEATERS

A WIRE BEATER.—Take a piece of wire ten feet long, and one-eighth of an inch in diameter, and twist it around a small handle of a broom, making it the shape of a spring. Then bring the two ends together, which will form a loop. Leave a small portion of the ends straight, so as to fit them into a handle, which may be a piece of soft wood driven on those ends, and shaped so as to hold in the hand. This is a good thing to beat the carpet with when cleaning it.

A WOODEN BEATER.—Get a slender pole, about ten feet in length, of hickory or any other material that bends easily without breaking, and bend it into a loop like a lawn-tennis racket. Bring the ends together so as to form a handle; tie them together, and wrap it with something soft so as to make a good handle. A barrel hoop may be made into this shape, and used for the same purpose. This instrument is to be used in beating carpets so as to loosen the dirt, also to drive it out, when you have your carpets up at the time of house-cleaning. That is a very effective beater, and much used.

PADDING THE STEPS

A GOOD PAD.—Here is a good device to keep the stair carpet from grinding out on the edge of the steps. Take cheese cloth and cut it into pieces to lay well back on the steps, and fall down in front three inches. Make the pieces long enough to fold, put cotton-batting between the fold, and sew them together as you would a quilt. It could be done on the machine. Take a piece of pasteboard five inches wide, and as long as the cheese-cloth strip, and bend it lengthwise down over the edge of the step, lay the pad on it, and tack them both to the step. Fix all the steps that way, and then put down the carpet.

MORE ABOUT PADDING.—The sharp edge of the steps, with the pressure of going up and down, soon wear the carpet bare. Besides it is noisy, and not so nice to step upon. The housewife can find devices of her own effort to aid in saving the carpet, and make the going up and down stairs a matter of more comfort. Get a lot of old newspapers, and fold as many together as will make a soft pad, then tack them on the stair steps in the manner described above, then lay the carpet down on them. This will answer the purpose.

XV—WALLS

SELECTING PAPER

PAPER FOR SMALL ROOMS.—Care should be taken in selecting the paper for the small rooms. Do not lose sight of the size of the room you wish to paper, and select the paper accordingly. Do not paper the walls of a small room with a paper of dark ground and large pattern. Use papers showing small patterns, and grounds of retiring color. In any room, large or small, use such papers as will not make the walls conspicuous. Overshadowing pictures and other ornaments in the room with wall paper, should be avoided.

PAPER SAMPLES.—The small scraps of wall paper that are usually exhibited as samples from which to select a pattern for a room are deceptive. It is not wise to select paper from them, as a selection so made is just as likely as not to make your room look smaller, altho it did not appear that way when seen in the sample. If you are pleased with the sample, before you decide, take a good look at the roll, and have two or three of them opened out before you at one time, so that you may get their full effect. Then decide what you will take.

SUBDUED COLORS.—When the time comes to do the house-papering, take a survey of your rooms, and if you have an apartment that is small, and you wish it to appear large, cover the walls with a paper of subdued color, without any design, but of solid color. If that can not be had, select a paper without any particular design. This causes the walls to be unnoted, and apparently makes them retire, giving the effect of a large room.

TO REPAIR WALL-PAPER

USING GOLD PAINT.—Nothing is more unsightly to the eye of a tidy housekeeper than places where the wall-paper has accidentally been knocked off, and the white wall beneath shows plainly. As a remedy for this defect use gold paint. It is easily and quickly applied, and the eye at any distance can seldom detect the place that is mended. At any drug store you can get a ten-cent paper of the paint, and it will cover hundreds of such spots, and put off for a long time the necessity of putting on new paper.

BROKEN PAPER.—The wall-paper is often disfigured in carrying some large object up the stairs or through the hall. The corner of a trunk, the edge of a piano, may often tear unsightly holes in the wall-paper. When the paper is so torn off or bruised in small patches, it may be repaired by matching it with a piece of the paper that was left over from the general papering. If that can not be done, then it may be repaired with children's paints. Such paints may be gotten at any book store or novelty store. Mix the colors until you get as nearly as possible the shade desired. Then go over the broken places and paint them lightly. If needed go over the places twice. At a distance of two or three feet the broken place or the paint will not be much noticed, if at all.

TO CLEAN WALL-PAPER

TO REMOVE OIL STAINS.—Unaccountable are the ways in which the wall-paper may become stained with grease or oil. Such spots are unsightly, and give the impression of carelessness. To remove them, make a thick paste of powdered pipe-clay and water. If the clay is not at hand, use French chalk, making it into a paste, and spread that thickly on the wall-paper over the grease spot. Let it stand for a few days. Brush the chalk off, and if any trace of the grease remains, apply the chalk paste again and again until the grease is removed.

GREASE ON WALLS.—Grease may be taken from the wall-paper without much trouble. Take several folds of blotting-paper, and lay them on the wall over the spot; then hold a hot iron on the blotting-paper until the grease is absorbed. Be careful not to scorch the paper. Remove the iron once in a while to see if there is any danger of marring the paper. To help the process of absorption, change the blotting-paper about over the grease spot a number of times.

TO CLEAN WALL-PAPER.—Give the walls a good dusting. Then take yeast-bread, two days old, and cut it into thick pieces. With this rub the wall from the top down, making a stroke half a yard in length. Always wipe downward and not across the paper. Wipe lightly, being careful not to rub too hard, and hold the crust part of the bread in your hand, completely cleaning each part as you go. When the bread becomes dirty, cut that part off. Renew the bread as required.

TO CLEAN WALLS

BLACKENED CEILINGS.—A ceiling may be unavoidably blackened. Here is a simple application that may be used on papered walls, or on those unpapered. Make a strong solution of baking-soda and warm water. Dip a cloth in this, and wring it so it will not drip, wiping the ceiling well with the cloth so prepared. This may have to be repeated.

AMMONIA ON WALLS.—Hard-finished walls are pretty, and are preferred by many to papered walls, but being white, as a rule, they show dirt quickly, and then they are objectionable. To remove any stains or dirt spots from the hard-finished wall, take *aqua ammonia* and apply it with a soft cloth, or sponge, rubbing lightly.

TO MEND PLASTERING.—Small pits appear in plastering sometimes and spoil the finish of the walls. Accidents happen to the plastering, leaving small holes. In order to mend such defects, get plaster of Paris. Five cents' worth will mend several dozen such broken places.· Take one tablespoonful of plaster of Paris, add to it three tablespoonfuls of fine sand, and mix them well. Then make quite soft with water, as it hardens quickly; it might harden before you could use it, if not made very soft. Apply it to the broken places with a table-knife, smoothing the plaster as you apply it. The plaster without the sand may be used, if desired.

TO COVER BLACK WALLS.—The walls near the stove often become black, especially in the kitchen. Paint or kalsomine will not hide such spots, for the black will strike through either. The wall must be prepared for the application of any coloring matter like whitewash. The black spots must be covered with a coat of shellac, then the black will not come through. Take gum-shellac and dissolve it in alcohol. Put sufficient alcohol on the shellac to make it thin as paint, and apply the shellac with a varnish-brush, or any clean brush that painters use. When the shellac is dry, apply the paint.

PASTE FOR WALL-PAPER

GOOD WALL-PAPER PASTE.—When using this paste spread it well on the paper, then lay or fold the pasted sides gently together; this makes the paste even, and aids in handling the paper with ease, as it is not so long a piece when so folded. As you put it on the wall, let it unfold. Take three and one-half pounds of flour and one-fourth of a pound of powdered alum, and mix these well together. With a little warm water make them into a smooth dough, so getting rid of lumps. While stirring the mixture pour on the required amount of boiling water, making the paste quite thin. Then boil it well, and use when cold. Laundry starch may be used instead of the flour.

PREPARING THE WALLS.—The walls of a room that you wish to paper being dry and scaly, should first be washed with the following preparation in order to make the paper stick. Take one-quarter of a pound of common glue and one gallon of hot water; dissolve the glue in the water and apply with a whitewash-brush, rubbing it well into the wall. When it is dry, the paper may be hung.

WALLS IN GENERAL.—In case the wall has been whitewashed, the following will answer the purpose in the absence of other articles: Take strong soda-water (vinegar will do as well), dip a large sponge in either, and with it wash the walls. Now paper.

XVI—BEDDING

THE BEDROOM

THE MODEL SLEEPING-ROOM.—The model sleeping-room should face toward the east, and should not be less than fifteen feet square, having windows on two sides for ventilation and light. There should also be an open fireplace as an additional ventilation. Have the walls hard finished, and tinted a color that will be restful to the eyes. Finish the woodwork in natural colors, not allowing any paint on it. The floor should be of hard, polished wood, covered with small rugs for comfort; such rugs as may be shaken as often as desired. Any lodging-place for dust should be excluded; not even the furniture should have much carving upon it. The hair mattress should be of the best quality, and made in two parts for convenience in turning and airing, and that should be accompanied with a woven-wire spring. Let the bedclothing be light, and at the same time very warm, consisting of blankets and a white spread. All extra adornments, such as lambrequins and fancy articles that are of no practical use, should be omitted. Let the curtains be of some thin washable material. The bed should be set away from the wall for health, as well as for convenience. Do not have a stationary wash-basin, such as is connected with the waste water; the common portable basin is preferable, as you then run no risk of being poisoned with foul gases. Have a good-sized closet in the sleeping-room, with a window or transom for ventilation, this closet being well furnished with hooks placed at the proper height to be reached by adults, and some within the reach of children.

180

THE BED DRAPERY.—Away with heavy curtains for the bed; they are unhealthy. Yet there can be no objection to an airy canopy of dotted muslin; this imparts such an inviting air to a pretty bed, and it may be shaken up and cleaned as often as desirable. The frame for a canopy may be easily made. Take a rod of wood, or such a pole as is used for hanging portières, and brace one end of it to the wall, letting the other extend out over the bed. Have a brass ball to finish it. Now take a long piece of ruffled, dotted muslin, throw it over the rod, and draw it down at each side, where it should be held in place by ribbon bows fastened to hooks set in the wall.

A RING CANOPY.—A simple way to suspend a canopy is to fasten a hook in the ceiling at the right place over the bed, fasten a nickel chain to the hook, allowing the chain to fall the proper length to the end of the chain, and suspend a wooden barrel-hoop, the size you prefer. The canopy may be made of any light material. Cheese-cloth makes pretty drapery, as it falls in soft folds, and can be found in desirable light colors. The canopy is drawn about the hoop, and hemmed on to it, then drawn back over the headboard of the bed, and allowed to fall down at the sides, where it is fastened to the headboard with bows of ribbon of the color of the material used. The bedstead may be given a coat of some desirable colored paint, and then penciled to match. Green enamel, with gold, is pretty.

THE BED CLOTHES

MARKING PILLOW-CASES. — Should the bolster and pillow-cases need marking, indelible ink is lasting, and easily applied. The name should be written in full on the inside of the hem, at the center. In marking with embroidering, use an initial or single letter, or a monogram would be better. Put the embroidery on the open end of the case, in the center, about an inch back from the hem, and let the lettering be large, as that would be much prettier than small letters. Any color may be used; white is always appropriate and pretty.

EIDERDOWN.—By a little bad usage eiderdown loses its beauty. When the eiderdown-quilt has become hard or packed, and has lost its elasticity, it may be easily restored. Brush it as well as possible, then hang it out doors in the sunshine, letting it remain out a few hours. In the meantime take a whisk and give it a good going over, loosening up the fiber, so aiding the sun to lift the nap. In that way it is renewed, and all the life comes back to it, making it soft and downy.

A WARM QUILT.—It is getting to be generally recognized that old newspapers may be put to many good uses in house-keeping. A new use to which they may be put is to make them into bed-covers. Newspapers placed over or under the bed-quilt will keep one as warm as an additional pair of blankets, and where there are no blankets, they are an excellent protection. Of cou.se, the larger the papers are the better they answer the purpose. Large sheets of tissue-paper are softer, and make less noise. Spread the papers out over the goods or the quilt, as the case may be, having them laid on in single sheets, or two or more deep. Then stitch them down to the article used, as that holds them in place, and gives it a substantial form.

OLD SHEETS.—Old sheets may still be made useful, even if they are worn. When sheets have become thin in the center, cut them in two through the middle lengthwise. Now sew the outer edges together, forming the middle, and put a hem on the new edges. This makes them last double as long as they would without such a change.

PAPER PILLOWS.—Pillows of paper are very useful, as they do not retain the heat, and on that account are desirable to rest the head upon in hot weather. They are not expensive, and, therefore, may be left carelessly lying around indoors, or out of doors. It is not expected that they are as soft as down, and while they are quite elastic at first, yet that wears out like everything else. The paper in the waste-basket would answer admirably for such pillows. A bag should be made of some soft

material, that will not be injured if rained upon. Make it the
size that suits you. The paper should be torn into strips about
four inches long and half an inch wide. Then draw them over
a penknife or scissors until they curl, and put them into the bag
that has been prepared. If you choose, put some pine tag in
the pillow, as it will give it a pleasant odor, and remind one of
the woods.

A PRETTY SPREAD.—A pretty spread for the baby's
crib may be easily made in what is called embossed work. The
material may be cashmere, sateen, or silk, and may be lined to
suit one's notion of appropriateness. Draw on the inside of the
lining, or have it stamped, any pretty pattern in parallel lines
about one-fourth an inch apart. Waving or twisted lines look
well for a border. After the pattern is drawn, tack candle-
wicking all over between the parallel lines, thus outlining the
design. Then lay the outside on; baste through the wicking
and cloth with white thread to bring the figure on top. Now
put the work on the sewing-machine, and stitch each side of the
wicking, which will bring the pattern or design out in bold
relief very much like embossed figures. Such a spread is especially handsome in pale blue or rose pink, or in pongee silk out-
lined in blue or rose. For an infant's crib the spread may be
finished with cream-lace edging. A wine-colored scarf made in
that way does good service, and looks well over the foot of a
bed or settee in readiness for a short sleep in the afternoon, or
at any time when one is in need of a few moments' rest.

PILLOW-TICKING.—Pillow-ticking is not sufficiently close
in weave to entirely prevent the down from feathers working
through. Any stiff, board-like qualities are wholly undesirable
for the dainty sofa and divan cushions so much admired. The
approved way to prepare the ticking is simple. A light quality
of ticking is made perfectly downproof by the use of beeswax.
Rub beeswax on the face of a hot smoothing-iron, and thoroughly iron over the inner side of the ticking. Apply the wax
to the iron when it has been rubbed off; that may be again and

again. The thinnest possible coating of wax is sufficient for the purpose. Put a case of white muslin over the ticking, sewing it on. The pillow is then ready for the outside cover, which may be a daintily-embroidered silk or pretty chintz.

FEATHERS

TO PURIFY FEATHERS.—It is a common experience with housekeepers to have trouble with new feathers. They become foul as the grease on the ends of the quills decays, and then they are anything but inviting to sleep upon. While sunshine is good for most anything, it seems not the best thing for feathers. It has no effect upon foul-smelling feathers, nor does it do any good to put such feathers in the oven of a stove and bake them. Besides new feathers there are the old, old feathers. The feather-bed that has done service for one generation or more, and has not been renovated, is hardly a desirable thing upon which to sleep. All such feathers should be thoroughly cleansed before being slept upon. The approved manner of purifying and preparing feathers is simple. Put the wash-boiler on the stove, and fill it half full of water; then add to it half a cupful of powdered borax. Put into this borax water about five pounds of feathers; immerse them well, and weigh them down; a heavy rock will answer for the weight. Bring the water to a boil, and let it continue during four hours. Lay the washboard across a tub; on removing the feathers put them on the washboard to drain. When they are cool enough to handle, squeeze them dry, taking a handful at a time in the operation. Put the feathers into the case, and fasten it at one end to the clothesline. Give them a thorough shaking up four or five times a day until they are dry, changing end for end every time they are shaken. It may take three or more days' airing to dry them. It would be well to put the feathers through that process every summer, as then they would be clean and fresh. The pillow-feathers could be boiled in the ticks, and, if squeezed dry, it will not disfigure the ticking in the least. Do not put soap with the borax.

FEATHER PILLOWS.—There are many methods of treating feathers to bring them to a proper state to be used. The following is a simple one. To clean the feather pillows put them out upon the grass in a drenching rain storm. When they have been thoroughly soaked squeeze them so that no water will run from the tick, and then hang them up in a shady place to dry, shaking them every now and then.

AIRING BEDS

STIRRING THE BED.—Thoroughly air the sleeping-room every day, air the beds and bedding as often as possible. Not only should mattresses be turned and aired, but pillows and bolsters should be beaten, shaken, and exposed to the fresh air. This should be done at least three times a week. Some such process is absolutely necessary to keep the feathers loose and fluffy, and the ticking fresh and clean. In case you have a folding bed, do not think that it does not need the same attention as others. Manage some way to keep it aired and wholesome.

THE CARE OF BEDS.—The importance of taking care of the bed should be well understood, as much of health and happiness depends on the proper care of beds. The first duty of the morning should be to spread open the beds, stripping them of all belongings, allowing the sunshine and air to come upon them, doing their part in cleansing and purifying. Do not, however, leave the windows open directly upon the bed and belongings when there is a fog or rain in the air. It sometimes happens that sheets and bedding are hung out of windows when the rain is not exactly falling, but the atmosphere is so charged with moisture that it is almost ready to fall in rain. Any person sleeping in that bed that night will wonder next morning how he got such a cold. The bed should not be in the least damp when slept in. The bedroom may be aired during damp weather, but the bedclothes must not be allowed to absorb any moisture. Should you find the sheets damp, do not hesitate because of the trouble to run a hot smoothing-iron over them before putting them on the bed. If a bed has been unused for some time, run a hot iron over the sheets before putting any one in it. The last duty of the morning should be to make up the beds.

TO CLEAN BEDS

THE FEATHER BED.—When the feather bed has been properly constructed in the first place, and then used with ordinary care, it should last two or three years without having to be cleaned. But at the end of two or three years' service it should be cleansed anyway, on general principles of neat housekeeping and precautions against disease. The tick should be opened, and the feathers put through the process described in the above method called "To Purify Feathers." Then the tick should be thoroughly dusted and washed. When it is dry, rub it well with wax on the inside surface, and go over it with a hot smoothing-iron. When the feathers are dry, return them to the freshened tick. The feathers may be put into any clean sack while they are drying.

TO SCOUR BEDTICKING.—Where there are small children, the bedticks often become soiled and stained. It is an easy matter to remove such marks. Take the required amount of dry laundry starch, add to it enough softsoap to make a paste (do not have it too wet), spread this upon the spots on the ticking, and let it remain until thoroughly dry. Then take it off dry. Dust the spot well with a whisk. You may have to make another application. Wipe the spot with a damp cloth when through with the other.

XVII—BRUSHES

TO CLEAN BRUSHES

BORAX ON BRUSHES.—A nice clean hair-brush is a luxury, and yet it is within the reach of all. Take the greasy, gummy, old hair-brush, that has been laid aside as useless, and clean it. Sprinkle powdered borax on the bristles, rub it in well. Then wet the borax with hot water, and comb the bristles. Pour hot water on them as you hold the brush over a basin; if it is not clean after that, wash them in the borax water, and put the brush out in the sunshine to dry. This will not injure the bristles or soften them, as the process is a quick one.

TO CLEAN WITH AMMONIA.—To clean a hair-brush is a simple matter. Hold the brush with the bristles up, and pour a mixture of hot water and *aqua ammonia* on the bristles, making the solution medium strong. Then take a whisk, and brush the bristles with it as if you were dusting. The ammonia and hot water soften and cut the dirt and grease. Brushing with the whisk removes that dirt from the brush which has gotten down between the bristles. The brush should be as good as new after such treatment.

CARE OF HAIR-BRUSHES.—Hair-brushes should often be cleansed. Indeed, it would be best to clean them every time they are used. Comb the loose hair out of them, using the coarse part of the comb. Then turn the bristles down, and strike them gently on something solid, which shakes the dandruff and dust out. Still holding the bristles down, run the hand over them several times; as you bend the bristles and they fly back in place, the dirt is thrown off. Every month, or as often as convenient, the brush should have a good washing after

187

going through the above process. Put one tablespoonful of ammonia in a pint of cold water. Have two basins. Pour the mixture on the brush as you hold it slanting, letting the mix· ture drop into the other basin. Pour it over the brush again and again, letting it fall as you pour. Then rinse it with clear cold water in the same way. Make a solution of water and alum, a tablespoonful of alum to a pint of cold water, rinse with that, and shake the brush vigorously to dry it. Double a towel across your hand, and strike the bristles on that several times, which will dry it as quick as anything that could be done without injury to the bristles. Wipe the back and handle dry. Lay the brush in a draft somewhere, and it will soon be perfectly dry and ready for use.

HAIR-BRUSHES.—Comb the hair from the brush, and shake out particles of loose dirt. Do not put soap on bristles, as it is apt to make them soft. Do not rub bristles when they are wet, as that breaks and softens them. So never attempt to dry wet brushes by wiping them. Take a piece of washing-soda, the size sufficient to make a tablespoonful when powdered, put it into a quart of hot water and dissolve, using a basin to hold the water. Turn the bristles downward, and dip them into the water and out again. Repeat this until the bristles look clean, and then rinse in clear cold water, keeping the back and handle of the brush as free from water as possible. Shake the brush well, driving off the water that adheres, and wipe the back and handle, but do not wipe the bristles. Set the brush to dry in the sunshine or near a fire.

PAINT-BRUSHES. — When a paint-brush has become gummed with oil and paint, or even hard with paint which has dried on it, clean it in the following manner: Put such brushes into softsoap, and let them remain two or three days. Then dip them in hot water and wash the paint out. Keep the soap from where the bristles are fastened, as it will cause them to rust and drop out.

TO CLEAN SPONGES

TO WASH WITH LEMON.—By continued use at the washstand by everybody, a sponge will become sour, and then it is objectionable; yet it may be all right otherwise, and you do not feel that it should be thrown away. It must be sweetened. Squeeze a lemon on the sponge, and thoroughly work it into the fiber; then rinse it in warm water until it is clean of any part of the lemon. After that process it will be as sweet and clean as new, and ready for use again.

THE TOILET SPONGE.—The washrag and sponge are indispensable in making the toilet; but where there are small children, such articles get much used and as much abused. Children, as well as some grown folks, will leave the sponge in the dirty water in the basin; then, perhaps, it will be taken out and squeezed dry without being cleaned well. The result is that such a sponge soon becomes too sour to be used. The toilet sponge should be thoroughly washed and sweetened every week, as there is nothing so comfortable and grateful to the face and hands as a good washing with a nice sponge. Put a teaspoonful of *aqua ammonia* and a teaspoonful of powdered borax in one pint of warm water, and wash the sponge in that until clean and sweet. Then put it out in the sunshine and air until it is dry.

TO CLEAN COMBS

HORN COMBS.—Horn has a grain, and on that account it easily splits under certain circumstances. Yet a horn comb is pretty and serviceable. But it must not be dipped into water, as that will cause it to split after a while, and then it will not be of much use, as it will be catching, and hanging in the hair. There are brushes made for cleaning combs, obtain such a brush, and with that clean the dirty combs, then wipe them with a cloth, without putting the comb in water.

COMBS.—They will become gummy between the teeth if not properly cared for. Grease and dandruff adhere to each other, and both will stick to the comb, and it is very tedious to remove such dirt in any ordinary way, such as taking a tooth at a time, and picking the dirt away. It is very desirable to have a clean comb. A dirty comb will leave particles of dirt on the hair. A good but simple remedy is to take a soiled towel under one arm, and take four or five strands of the fringe in the hand of the same arm, then holding the fringe out tight and straight, run the teeth of the comb through them. You will see from experience how the towel should be held, and the comb managed in order to succeed.

A DEVICE FOR COMBS.—Take a small stick about six inches long; a lead pencil will do. Tie to that ten cords, putting them close together. Let them be a foot long. Catch the loose ends in one hand, and have the other end caught over something. Then draw the comb over those cords, and the dirt will be removed. This device may be kept for use many times. It is easily made, and can be replaced at any time.

TO CLEAN COMBS.—You will notice the teeth of a comb seem to be sawed out, or cut out with machinery, and they are flat where they join the back of the comb. Something square that would pass between the teeth, would remove the dirt with it as it went through. Down near the base of the teeth is where that gummy dirt adheres, and such a device would reach that. Select a square-pointed nail, something like a lath nail, and fit it between the teeth of your comb; make a snug fit. Take a small piece of wood the length of the comb, lay the comb on it, and mark along the center of it the spaces between the teeth. Drive the nails all the way through that strip at each place marked. That will form an iron-toothed comb to correspond with your hair comb. Pass those iron teeth between the teeth of the comb, and clean it.

THE CARE OF BROOMS

TO PREPARE BROOMS.—When the straws of a broom become thoroughly dry they are brittle, and are easily broken. Besides, when the straw is dry it is stiff, and by much using it will wear the nap off the carpet; so in order to save the carpet, and make the broom do good work, dip the straw into a basin of boiling water each time you are going to use it in giving the rooms a sweeping.

NEW BROOMS.—You want to make the broom last long, and be pleasant to use. So, when you get a new one, put the straw into boiling water, and let it remain there until the water is cold. Then put it out in the open air until it becomes dry as far as you can see. When ready to use it, dip it into water and out again quickly; then it may be used. Frequently wetting the broom adds to its usefulness, and is better for the carpets. Besides, it catches much of the fine dust when wet.

TO KEEP BROOMS.—To make a broom last longer, make the straws tough and pliable. This can be done by dipping the straw on the broom into boiling soap-suds, letting it remain one minute only. Do this with the broom at least once a week, on wash days.

WHEN THE BROOM IS NOT IN USE.—While the broom is useful and can not be dispensed with, yet it often seems in the way. If put into a corner something is sure to knock it over, and then it is under one's feet and in the way. It is annoying to have the broom always laying about on the floor. And yet it can not stand of itself; it must be made to keep out of the way. Take two wire clothes hooks with a screw on one end. Put them up in your pantry, or where you want them. Put them far enough apart, so that one end of the broom may rest on one, and the other end of the broom on the other. The under part of the hooks may be used for other things as occasion may require.

THE BROOM RING.—It is trying to a housekeeper's patience to make a search to find the broom that the children have misplaced. And yet you can not always watch the broom to keep it where it should be when needed. Get a small staple and an iron ring large enough to admit the handle of the broom. With that staple fasten the ring somewhere. Put the broom-handle in that ring. The children can not take it down.

TWO NAILS FOR THE BROOM.—Drive two picture nails close enough to squeeze the straws of the broom between them. This holds the broom and keeps the straws together.

XVIII—PAINTS AND WASHES

MAKING PAINTS

A RED PAINT.—Red paint is lasting and looks well as long as there is any trace of it. There is nothing better for gates and out-buildings, if something inexpensive is wanted. Take as much skimmed milk as you want quantity of paint, then add to it enough Venetian red to make it the consistency to be applied with a paint-brush, and it is ready for use.

ANOTHER RED PAINT.—Good paint is made from oxide of iron, which may be gotten at any drug store. It is a deep red, and lasts wonderfully well. The iron in it is what makes the stain, and gives value to it. For a cheap lasting paint there is nothing better to be obtained. Put as much of the powder in a can as you think you will need, then put boiled linseed-oil on it until thin enough to apply with a paint-brush; then it is ready to be used when needed.

AN ACID-PROOF PAINT.—There are times when a housekeeper needs a paint that will not succumb to acid. When such is wanted, here is a good mixture : Take pure asbestos, finely pulverized, as much as is required. Mix that into a paste with a small amount of syrup solution of water-glass, taking care to work out all dry lumps; make a smooth mixture. Now thin that paste to the consistency of paint by the addition of a solution of water-glass, having in it as little free alkali as it is possible to make it. When brought to the right consistency it is ready to be applied, which is done with a paint-brush. The water-glass becomes as hard as glass when exposed to the air for some length of time, and it can not be softened again.

A PAINT BASIS.—A simple basis for paint is lime, as any color can be added to it. It may be applied to any surface where paint of such kind is used. Take lime that has been slaked with water and has dried to the consistency of paste. To the amount required add skimmed milk until it is reduced to the thinness of paint. Then apply it with a good clean paint-brush.

WHEN TO PAINT.—The time for painting should be carefully considered, for there is a good time and a bad time to do such work. Painting for the outside of a building is best when done in cold weather, as it hardens on the surface, and protects the wood. In warm weather the wood absorbs the oil, and there is less protection afforded the surface.

A BLACK PAINT.—Good black paint may be made as follows: Get the required amount of lampblack. If you have no lampblack, use finely-powdered charcoal. With a little linseed-oil make the black into a smooth paste to avoid any small, dry lumps being in the paint. Put sufficient litharge into it to cause the paint to dry well after being applied. When ready to use, thin it to the proper consistency with linseed-oil. Always use boiled oil in paint.

A GREEN PAINT.—To make a good dark-green paint, follow the above form, with this addition: When you have made the black paste, add to it a little yellow ocher, a little at a time, until you reach the shade of green desired, mixing them into a smooth mass. Thin it with boiled linseed-oil to the consistency required for use with a brush.

LAMPBLACK.—If you can not get lampblack, and yet need it, make it yourself. Take an iron pot, small enough to handle easily (it must not be greasy on the outside). Put water into it, and suspend it over a gas-jet or an open lamp-flame. The black will accumulate on the bottom and sides very rapidly. Scrape it off into something where it may keep for use as needed.

A GOOD CHEAP PAINT.—Here is a paint that is really cheap. It sticks well to wood, brick, stone, mortar, where there is nothing oily or greasy. It is durable, as it may be rubbed with a damp cloth. If desired, any coloring may be used. The following are the proportions and the material used : Two ounces of new water-slaked lime, five pounds of Spanish whiting, and two quarts of skimmed milk. Put the lime into a wooden vessel. Add enough milk from the above amount to make the mixture the appearance of cream, and then add the remaining milk, mixing it well. Sprinkle the whiting over the top. It will gradually sink. Then mix it well, as in the case of other paint, and it is ready for use. Apply as many coats as necessity requires. It dries quickly.

FINE PAINTS.—About the house there are many delicate decorations that may be greatly improved and made doubly valuable by a little artistic painting. The paint for such purpose may be gotten at any store that deals in the manufactured dyes now on the market, and come in a powder done up in small packages. They may be gotten for use in gilding, silvering, bronzing, and ebonizing. Full directions are given with each package. They may be used on any kind of wooden ornament, also on metallic ornaments, letters, emblems, statuettes, paper mottoes, and other such things where paint may be used to advantage.

WATER-COLORS.—Water-colors seem to be used in every form of fine art work, from elaborate paintings to colored photographs. The fascination to paint in water-colors, for various reasons, is very great. To obtain the best colors is a matter of importance, and, therefore, special attention is called to the fact that there are no more desirable colors than those made from the prepared dyes that may be obtained at any drug store. The best materials are used in making them, and for all practical purposes, they are equal to any of those paints bearing great names and fame.

A RULE FOR QUANTITY IN PAINT.—As a rule it is easy to ascertain how much of the best oil and paint is required to paint a house. Yet there are exceptions to this rule in common with others, as, for instance, the weather-boarding may be dry and old, and so absorb an unusual amount of paint. The wood may be of an open and thirsty kind. The surface may be of metal, the paint may be thin or thick, and so the amount used would vary according to these exceptions. But a good general rule is to divide the number of square feet of surface by two hundred. The result is the number of gallons of prepared paint sufficient to give two coats to the surface. If you would know how many pounds of pure ground white lead is required to give three coats to the surface, divide the number of square feet of surface by eighteen, and the result will be the number of pounds of simple white lead.

PLAIN PAINT.—It is very easy to make paint from simple colors, where there is no combining of colors to be accomplished. If there is need of brown, yellow, red, at any drug store buy Spanish brown, yellow ocher, oxide of iron, or Venetian red. Take any of those powders and mix them with the proper amount of boiled linseed-oil, and you have as good a paint as can be bought ready mixed, at much less cost and little trouble.

WHITEWASH

A VERMIN WHITEWASH.—When vermin of any kind gets into the cellar it can be subdued, or exterminated, in a simple manner by the use of whitewash prepared with copperas. To an ordinary water bucketful of whitewash, add one handful of powdered copperas. If preferred, dissolve the copperas in a little hot water, and add it to the wash. Apply it to the cellar walls in the usual manner.

A FAST WHITEWASH.—Whitewash comes off easily, if touched or rubbed slightly, and on this account it is objectionable to most housekeepers, as it causes extra work in dusting

clothes, and sweeping away the fallen particles. A whitewash
that will stick fast should be used. Here is a good formula for
a stick-fast whitewash. Take the amount of kalsomine usually
bought for ten cents. Get five cents' worth of common glue,
and two quarts of softsoap. Put the glue in some small vessel,
and put that vessel in hot water on the stove, adding a few
spoonfuls of water. Now mix the soap with the kalsomine,
making it into a smooth paste, leaving no dry lumps. Put the
dissolved glue into that, mixing it well. Coloring may be added
if desired. Venetian red, burnt umber, bluing, according to
the effect desired. Apply with any brush.

ANOTHER GOOD WHITEWASH.—Take four pounds of
Spanish whiting, and add cold water to it until of the proper
consistency. Take two ounces of plain glue, put it in a small
vessel, and put enough water on it to cover it well. Let it stand
over night, and then put the vessel into warm water, and let it
remain until the glue is dissolved smoothly. While hot, pour it
into the whiting, stirring and mixing it well. It may be used at
any time after being so mixed. Use a painter's large brush, or
regular whitewash brush.

A SUPERIOR WHITEWASH.—Here is a whitewash that
almost equals oil paint. The formula was indorsed by the
treasury department of the United States, and sent out by that
department to all our lighthouse keepers, to be used on the
lighthouses. It is good on wood, brick, and stone, answering
equal to paint, and it is not so expensive. Take one-half bushel
of unslaked lime, and slake it with boiling water, keeping the
lime covered during the process. When slaked, strain it, and
add a peck of common salt that has been dissolved in warm
water. Put three pounds of ground rice into boiling water, and
boil it to a thin paste. Dissolve one-half a pound of powdered
Spanish whiting in warm water, and half a pound of common
glue in warm water. The whiting and the glue should be well
mixed together. Then mix all these thoroughly, forming the

compound. Let the mixture stand for three or four days, stirring it each day. Keep that whitewash in a kettle, or anything that may be heated, and when it is used apply it as hot as possible. Use either a painter's brush or whitewash brush. If it requires thinning before using, add hot water to it.

KALSOMINING.—Before kalsomining, the cracks and nail holes in the walls should be filled with plaster of Paris. If the plaster of Paris is mixed with paste it will not dry before you can use it. All colors and shades are made by adding the dry colors to the kalsomine. If after the color is added the kalsomine is too stiff to work well, add softsoap until it is of the proper consistency. Dissolve ten pounds of powdered Spanish whiting in half a gallon of hot water, and a half pound of white glue, dissolved, and add it to the whiting. Dissolve half a pound of alum in hot water. Also dissolve enough ultramarine blue to increase the whiteness of the mixture when added. Mix, strain and use.

INK

A COPYING-INK.—A good copying-ink is easily made by using a good quality of ordinary ink, and adding to it white granulated sugar. Into one pint of ink put one tablespoonful of sugar, stirring it until dissolved. A copy of the writing may be taken by laying on it a sheet of unsized paper, or a sheet of tissue-paper that has first been dampened, and then gently pressing over it a moderately-heated smoothing-iron, which presses the paper on the writing.

TO KEEP AWAY MOLD.—To keep mold from forming on ink, put four or five cloves into the bottle, according to the size of the bottle. The oil in the cloves is of that nature that will keep mold away.

AN INDELIBLE INK.—Take powdered soluble nigrosine and dissolve four parts in fifteen parts of hot water. Strain the hot solution four or five times through closely-woven silk, or filter it through regular filtering-paper, that can be gotten at any drug store. If a funnel is used, have it hot.

ANOTHER INDELIBLE INK.—Take two and one-half drams of gum arabic and dissolve it in one hundred and seventy drams of water. Then get two hundred and forty drops of strong hydrochloric acid; add to it forty-two drams of strong alcohol, and in the acid and alcohol dissolve one and three-fourths drams of aniline black. Mix together, stirring them well, and the preparation is ready for use.

AN INK FOR STAMPING.—Many people use a rubber-stamp for their post-office address, and in other lettering as well. For such purposes a good ink may be obtained in this way: Get a package of prepared dye (any color that suits); mix it with four ounces of glycerine, and stir well.

A PAD INK.—Take one ounce of aniline blue, or violet, and put in seven ounces of hot water to dissolve. When cold, add one ounce of alcohol, one-fourth of an ounce of glycerine, five drops of ether, and one drop of carbolic acid, and mix well. Keep this ink in a well-corked bottle when not in use.

A COPYING-PAD.—Take one ounce of gelatine and soak it over night in cold water. In the morning pour off all of the water possible. Take six and one-fourth ounces of glycerine and heat it almost to the boiling point; then add to it the soaked gelatine, and continue to heat the mixture, during a few hours, over a slow fire, in order to expel as much of the water from the gelatine as possible. This will produce a nice clear solution. Pour the solution in a shallow tin, the length and breadth the pad is to be. The top of a pasteboard box will answer instead of the tin. Place it level, and let it stand six hours, protected from dust. To copy, use "Pad Ink," described above, on any paper desired. Let the ink dry, and moisten the pad slightly with water, and let it almost dry; then press the writing gently on the pad, allowing it to remain a minute, so as to allow the pad to absorb most of the ink from the paper. Remove the paper, and the gelatine is ready to give impressions. Place the writing-paper on the prepared pad, then smooth it with the hand, and remove the paper immediately. Other copies may be taken until the ink on the pad is exhausted. When through with the pad, wash the inked surface with cold water, using a sponge. Continue to wash it until the ink is removed sufficiently to give no impression. Let it dry, and it is again ready to be used as before.

A GOOD BLACK INK.—To make a nice black ink, get one ounce of aniline black, and put it into seven ounces of hot water. Stir the powder until it is dissolved. If this amount of water does not make the ink thin enough, add more, little at a time, until sufficiently thin.

A STENCIL INK.—For the purpose of marking, and also for use with a stencil, any good common staining substance will answer the purpose. Should you use a stencil, put a sponge in an old cup, and saturate it with the marking fluid. Touch the brush to the sponge for ink. Take an ounce of aniline blue, and dissolve it in a pint of water or more, according to the thickness needed, and it is ready for use.

STAIN FOR BRICKS

BLACKING FOR HEARTHS.—Perhaps the best color for the hearth is black of some kind, and a very good black is black-lead. It may be obtained at a drug store, in bulk or in a stick, put up for use on stoves. Take the quantity needed, and beat into it the white of eggs; mix them well. Rub on the hearth with a painters' brush, and then brush it bright with a polishing brush.

A WASH FOR BRICKS.—Take one ounce of common glue and dissolve it in one gallon of water (on the fire). Put into this one tablespoonful of alum while the glue is hot. Add one-half pound of Venetian red, and one pound of Spanish brown. If the mixture is too light add more red and brown, if too dark, add water, a little at a time, until the desired color is reached. Mix well. Apply with a paint-brush.

STAINS FOR WOOD

A RED STAIN.—For a good, bright, cheap red stain, use archil dissolved in water or in oil, according to requirement. If dissolved in hot water, let it get cold before applying. Apply one or two coats and let them become perfectly dry. Then make a saturated solution in pearlash in hot water, and brush the stains over with this.

TO EBONIZE PINE.—Make a saturated solution of alum and hot water in sufficient quantity to immerse the object to be stained. Put the pine into this and let it remain during forty-eight hours. Boil one part of logwood in ten parts of water until they are thoroughly mixed, and then strain it through linen, and let it boil at a gentle heat until the quantity is reduced to one-half. To every quart of this add ten drops of a saturated solution of indigo and water. Apply several coats of the logwood to the pine after being in alum. Make a saturated solution of verdigris and hot concentrated acetic acid, and apply until a black of the desired intensity is obtained. Let the wood dry after each application of the various chemicals employed in the process of staining.

VARNISHES

BROWN VARNISH.—The following is a nice quality of varnish, such as is used to finish paper water buckets, and can be used for various other purposes about the house where a colored varnish is needed. Get sixty grams of shellac, and dissolve it in sixty grams of alcohol; then heat the mixture until it becomes quite thick. Put into that a few drops of alcoholic solution of aniline brown, and twenty-five grams of castor-oil; mix well, and it is ready to use.

TURPENTINE VARNISH.—Turpentine varnish is very easily made,. and it will not destroy the beauty of a painting or picture in any way. It will bring out the colors in colored prints when they begin to fade from age. Take pale resin, and dissolve it in oil of turpentine, making it the consistency required for application. Use it like other varnish, applying with painters' brush.

MAHOGANY VARNISH.—Any piece of furniture may be colored with this varnish. Soiled wicker chairs, or any article of wickerware may be made to look handsome with a coat or two of it. Take one ounce of aniline cardinal dye, and dissolve it in one pint of good shellac. Apply it with a soft bristle brush or a camel's-hair brush, giving one coat.

BLACK VARNISH.—For beauty of appearance there is no varnish better than this when it is dry. It gives a beautiful gloss, and is especially useful in painting baskets, and all ornamental work requiring a black, glossy finish. It is easily made, and easily applied. Take one ounce of powdered black sealing-wax, put it into four ounces of alcohol, put them into a bottle, and set in a warm place. Shake the bottle once in a while until the wax is dissolved. It should be applied while warm with a soft bristle brush.

A LIQUID FOR BRONZE.—Here is the liquid with which the bronze powder is mixed. Take one-half ounce of ordinary varnish, and add to it one ounce of spirits of turpentine. Shake well, and keep tightly corked. Put a small quantity of the powder into a saucer (never mix more than is required for the work in hand), add enough of the liquid to make the powder slightly liquid, stirring it with a brush, and it is ready for use. Stir it each time the brush is put into it, for the powder sinks when not disturbed, hence the reason for using small amounts at a time. Apply with a camel's-hair brush.

XIX—CEMENTS AND GLUES

CEMENT FOR CHINA AND GLASSWARE

FOR GLASSWARE.—Take ten parts of gelatine, and dissolve it in two parts of a saturated solution of acid chromate of lime and water. When thoroughly dissolved it is ready to be used. Apply it to the broken edges, then put it in the light, as this cement is hardened by the action of light.

PLASTER CEMENT.—Here is a cement that will mend broken marble, as well as broken china, and the like. Where this is applied, in three days after, the article will not break in the same place without a hard blow, sufficient to break any part of the article. Make a solution of gum arabic and water to a fluid state, then stir into the dissolved gum sufficient plaster of Paris to make a mixture the consistency of cream. Apply it with a small brush to the broken edges of the article, then join them neatly together, and lay the article away for about four days to dry. Mix no more of this than is needed at one time.

ACACIA CEMENT.—This is also a simple cement, not requiring any trouble to make, and it is easily applied. It is used on china, or any such white goods. Take half an ounce of acacia gum, and dissolve it in two tablespoonfuls of boiling water. Take as much plaster of Paris as is needed for the one time, and pour into it enough of the gum solution to form a thick paste. When thoroughly mixed apply the cement to the broken edges with a brush, taking care not to apply it too thick. Let it dry well before using.

LIME CEMENT.—Lime and the white of an egg make one of the simplest and best cements for crockeryware. Take a lump of unslaked lime, and scrape off a small amount of it into the white of the egg, mixing them thoroughly. Make it the consistency of paste. Do this quickly, as it hardens in a few minutes. Apply it to the broken edges quickly, and place them firmly together. It will dry in a few hours, when it will be set and strong, ready for use.

WATERPROOF GLUE.—This is one of the best cements for repairing marble or porcelain. It becomes perfectly hard, and is a good imitation of ivory, for it is hard as bone, and has the clearness of ivory when dry. Take one-half a pound of the best plain white glue, and add to it two quarts of skimmed milk. Put them into a vessel, and put that vessel into another containing hot water. Set on the stove, and let the mixture evaporate until it reaches the consistency of ordinary glue. By still further evaporating it becomes one of the hardest of cements.

CEMENT FOR METAL AND GLASS.—Here is a cement that will resist water and acids. It is used to fasten any kind of metal to glass. Take three teaspoonfuls of finely powdered litharge, and three teaspoonfuls of fine dry white sand, also three teaspoonfuls of plaster of Paris. Then take one teaspoonful of finely pulverized resin. Put these together, and add sufficient boiled linseed-oil to make them into a paste. Let the mixture stand four hours before using it. Do not let it stand too long before using, for after it stands fifteen hours it loses its strength. Apply it by smearing the metal and the glass, and put them together firmly, and let the articles stand and dry.

GLUE FOR GLASS.—A good cement for mending broken glassware is gum from a peach tree or a plum tree. It holds firmly, and when well dried it does not show. It may be gotten from the tree where it has oozed out of the bark.

ISINGLASS CEMENT.—Isinglass is a simple and good cement. It is an animal matter, and dissolves readily in water. It may be obtained at any drug store in quantity to suit. Put sufficient Russian isinglass in hot water so as to melt it. Set it on the stove, and let it remain until dissolved. It may take a few moments to dissolve, when it is ready for use. Put it on the broken edges of the article to be mended, whether of glass, china, or marble. Put the broken parts together, and do not use the article until the cement is dry and apparently completely hard and tight.

WHITE-LEAD CEMENT.—There is nothing better for mending broken crockery than white lead. Smear it thinly on the broken edges of the article; press them together, and let the lead get dry. It resists water and heat.

CEMENT FOR KNIFE-HANDLES

COLOPHONY CEMENT.—Take one pound of colophony (a dark-colored resin obtained by the distillation of turpentine). It may be bought at any drug store. Take eight ounces of sulphur, and melt the two together. The mixture may be made into bars, then, when needed for use, as much as is wanted can be reduced to a powder. Take one teaspoonful of the powder and mix it with one-half a teaspoonful of one of the following, iron filings, fine sand, or brick dust, whichever is convenient, and fill the cavity in the handle with this mixture. Then heat the stem of the knife or fork; get it as hot as possible and put it into the handle. When the mixture is cold, the knife will be fixed as firmly as possible.

FASTENING KNIFE-HANDLES.—If the handles of the knives should become loose, melt a teaspoonful of resin, and add to it a little brick-dust. Mix them well. Powder it when cool. Put this powder into the cavity until it is full. Have the piece to be inserted quite hot, and press it into the handle, allowing it to cool, and the handle will be fixed as well as when

new. "Plaster Cement," described above, can also be used for
that purpose.

CEMENT FOR BOTTLES

WAX CEMENT.—Bottles of catchup, and such preparations,
may be sealed with this cement. It keeps the corks in the bottles, and prevents leaks. Take one-quarter of a pound of sealing-wax, one-quarter of a pound of resin, and two ounces of
beeswax, and melt together. When the mixture froths, stir it
with a tallow-candle. When the ingredients have melted, dip
the mouths of the bottles into it, having first put the corks in.

RED SEALING-WAX.—For making your own sealing-
wax, you will find nothing better than this: Take four pounds
of resin and two pounds of shellac, and melt them over a heat.
When they are melted, mix with them one and a half pounds of
Venice turpentine, and one and a half pounds of red lead. Mix
them thoroughly. It may be molded into sticks or any shape
one may desire. When cool, the wax is made and is ready for
use.

PARAFFINE.—For sealing bottles and jars and other like
things nothing is better than paraffine. It keeps out the air,
and holds the stopper in. Melt the paraffine, and when it is in
a liquid state, dip the part into it that you want sealed, holding
it down until it sets.

RUBBER CEMENT

A GOOD RUBBER CEMENT.—A good rubber cement that
may be used for sticking rubber together, or patching and
mending rubber goods, is made in the following manner: Take
fifteen grains of India rubber, and dissolve it in two ounces of
chloroform, mixing them well together. Then add to that
four drams of a resin called mastic, obtain it in the powdered
state. Mix them all well together. Let the mixture stand during a week or more before using.

A CEMENT FOR LEATHER.—Sometimes a piece of ornamental leather is attached to wood, and by some means it may come loose, thus showing an ugly defacement. That may be easily remedied by using this cement : Dissolve seven grains of India rubber in one ounce of chloroform, and then add to it two drams of shellac varnish. Mix them well together, and the cement is ready for use as indicated.

CEMENTING RUBBER AND METAL.—This cement will make rubber in any form adhere to glass, metal, or other surfaces. It resists gases and liquids. Take ten grains of powdered shellac, and put it into one hundred grains of strong *aqua ammonia*. The mixture will become a transparent mass. Let it stand three or more weeks, and the mixture will turn to a liquid. Have the bottle well corked. When applied it softens the rubber, but as soon as the ammonia escapes, the rubber hardens again. Apply the cement thinly with a stick.

VARIOUS CEMENTS

A GOOD CHEAP CEMENT.—This is a useful cement, and may be used in many ways in patching crockeryware, stopping holes in kettles, mending leaks, and many other ways. Should you have no plaster of Paris, take oyster-shells, and burn them well in the stove, or open fire; then pulverize them to a powder. Take as much as is needed of this powder, and mix it with white of egg to the consistency of cream. Apply by smearing it on the article. Let the cement become thoroughly dry before using the mended article.

LITHARGE CEMENT.—This cement may be used to line the basin of a fountain, connect blocks of stone, or cover terraces; stop the leak in the roof, close holes in pots, and such like. It sets so hard in a week that it will scratch iron. Take brick, or well-burnt clay, and pulverize it to a powder. Pulverize litharge. Take ninety-three parts of the brick, and seven parts of litharge, mixing them well. Now add linseed-oil sufficient to form the mixture into a kind of mortar. Apply as mortar. Before applying the object to be covered must be dampened. A wet sponge would do that as well as anything you could use. The cement must be allowed to thoroughly dry before going upon, it, or using it in any way, then it will be found like iron.

TO SOLDER IRON.—For soldering cast-iron to wrought-iron, take cast-iron filings, about one handful, and one handful of calcined borax, put them in a crucible and melt them. Then pulverize the product. It will be found a black vitreous substance. Sprinkle some of the powder over the parts to be welded, then heat the irons, and weld them together on an anvil, striking only very light blows.

A HEAT AND MOIST-PROOF CEMENT.—Here is a cement that may be made very useful in mending many things, such as to fasten the brass on lamps and lamp-standards, to fill the cracks in kettles, close leaky seams in pans, and almost any purpose where a cement is needed. It is proof against heat and moisture. Take powdered litharge and put sufficient glycerine in it to make it the consistency of putty. Mix well and apply.

LIQUID GLUE

GLUE FOR WOOD.—To patch and mend woodenware, the following glue is good: Take one ounce of clear gelatine, one ounce of cabinet-makers' glue, one-quarter of an ounce of alcohol, and one tablespoonful of powdered alum. Mix these, and add two ounces of twenty per cent. acetic acid. Put in a vessel, and put the vessel in hot water and heat it for six hours, and it is ready for use. Keep covered from dust and air.

A GOOD LIQUID GLUE.—A simple, good liquid glue may be made as follows: Take a Mason's glass jar and make it half full of broken pieces of the best quality of glue, then cover it with vinegar. Put it in hot water and let it remain a few hours until the glue is melted, when it is ready for use.

A GLUE FOR ALL THINGS.—It is good to be used on furniture, marble, glass, china, and elsewhere. Dissolve twelve ounces of glue in one quart of water. Add one ounce of white lead, stirring it into the glue. Then add twelve ounces of whisky or alcohol, either will do, as it answers the purpose of keeping the glue soft. When using that glue, put it on the fire to heat, and stir it too, whenever dipped into.

A GOOD GLUE FOR PHOTOGRAPHS.—Take six ounces of chloral-hydrate, nine ounces of gelatine, and twenty-five ounces of water, and mix well. Let the mixture stand for forty-eight hours, and it is then ready for use. Apply with a brush as in using any other paste or glue.

MUCILAGE

GUM ARABIC.—Mucilage is easily made, and the ingredients are simple. This is as good as any that can be made. Take equal parts of gum arabic and gum tragacanth, and dissolve in hot water. Both of those gums expand greatly in water, so a small amount will make much mucilage. When dissolved the mixture is ready for use.

GOVERNMENT MUCILAGE.—At any drug store get an ounce of dextrine, and add water to it sufficient to make the paste a thick cream or mucilage. Then add a few drops of oil of cloves or peppermint, in order to keep it from molding. When melted it is ready for use. Apply with a small brush or small flattened stick.

A GOOD MUCILAGE.—Take one ounce of common glue, and dissolve it by letting it stand in one ounce of water, one ounce of vinegar, and one ounce of alcohol, adding one-fourth of an ounce of alum water. That is ready for use when melted. Apply with a small brush.

GUM TRAGACANTH. — This mucilage will keep any length of time, and will answer all purposes. Take one ounce of gum tragacanth, and add to it as much corrosive sublimate as will lay on a dime. Put them into a jar, and add one quart of cold water. Let it stand twenty-four hours, then mix it well, and it is ready for use. Apply with a small brush.

WHITE MUCILAGE.—A good white mucilage is made as follows: Take one-quarter of a pound of white glue, and dissolve it in one quart of sweet skimmed milk, then evaporate it to the right consistency and add a few drops of nitric acid.

PASTE

STICK-FAST PASTE.—Here is a good paste that will hold fast on almost anything. Take two ounces of gum arabic, and dissolve it in a pint of water. When dissolved, add one-half an ounce of laundry starch, and one-half ounce of white sugar. Mix them well, then put the vessel in boiling water, and cook the mixture until the starch becomes clear. It should be thick as glue when done. Keep it from spoiling by adding a few drops of camphor or oil of cloves.

A FLOUR PASTE.—This paste will keep for any length of time if a germicide is added to it, as that will keep mold from forming. In one quart of warm water dissolve one ounce of alum, add sufficient flour to make it the consistency of cream, and then add a level teaspoonful of powdered rosin, and six cloves. Boil the mixture until it is a thick paste, as thick as tar. To keep mold from growing on it, add a few drops of oil of cloves, or a few drops of carbolic acid.

A WALL PASTE.—If you should want a good, smooth paste, such as many use in hanging wall-paper, it may be made in the following manner: At any grocery store buy as much laundry starch as you need, and mix it with water until it is as thin as milk, then cook it until it assumes the pasty condition needed. If preferred, use only one-third dry starch, and the other two-thirds flour, which also makes a good, smooth paste. Apply with a clean whitewash-brush, or regular paste-brush.

SIMPLE PASTE.—For a simple paste that may be used for sticking labels and wrappers for papers and the like, take a tablespoonful of flour, add to it a teacupful of cold water, mixing them well. Then add a few drops of carbolic acid, which will preserve it. It is then ready for use.

PASTE FOR LEAKS

WHITE LEAD.—When some crack or crevice about the roof leaks, it may be easily stopped by the application of a little white lead. Take the thick portion of lead and daub it into and over the crevice. It will dry perfectly hard in a few days and prevent all leaking.

A FIRE-PROOF COMPOSITION.—This has been found to be a good fire-proof paint for roofs and outside buildings, as barns and mills. Take one-half a bushel of unslaked lime, add enough water to form a solution of ten gallons, and mix well until a creamy substance is formed. To every ten gallons of this liquid add each of the following ingredients separately, stirring well. Take two pounds of powdered alum first, and the others in their order as named, twenty-four ounces of carbonate of potassium, and one pound of common salt. Mix well. If white paint is needed, nothing else need be added. With lamp-black several dark shades may be had. The color desired is not added until the last thing. Sift well, and when ready to apply it, bring it to the boiling point, and apply while it is hot. If it is needful to make it thicker, add a few ounces of plaster of Paris, which will also add to the whiteness of the composition, should it be white.

XX—BOOK LEAVES

TO TAKE OFF GREASE

OIL ON BOOKS.—To remove grease spots from a book take a little powdered pipe-clay or fullers' earth, and mix it with water to the thickness of cream. Then apply it to the spot, laying it on a quarter of an inch thick. Let it remain during four hours and then scrape it away. If the spot has not been absorbed by the clay, put the wet clay on it again and repeat as before.

TO EXTRACT GREASE.—Lay blotting-paper on it, then press the blotting-paper with a warm iron, repeating the process several times, so as to absorb as much of the grease as possible. Then take a little essential oil of turpentine and heat it almost to the boiling point. Have the greasy leaf warm, and then with a clean brush wet in the warm turpentine; go over the grease spot on both sides of the paper. Repeat this process and the stain will soon disappear. Lastly, apply the blotting-paper and warm iron.

A SIMPLE METHOD.—If oil or grease has got on your best book, use this simple method: Apply spirit of turpentine to the spot, smearing it on thin with a small swab. Let the turpentine dry, then moisten the spot with alcohol with a clean swab, and the grease will disappear. The paper will not be discolored. If necessary make a second application.

TO REMOVE DIRT FROM BOOKS.—A good book may be so thumbed by constant use as to become dirty on the margin, or even on the entire pages. Such dirt may be removed easily without injuring the printing. Take the soft part of stale bread, and with it rub off what dirt is loose. Then make a saturated solution of oxalic acid and water. Citric acid or tartaric acid may be used if preferred. None of them injure printing ink. They will remove margined notes if in writing ink, so care must be used in that respect. When the acid solution has been made, apply it with a small swab to the dirt. Let it evaporate, and the dirt will also disappear. It might not be best to make the paper too wet, as it may pucker when dry. Simply moisten the book leaf with the solution of acid.

TO MEND TORN PAGES.—Children sometimes get hold of valuable books and make playthings of them, and often tear the leaves. To mend the torn pages, take a piece of white tissue-paper and cut it to the right size, then smear mucilage on it thinly, and lay it on the joined parts of the torn page. Apply the paper on both sides of the page if that is needed. The printing can be read through that kind of thin paper, so there need be no fear to injure the book with it.

TO REMOVE GREASE.—A simple but effective method for removing grease from book-leaves is as follows: Take powdered French chalk and lay it on the grease spot, at least one quarter of an inch deep, then put a warm smoothing-iron on that. Be careful not to scorch the page with the iron.

TO TAKE INK FROM BOOK LEAVES

TO REMOVE INK STAINS.—The following will remove ink marks, whether blots or intentional writing, so care must be exercised not to get the remedy where it is not wanted. If one application is not sufficient, make a second. Take one tea-spoonful of chloride of lime; add to it enough water to barely cover it, and let it melt somewhat. Then take a soft cloth; moisten a corner of it in the lime, and pat the ink spot with it. Be gentle, and do not rub the paper. Under that process the ink marks will slowly disappear.

A GOOD ERASER.—Here is a good mixture to be used in removing ink marks of any kind. Take one pound of chloride of lime, thoroughly powdered. Put this into four quarts of water. Shake, and mix them thoroughly. Then let the mixture stand during twenty-four hours, so as to dissolve the lime, when it should be strained through a cotton cloth. For every ounce of the solution add one teaspoonful of acetic acid, and allow it to dissolve. It is then ready for use. When applying, dip a splinter, or the blunt end of the penholder, into it, and touch it to the blot. Do not rub the spot. When the ink has disappeared, place a blotter on the spot so as to absorb the erasing fluid. It may be written on again.

TO REMOVE INK BLOTS.—Take a teaspoonful of oxalic acid, and add enough water to it to make a saturated solution. Dip the tip of a finger in the solution, and touch it to the ink spot; then touch it repeatedly and gently, as if pressing the acid into the blot. Do not rub, as that would deface the paper.

TO ERASE INK.—Take a large crystal of tartaric acid, and smooth off the sharp corners. Dip the crystal in water, and shake nearly dry. With the moist crystal rub the ink marks slightly. Wait a moment to see if the ink will disappear. Do not apply it where it is not intended to remove the ink. After the application, dry the spot with blotting-paper, and it may be written over at once. This is better than to scratch the ink out with a knife.

TO CLEAN ENGRAVINGS

TO REMOVE YELLOW STAINS.—An engraving, otherwise attractive, may be marred by ugly spots or yellow streaks, or even a margin that has turned yellow from exposure. Such yellow stains should be removed, and the picture will be as clear and attractive as ever. Here is a good substance to use, but be careful not to get it on the ink of the engraving, as it will take it out. Take a teaspoonful of hydrochloride of soda, and add enough water to it to make a saturated solution. Apply with a small piece of cotton cloth. Wet the cloth with the solution, and with it pat the stain. Do not rub the paper.

TO REMOVE CREASES.—Place a piece, the amount needed, of unsized white paper on something solid; then lay the engraving or paper face downward on the unsized paper. Cover the engraving with another sheet of unsized paper that has been slightly dampened; then take a moderately hot smoothing-iron, and go over it until the crease is removed.

A GOOD BLEACHER.—Here is a good means by which to bleach paper of any kind without injuring it in the least. It acts perfectly on mildew and other stains that have gotten on engravings and such paper. Take a tight barrel, and in the bottom of it, inside, place a small crock, or jar, in which put a piece of clean phosphorus, and partly cover it with water. This combination will form ozone. Let the barrel get full of ozone, and then suspend the engraving in it, covering the top of the barrel to close the ozone within. Watch the process, and when the article is sufficiently bleached, remove it from the barrel.

TO RESTORE WRITING

TO RENEW MANUSCRIPTS.—Many important papers containing old writing are hard to read, on account of the faded state of the ink used. Should it be important to bring out the characters so that they may be read again, some such method as the following may be used to great advantage, if the paper of the manuscript has not been destroyed. Make a saturated solution of prussiate of potash and water. Dip a camel's-hair pencil in the solution, and moisten the part that has been effaced. Under that treatment the writing will again appear, when a copy of it had better be taken, as it may not last long.

TO PREVENT MOLD

TO KEEP BOOKS FROM MOLDING.—Books that stand on the shelves in a damp closet, or against a moist wall, are apt to become moldy in a short time. Any of the above methods applied would remove the ugly mold spots, but it would be better to prevent the growth of mold than to undertake to remove it when once grown. A simple method, such as the following, might answer in any ordinary case that may arise. Get one-half an ounce of oil of lavender, and sprinkle or spray a few drops of it on the book shelves. If lavender is not agreeable, try oil of cloves or peppermint.

XXI—CLEANING WOOD

TO REMOVE STAINS FROM WOOD

PAINT STAINS.—Paint may be carelessly handled, and allowed to get on the floor. When a house is being painted, one of the rooms is usually made to answer as a paint shop; in that case the floor is apt to be very much soiled with paint that has been spilled. To remove this, apply on them spirits of turpentine or benzine, letting the application soak in and soften the paint. Remove what can be taken off, and then rub the spots with fine sand, or fine sandpaper.

TO REMOVE GREASE FROM FLOORS.—Do this with the floor that has been soaked with grease, in case it is to be stained, or painted, and the paint or stain will stick to the wood, as this process removes the grease from any board floor. Put slaked lime on the grease spot. Let it be well covered, then slightly wet the lime, and let it stand on the spot over night; next morning lift the lime up, and wash the floor as clean as possible.

GREASY FLOORS.—Should the floors be spotted and marred with grease stains, a simple method to use for cleaning is the following: Put on the stains a thick coating of softsoap. Let it remain there during an hour or two, as you have the time to spare. Then take a hot smoothing-iron, and rub it over the spot, soap and all. Do this about five times. Then take hot water, and with it wash the spot well.

TO REMOVE DRY PAINT.—Take a hot stove-lid, and lay it on the paint. When it begins to blister, take an old knife and scrape it up; be careful not to scorch or burn the floor.

CHLORINE FOR STAINS.—Ink stains, lime stains, stains from coloring matter of any kind, may be removed by an application of a saturated solution of chlorine. Let it stand on the wood until the object is accomplished, then remove it.

TO POLISH FLOORS

A GOOD POLISH.—Take one pound of yellow beeswax, and melt it slowly. When melted, add one quarter of a pound of common rosin, and let that melt slowly. Then add one-quarter of a pound of oil of turpentine. Stir the ingredients constantly while heating. When they have become united, making one mass, take them from the fire, and continue to stir them until the mixture is cold. Dip a woolen rag into this mixture, and apply it to the floor, rubbing hard and thoroughly in order to give the luster so desirable. On a new floor more than one application may be required to give the proper finish. Every now and then give another application. In this way the floor may be brought to perfection in polish.

WIPING THE FLOOR.—When a floor has been polished it may be kept in order without much trouble. Many new things are advised for keeping the floor looking nice, but nothing is better than this: Take a flannel cloth, and saturate it in sweet unskimmed milk; with that wipe over the floor whenever it needs cleaning or brightening.

PREPARING TO PAINT

TO REMOVE DRY PAINT.—Before repainting it is often better to remove the old, dry paint, as then the new paint will appear better and smoother ; besides, the amount of paint required to do the work will be less, for then there will be no cracks and crevices to fill before a smooth surface is reached. To remove the old paint, make an application of oxalic acid. Make a strong solution of oxalic acid and water; then apply it to the paint, using a clean, large paint-brush. This will soften the paint so that it may be easily scraped or rubbed away.

REPAINTING.—Preparatory to repainting, go over the old paint, and give it a cleaning. Especially about the kitchen such a preparation is almost necessary. Take two ounces of soda and dissolve it in one quart of hot water. If more is required, make the amount in the above proportion. Apply while hot to the woodwork about to be repainted, then take clear water and wash away all traces of the soda. This is a good preparation, and it can always be employed without trouble.

TO REMOVE OLD PUTTY.—Old putty on a window has to be removed when a new glass is put in. A good way to accomplish that is to heat a poker red hot, and pass it slowly over the hard putty; the heat will soften it for removal.

BEFORE PAINTING.—All grease spots should be removed from woodwork before it is painted, as otherwise the paint will not adhere. If soap-suds are used to clean with, they should be thoroughly washed off the wood, as soap will not let the paint dry hard and smooth. Scour the grease spots away with water and marble-sand, or use sand and soap. When the scouring is done, rinse the work well.

AMMONIA.—When paints need washing preparatory to putting on a new coat, nothing will be found better for the purpose than ammonia. Take a basin of warm water and make it quite strong with *aqua ammonia*. With this go over the paints, and they will be in good condition for receiving the new paints. Ammonia evaporates quickly, so there is no injurious substance to be washed away.

LYE FOR CLEANING.—If a thorough cleaning is necessary, and nothing that has been used seems to answer the purpose, use concentrated lye. Dissolve the usual size can of lye in four quarts of cold water. This gives a strong solution. When used, dilute with warm water, and apply to the paint. If old paint is to be removed, apply the strong solution, which will soften it at once.

TO CLEAN PAINT

VARNISHED PAINT.—When varnished paint or grained woodwork is to be cleaned, use cold tea for the purpose. Take what cold tea may be left over from any meal and warm it slightly. Put it in a basin, then dip a flannel cloth into it, and in the usual way rub the paint clean. The tannic acid in the old tea does the cleaning.

TO WASH PAINT.—In washing the painted woodwork, do not use much soap. The less used, so as to make a clean work, the better. Much soap is apt to streak or remove the paint. When washing paint, keep the water warm and clean by frequently changing it. Use a flannel cloth, as it is better than cotton in rubbing off fly specks and other particles that may adhere to the paint.

FULLERS' EARTH.—The wainscot should be scrubbed often enough to keep the paint clean. So with other painted wood where there is not a fine varnished finish. Fullers' earth answers well on such paint, and is a perfect substitute for soap on wood surfaces where there is no paint. Rub a cloth into the fullers' earth and apply it to the object to be cleaned, using clean warm water.

TO CLEAN WOOD.—Where extreme niceness is required in cleaning use the following mixture. It will clean painted wood without removing the paint. Take one pound of softsoap, two ounces of pearlash, one pint of lard, and one pint of cold tea. Put these ingredients into an earthen or porcelain kettle, and let them heat slowly on the stove until they are entirely mixed. Apply by putting a small amount on a flannel cloth, and with it rub the paint. Wash the mixture off with warm water, and then dry the wood well with a clean soft cotton cloth.

TO REMOVE SMOKE STAINS.—In the kitchen the door facings and doors often catch the smoke that gets into the room when kindling the fire. To remove this, take wood ashes sifted fine. Dip a wet cloth into the ashes, then rub the smoky paint with that. Repeat the operation until the paint is clean.

TO SCRUB FLOORS

MUSTY FLOORS.—If a damp room is closed any length of time, the walls and floor will become musty. Scrub the floor, and make it as clean as possible. Then make a strong solution of chloride of lime and hot water. Pour this on the floor, rub it in with the broom, thoroughly wetting every part of the floor with it. Then dry the floor.

THE KITCHEN FLOOR.—The kitchen floor usually has no cover upon it, that being the best way to keep away disease that might arise from a greasy and dirty kitchen carpet. On the bare floor there is nothing better to apply in order to clean it than ordinary soap. Take lukewarm water, dip a scrubbing brush in that, then rub it upon the soap and apply it to the floor, cleaning a section at one time, and wipe it dry as the work advances, thus leaving it clean.

A SCRUBBING FLUID.—For cleaning old and neglected floors this is good. Make the mixture and put it in a bottle, and keep it for use. If the lye from ashes is at hand, put as much of it as is required into a vessel, and then add to it unslaked lime, as much as the lye will dissolve. When using, dilute to the strength needed. Put into the water with which the scrubbing is to be done, and then it is ready for use. It will bleach the ordinary wood floor.

UNCOVERED FLOORS.—Hard pine floors, those also of oak, are very attractive for a hall, as well as for the kitchen. Wherever they are, when they need cleaning use sand and soap upon them. Dip the scrubbing-brush in water, rub it on the soap, sprinkle marble-sand on the floor, and with the soapy brush rub it clean. Mop up the sand and water. When the floor is dry, give it a nice rich color by applying linseed-oil in hot water. Put a little oil in hot water, and put it on with a mop as when the floor is being washed. This imparts an even color to the floor, and one that is very attractive, being rather dark.

TO RESTORE WAXED FLOORS.—To remove old wax and dust from a floor, wash it with this mixture: Take one-half a pound of calcined soda, and one-half pound of slaked lime, add to them seven quarts of water. Then scrub the floor with sand and water, and let it dry well. Take eight pints of water, add to it one pint of sulphuric acid, wet the floor with that and let it dry again. Then scrub the floor with clear water and wipe it dry. The floor will look like new and may be coated with wax again.

XXI—CLEANING PIPES

STOVE PIPES

A SOOTY CHIMNEY.—Here is a very good and effective remedy, but one that must be used with judgment. The soot may be cleaned from the chimney very quickly with it. Take a gun, and charge it with the usual amount of powder, but no shot. Put the gun up the chimney, and discharge it. The concussion dislodges the soot, and it falls down. A pistol will do if you use blank cartridges, otherwise be careful of the rebound of the ball. If a stove is used, and the stove pipe is sooty, before the fire is kindled put a good charge of powder in it, then drop a match on the powder, close the door quickly, and hold it so that the force may go up the pipe. The effect is quick, and complete.

SOOTY PIPES.—This may be used by those who do not wish to set the chimney afire to clean out the soot. It is simple and effective, being unattended with any danger. It works to perfection where a stove is used. Have the stove hot, then place a good-sized piece of zinc on the live coals, and close the stove. The vapor caused by the zinc will decompose the soot, and carry it away in the ascending smoke.

WASTE PIPES

TO CLEAN THE SINK.—Proper care should be taken of the kitchen sink. To neglect the proper precautions may give rise to unpleasant odors and much annoyance. Keep it fresh and clean by washing every day with the following preparation, as it is one of the best substances for cleaning the sink: Take one pound of copperas, and dissolve it in one gallon of boiling water. When using it put a pint of the solution in two quarts of hot water.

AMMONIA.—The sink in the kitchen, or outside, and any waste water-pipes or drains, may be properly cleansed by pouring into them the strongest and cheapest ammonia. There are brands of ammonia sold at the grocer's, commonly used for washing clothes, that will answer the purpose. Use it at its full strength. Apply it by pouring it into the sink or pipe.

THE DRAIN-PIPE.—The waste pipe that receives the kitchen water often becomes stopped up. The remedy is to flood the pipe with boiling water once a week. Then lay a lump of washing-soda upon the drain-pipe down which the kitchen waste water passes. This will prevent the pipe clogging with grease and such waste matter.

THE CARE OF SINKS.—The hot water with which the dishes and pans are washed is usually full of grease, and this is poured into the sink, where it becomes a source of danger, as it produces conditions favorable to the growth of the germs of fevers, diphtheria, malaria, and other such diseases. One of the very best disinfectants is strong carbolic acid. A good-sized bottle of it should be kept on hand; be careful to put it out of the reach of children. Once a week put a few drops of it in the sink, and down in the drain pipe, and where the washsuds are poured, and anywhere from which there is fear of contamination.

TO BRIGHTEN THE SINK.—Besides the fact of cleanliness, it adds to the attractiveness of the kitchen to have the sink looking clean. When the sink is painted it will get dirty, and requires cleaning, yet the paint keeps the rust away. But with a painted sink strong acids, or alkali, must be used cautiously, as they would eat the paint off at once, and cause rust. When the sink gets dull and dirty, rub it well with kerosene oil, or use spirits of turpentine; they are innocent and effective.

THE BATH-TUB.—Keep the bath-tub clean. Scrub it often and rinse it well, using a dilution of carbolic acid as a cleanser and disinfectant. The bath will then be a source of joy and health.

FROZEN PIPES.—If water-pipes are in the wall when they are frozen, one used to handling them should be called in; but if they are accessible, a little home talent may be all that is required. It is not necessary to let them burst while waiting for some one to come and fix them. Wrap the pipes thickly with old flannels, or a piece of woolen carpet, then pour boiling water on the wrapping, which holds the heat and gradually melts the ice in the pipe. With that process the pipes may be kept from bursting.

XXIII—DAMPNESS AND ODOR

SWEET ODORS

A ROSE JAR.—In the early morning gather the rose petals of some sweet-smelling variety. Let them remain spread out in some cool place, stirring them until they are free of the dew, which may take one or two hours. Put a layer of the leaves in a large covered dish, and sprinkle a little salt over it. Then make another layer, adding salt, until the leaves are all in. This may be added to many mornings, until enough has been gathered to fill the jar that is to be used. Let that stand for ten days, stirring it every morning. Now take a glass fruit-jar of the size desired, and put in the bottom of it two ounces of coarsely-ground cloves, the same amount of broken allspice, the same of broken cinnamon, and one grated nutmeg. Then put the rose leaves in the jar on the spice, and let the mixture stand for six weeks. Have it closed as tight as possible during the time. In preparing the composition see that the ingredients are free from moisture before being closed up in the jar. When it has stood the desired length of time, then it is ready for use. When the room is to be scented, remove the top from the jar for a few moments.

A ROSE HOLDER.—Instead of using the jar for the rose mixture, make small sacks of stout cotton cloth. Put the mixture on a small piece of cotton-batting˜ so as to surround it, then put the batting in the sack and sew it up. Take a piece of silk of any kind, the smallest silk handkerchief would be pretty; into it put the sack, and tie it up with narrow colored ribbon, making the loops as many and pretty as possible. Various colored ribbon may be used for that.

226

COLOGNE WATER.—This is commended as a good cologne. It may be used to scent the best room, or used upon the handkerchief. The ingredients may be gotten at any drug store and mixed with little trouble. One pint of alcohol, fifty drops of musk, eight drops of oil of cinnamon, eight drops of oil of cloves, two drams of oil of rosemary, two drams of oil of lemon, one dram of oil of lavender, and one dram of oil of bergamot. Put them all into the alcohol, having it in a good-sized bottle; then shake them well until mixed. It is then ready for use. Keep the bottle well corked when unused.

SPECIAL PERFUMES.—Many persons prefer to have a perfume that is different from any other scent. Women often desire to be known by the special perfume they use—a kind of individuality in perfumery. To have such an individuality is not always an easy matter, for others can obtain the perfumes that are usually employed, such as violet, heliotrope, mayflower, and others. The way to secure a special perfume is to experiment with two or more kinds of scents, taking a few drops and mixing them, blending them until a new fragrance is found. Make a note of the ingredients and proportions. Then, of course, you must not reveal that to others, for they would use it.

GERANIUM PERFUME.—A good perfume may be made from the leaves of rose geranium, nutmeg geranium, or any of the many sweet-smelling geraniums. Gather the leaves when there is no dew or wet of any kind upon them, then lay them flat in a wide-mouth bottle, or Mason's fruit-jar. Pack the leaves into the vessel, making it full, then pour all the alcohol on the leaves that the bottle will hold. Let it stand two weeks tightly corked, then at your discretion the leaves may be renewed. After standing long enough to allow the alcohol to extract the oil from the leaves, it will be perfume, and will be ready for use as you may desire.

BATH PERFUME.—Take rose-geranium leaves as above described, and put them into a wide-mouth bottle, then fill the bottle with glycerine, cork it tight, and let it stand four weeks. The glycerine will extract the perfume from the leaves. It may be used in the bath.

A TOILET WATER.—This is a fragrant and lasting perfume, to be used as you please, after the bath or upon your handkerchief. Take one pint of alcohol, one ounce of oil of neroli, and one ounce of essence of violets, and put them into a bottle, shaking them well until thoroughly blended. When not in use keep the bottle well corked.

VIOLET PERFUME.—Take a two-quart Mason jar, and lay in the bottom of it a piece of cotton wool that has been wet in olive-oil, on that put a layer of fresh violets, and so alternate the layers until the jar is full. Screw the top on tight, and let it stand all night. In the morning take out the old flowers and add new ones, changing the flowers every day until the olive-oil has become strongly scented. Lastly, take out the flowers and put one pint of alcohol on the cotton. Put some of this liquid into a small bottle for use, and always use it out of the jar. When exhausted put more alcohol on the cotton, and use as before.

VIOLET WATER.—This is a good way to make an excellent quality of essence of violets. It will be equal to any violet perfume you can buy. Take one pound of powdered orris-root, and mix it with one pint of alcohol. Get a sheet of filtering-paper from a drug store. Get the druggist to fold it for you so as to put it in a funnel which is sufficiently large to prevent the liquid from flowing over. Put the funnel in a bottle. Put the mixture into the funnel, and let it strain into the bottle slowly, a few drops at a time. It is then ready for use.

ESSENCE OF VIOLETS.—One can easily have a perfume that smells like fresh violets. Take one-half an ounce of orris-root, and break it into small lumps, then add to it two ounces of alcohol. Put them into a tightly-corked bottle, and let stand for a week.

LAVENDER WATER.—Take one pint of alcohol, one ounce of oil of lavender, and two and one-half drams of essence of ambergris. Put these into a bottle of the proper size, and shake them until they blend. Keep the bottle well corked.

FLORAL PERFUMES.—Any kind of floral perfume may be obtained by putting the flowers into alcohol. Where a person has flowers of jasmine, violets, jonquils, heliotrope, let a quart Mason jar be filled with them, or only one kind if desired. Then put as much alcohol into the jar as it will hold. Let them stand for two days, and then renew the flowers. Do that every two days until the liquid is sufficiently strong for a perfume.

TO FUMIGATE A ROOM

SALT AND ACID.—When there has been sickness in a room, it is well to purify it. Dampness and mildew also cause a disagreeable odor that should be abated. Be careful in handling sulphuric acid not to get it on your clothes or hands, as it eats rapidly. Take half a teacupful of common salt and two ounces of sulphuric acid. Put half an ounce of the acid on the salt, and stir it with a stick. After fifteen minutes put more acid on the salt, and stir it. Repeat until the acid is used. Let the process take place in the room to be purified.

THE PROCESS OF FUMIGATION.—Six hours should be allowed for fumigating a room. At the end of that time the room may be entered, and the windows opened; but one should leave the windows open as long as convenient—for a whole week if possible. When the fumigating is over, thoroughly clean the room—rub down the walls and ceiling. It would be better to whitewash or paper them. Scrub the floor and the woodwork, also the furniture, with a solution of carbolic acid. Close the windows of the room, and chink the cracks; close the fireplace, and all extra openings. Take two pounds of sulfur for a room of ten or twelve feet; divide it into three parts, putting each part into a separate pan, with a brick or something to hold the pan from the floor, so as not to burn it. Place the pans about the room; pour a little alcohol over the sulfur, and then set fire to the sulfur farthest from the door. Then fire the next, and the last near the door. Then close the door; chink all the cracks, and let the work proceed.

TO REMOVE PAINT ODOR.—The unpleasant odor that arises from new paint has the effect of making some people sick with headache or an unsettled stomach. Take water-buckets, or other vessels, and put water into them, almost filling them. Place them about in the room, or house, where needed. The water will absorb the odor. Renew the water if necessary. To add to the efficiency of the method, put one handful of chloride of lime into the water of each bucket, or you could use an ounce of sulfuric acid in each room in the water to absorb the unpleasant new paint odor.

TO FUMIGATE CELLARS

AMMONIA IN DISINFECTING.—If there is any reason to think that the cellar floor or walls may cause disease, a simple and effective method could be employed to stop it or remove the cause. Take the ordinary *aqua ammonia*, such as is used in the laundry, and dilute it one-half, then sprinkle it around, using plenty of it where it seems most needed.

PURIFY THE AIR OF THE CELLAR.—The foul air in the cellar may be easily purified, at the same time the parasitical growth may be destroyed with the same process. The simple use of sulfur is one of the best remedies, where all crevices may be stopped sufficiently to keep the fumes from escaping. Put a pan upon the cellar floor, and put two tablespoonfuls of sulfur into it. Then put a coal of fire in the sulfur, or set it

ablaze by putting a few drops of kerosene-oil on it.   Then
touch it with a match; close all windows and doors for three
hours. Repeat when needed.

NITRATE OF LEAD.—Here is something effective and
very inexpensive for use in destroying bad odor. A little of it
may be used at one time. It is good for use in the cellar, the
barn or outhouse, also the cesspool. Take one dram of nitrate of lead. Dissolve it in two gallons of soft water. Take
one dram of common salt. Dissolve it in one quart of soft
water. When they are dissolved, mix them. Then take the
mixture and sprinkle it where the odor arises, or where mostly
needed.

CHLORIDE OF LIME. — One of the best disinfectants
known is simple chloride of lime. It can be made in this way:
Into a barrel, or kettle, put one bushel of unslaked lime. Pour
onto it enough kerosene-oil to saturate it, then let it stand during two hours. Now fill a water-bucket with water, and add
salt enough to make a strong brine. Pour the brine over the
lime, stirring it well into the mixture, making a smooth solution
of it all. Do the stirring with a long stick. Now let the compound stand during six hours, after which it may be used as
necessity requires. This preparation is the strongest kind of
chloride of lime. Sprinkle a little of it on the cellar floor, or
where slops are poured, and in the cessvault.

TO DEODORIZE A REFRIGERATOR

CHARCOAL.—If housekeepers better understood the good
qualities of charcoal, they would use more of it about the
kitchen and in the cupboard and refrigerator where food is
kept. It is one of the best known deodorizers. Take a few
lumps of charcoal about the size of an egg, and lay them about
in the refrigerator and cupboard. They will prevent that strong
smell of cooked food so offensive to many. They will also
absorb that sour smell of old and moldy food.

QUICKLIME. — The unpleasant smell in the refrigerator may arise from dampness. Such odors are often absorbed by the wood, and are a constant source of annoyance. Whatever the cause may be, use this simple remedy: Put a plate of unslaked lime in the refrigerator; it will absorb the dampness and the air, so doing away with the unpleasant smell. Besides it adds to the coolness of the air in the refrigerator.

TO DEODORIZE VESSELS

TO SWEETEN VESSELS.—Any kind of a vessel that has a bad odor may be easily made sweet and fit for use again, or made ready for a new use. Take powdered charcoal, and with it scour the vessel thoroughly. Then rinse it out with clear water, and if the odor has not been removed, scour the vessel again with more charcoal.

LYE.—About the house there are many old wooden vessels that need deodorizing now and then. There is the slop-bucket, the bread-bucket, the butter-bucket, and barrels, besides the stone jars that are used for pickle, sauerkraut, and such things that leave an odor. Here is a good simple cleaner: Take one can of concentrated lye and dissolve it in four quarts of water. If the vessel is very dirty, put into it a teacupful of the solution of lye, and rinse it around. Do not touch the solution with the hands. After a proper rinsing add enough water to neutralize the lye.

WOOD ASHES.—A simple and good deodorizer and cleaner is wood ashes. Put the ashes into the vessel, then add enough water to make a paste; with that rub the vessel, add more water, and rinse well.

TO DEODORIZE CLOTHES

ALUM WATER FOR CLOTHES.—One can not always take the longer methods to remove odor from clothes that are scented under the arms. Here is a good and quick deodorizer: Make a saturated solution of alum and water, and apply it to the inside of the clothes where the perspiration is absorbed by the goods. It may also be put in the armpits after the bath, as it destroys the odor temporarily.

ONION ODOR.—After peeling or handling onions, the hands are scented with them. The odor is unpleasant to many persons. To remove it, rub the hands with celery tops, and if they are not convenient use mustard tops.

DAMPNESS

DAMP WALLS.—Spots of wall, and sometimes entire walls, are damp, and no cause can be found for it. Usually such walls are old, yet in a good state of preservation. Dampness strikes up through the wall from the ground, or the brick may be porous, and naturally hold moisture. It is disagreeable to have the rooms spotted with dampness, and to remedy it use tinfoil. Get a number of sheets, and with copper-tacks fasten them over the damp places. Then put the wall-paper on and the moisture will not show through. The entire wall may be covered in this way, if necessary.

TO ABSORB DAMPNESS.—To have the nice furniture and best room in the house made unsightly with moisture and mildew is a great affliction to a neat housekeeper. Put un-slaked lime in two or three plates or saucers, then place them about in the room where there is mildew and dampness. The lime will absorb the dampness, and also add a sweetness to the room. Renew the lime as often as it becomes slaked, if the condition of the room requires it.

XXIV — CARE OF LEATHER

TO CLEAN LEATHER

TAN-COLORED LEATHER.—A stain will often appear on a nice piece of tan-colored leather. A good and effective remedy is this: Take two or three crystals of oxalic acid and dissolve them in warm water, making a weak solution. Dip a rag into the solution, and with it rub the stain. Watch closely, and as soon as the stain disappears, apply clear water to overcome the acid, as it is a powerful bleacher, and may turn the leather a lighter color. Wipe the leather dry with a clean cloth.

TO BLACKEN LEATHER.—Tan-colored leather is pretty when fresh and new, but it stains easily. Dampness and mildew soon discolor it when on chairs or other furniture. Leather cushions, or chairs upholstered in leather, may be easily blackened when much disfigured by stains. Get some lumps of copperas and dissolve them in water, making a saturated solution. Tie a rag to a stick and dip it into the solution, and with it rub the leather. Let it stand; when dry it will be black.

TO CLEAN BUCKSKIN.—Buckskin-gloves may be cleaned in this way and made like new. Remove the dirt from them by washing in warm water, applying soap. Pull them into proper shape, and stretch them upon your hands. Then mix pipe-clay, or fullers' earth, with vinegar, making a thin paste. If the gloves are of a yellow cast, put a little yellow ocher into the clay Rub the paste on the outside of the gloves, and lay them out of doors in the shade, so that they may gradually dry. If they must be dried in the house, do not put them near the fire, as that will harden them. When the leather is almost

234

dry, rub it between your hands until pliable and soft, then stretch them on your hands. Take hold of the top and pull them wrong side out in the act of taking them off your hands; in that way they are not pulled out of shape again. Let them dry, turn them right side out, and give them a good brushing with a soft brush. Lay them flat and smooth on the ironing-board. Put a piece of cotton cloth over the glove, and then, with a moderately warm iron, go over them and press them smoothly. Raise the thumb of the glove and press under it. Press the thumb last, laying it down in the palm of the glove as it is pressed. Keep out all wrinkles, pressing them straight and flat. Then they are ready for use, as before cleaning.

TO RESTORE LUSTER TO LEATHER.—There are many fine grades of goods that are made up in morocco leather. When they are new the finish is glossy and attractive ; after a while that wears off, leaving the article looking rusty and dull. To restore the luster, take the white of an egg, dip a cloth or sponge into it, and with it rub the morocco until the gloss has returned.

TO REMOVE INK FROM LEATHER.—Accidents sometimes happen to the ink bottle with the result that some of the best leather-covered books become very much disfigured, as they are often lying on the library table when the accident happens. The best way to remove such stains from the leather cover is to make a saturated solution of oxalic acid and water, and apply it with a cloth to the sheepskin cover of light or brown color. If the color is bright red, or bright color of any kind, dilute the solution and watch the spot of ink as it is applied; as soon as it disappears apply a cloth wet in clear water, so as to neutralize the acid and keep it from bleaching the leather more than is needed. Should the bleacher do more than is desired and take out the color, the color may be restored again. Match the color with one of the dyes so common on the market, dilute it and touch the spot with it until the desired color is restored.

HARNESS

OILING THE HARNESS.—Before oiling harness give it a thorough washing with soap and water. To do this properly, take it to pieces. Have ready a tub of hot soap-suds, have the water as hot as possible, put the pieces of harness into the hot suds and let them soak during the night. In the morning wash the harness, scraping from it the sweat and dirt. Then take a coarse cloth, and with it rub the harness, removing what patches of dirt adhere. Get one-half gallon of neatsfoot-oil, and add to it five cents worth of ivoryblack (be sure it is not lampblack). The ivoryblack will give a beautiful finish to the harness when mixed with the oil. Warm the oil, and as the straps come out of the water run them through a cloth, then apply the oil to them, smearing it on two or three times and rubbing it in each time. Then wipe the piece off and hang it where it may dry, going over the harness in that way. When dry, if the harness is not soft enough oil it again. An ordinary harness should consume the half gallon of oil. Give the harness that kind of treatment about three times each year, if you would have it last as long by three times as it otherwise would. After the above treatment the harness should look as good as new, and last as long as tho it were new.

TO TAN LEATHER

SKINS FOR MATS.—The following is a simple way to cure sheepskins and other skins with the wool and fur on them for use in making foot-mats or rugs: Take off any piece of fat and meat left on the skin. Take one pound of alum, one pound of common salt, dissolve them in one gallon of water, and into this put the sheepskin as soon as possible after it has come from the sheep. Let it stand and soak during twenty-four hours. Then take it out of that solution and nail it to some outhouse. Stretch the skin as it is nailed, and turn the flesh side of the skin out to the sun. Let it get dry. Line the skin with a piece of ingrain carpet or anything desired.

TO TAN THE HAIR ON.—Here is the way to cure hides with the hair on them. Small as well as large hides and rattlesnake skins with the scales adhering are tanned in this way: Turn the hair or scales down, and stretch the skin tightly and smoothly on a board or door, then tack it in place, using as many tacks as are required to make it lay smooth. With a blunt knife take off any pieces of flesh or fat that cling to the skin, now rub prepared chalk into the skin, rubbing it hard and thoroughly; when the chalk will not adhere any longer and remains dry when applied, then remove the skin from the board and rub powdered alum into it; let the alum lay thick on the skin. Fold the skin through the middle, laying the two raw surfaces together, then roll it up tightly and put it away where it will keep dry. Let it stand one week. That treatment will make it pliable and also retain the hair or scales on the skin. It may be used as desired.

TO MOUNT SKINS.—To stuff the various kinds of skins, they must be prepared. The skins of birds, snakes, rabbits, squirrels, may be prepared in this way. Take off all the pieces of flesh that cling to the skin, then rub with a mixture of equal parts of salt and wheat bran. Apply it thoroughly. When the salt and bran fall off dry, then it has been sufficiently applied. The mixture preserves the skin from decay, and if properly treated it will be dry and pliable, which it should be before stuffed. For stuffing use sawdust or cotton, as they are not likely to be eaten by insects. Put a little camphor with the stuffing.

TO TAN THE WOOL ON.—Should the skin be old and dry, soak it in water until soft and easy to handle, then take a case-knife, and remove particles of flesh from the skin. Do all the hides that way, such as deer, sheep, calf, and fur skins. With the sheepskin make this difference: trim off the rough edges. Take one pound of pulverized alum, one-half pound of salt, one pint of wheat bran, mix them together, and add enough water to make them into a thick paste. Spread that evenly over the raw side of the hide. Now fold the skin in the middle, bringing the flesh sides together. Then roll up tightly. Lay it away for one week, where it will not get wet, rat-eaten, or frozen. At the end of that time unroll it, brush away the mixture, and rub the skin between the hands until it is pliable. The skin may be lined should it be used as a robe.

CARE OF SHOES

OINTMENT FOR BOOTS.—With this composition the boot is made soft, shining, waterproof, and durable. It is just what should be used in the winter on all shoes and boots that must be much in the rain, snow, and mud. Take four ounces of lard, four ounces of olive-oil, one ounce of caoutchouc, and melt together over a slow fire until they are thoroughly mixed. Now moisten the sole of the shoe or boot with water, and warm the boot before the fire. Then smear the ointment over the sole and the rest of the boot or shoe that is exposed to the wet.

TO REMEDY TIGHT SHOES.—In a hurry, or otherwise, a shoe may be gotten that is a little narrow, and while it must be worn, yet it is uncomfortably tight. In such cases, take a folded cloth, and wet it in hot water, and lay it over that part of the shoe that pinches; many times it will afford relief at once. In order to stretch that part of the shoe, and cause it to fit to the shape of the foot, change the wet cloth several times, so as to keep up the heat and moisture, while the foot presses it.

A COATING FOR SHOES.—This composition keeps the pores of the leather closed, and is an excellent coating for boots and shoes. It should be applied in the winter when there is an extra amount of moisture. Rub it over the soles and uppers of the shoes after they have been thoroughly cleaned. Take one tablespoonful of beef tallow, mutton tallow, or neats-foot-oil, whichever is convenient, one tablespoonful of beeswax, and one teaspoonful of raw rubber, commonly called caout-chouc. Melt them till they thoroughly blend. Then apply to the leather.

FOR TAN SHOES.—It is well-known that banana peel-ing contains a good amount of coloring matter and tannic acid, and is, therefore, useful in polishing red leather. Take a piece of banana-peel and rub the soft part on the shoe. Apply only a little of it, then take a rag free from lint and polish the paste.

TO SOFTEN BOOTS.—On a rainy day many shoes of men and women are almost ruined by being hardened from exposure to the wet. In many cases women's shoes are not fit to wear again after being once wet. But to restore the softness and pliability of the leather almost like new, rub the shoes with kerosene oil, pinching the leather between the fingers as you do so.

TO FRESHEN LEATHER.—Leather should be treated every now and then in such a way as to preserve and restore it. The shoes that are constantly worn gradually become hard from absorbing the perspiration of the feet, if in no other way. Once a week, at night, men's shoes should be rubbed with milk. Dip a cloth in milk, and with it rub the shoes; the next morn-ing they may be polished as usual. Ladies' shoes may be so treated any time.

KID SHOES.—Kid hide makes a nice soft leather, but it soon hardens and cracks when made into shoes. Proper care must be taken of them in order to preserve such shoes. Clean them well, and then rub them with castor-oil. If this is done once a week, kid shoes will keep soft and free from cracks.

TO DRY SHOES.—To dry wet shoes quickly and safely, put some small pebbles in a pan and heat them, but not too hot; then put them into the shoes. It may be necessary to repeat the process.

TO DRY RUBBER BOOTS.—When rubber boots become wet inside, the ordinary ways of drying boots will not answer, as such methods would destroy the rubber. One of the best ways in such a case is to use oats. Keep a peck or more of them at hand in case they should be needed. If oats are not convenient, use coarse sand, and even old rags would answer. Heat the article you intend to use until it is quite hot, then put it into the boot. If one application is not sufficient, try again, until the boot is dry inside as needed.

FOR LADIES' SHOES.—Ladies' shoes can be easily kept pliable and soft, and also nicely polished. There should be no danger of soiling the clothes in the use of this simple application, as in the case of many shoe polishes that are on the market. Take pure glycerine and rub it into the shoes, working the leather well between the fingers as the glycerine is applied.

LEATHER BELTS.—When a leather belt has been exposed to the wet it is likely to become hard and easily broken. It will many times become dry and break. As soon as it seems to be getting harsh, rub it well with kerosene-oil. Put the oil on a rag, and draw the belt through the cloth.

TO MAKE SHOES WATERPROOF.—If the shoes are not broken in any way, they may be rendered proof against water without much trouble; besides, this application makes the leather pliable, and causes it to wear well. Take equal quantities of beeswax and mutton tallow and melt together until thoroughly blended. While it is hot apply it to the shoes or boots. Take particular pains to fill all seams with it. Smear it on the soles and where the soles join the uppers, also put some on the uppers.

SHOE-OIL.—Here is something extra nice to keep the shoes of ladies in good condition, as it softens and cleans and polishes the leather. It may be made at home at little outlay and trouble, and will answer as well as any shoe-dressing on the

market, without the danger of hardening the leather and causing it to crack. In this combination the glycerine softens the
leather, and the ink makes it black and gives the polish. Take
one ounce of glycerine, one ounce of good black ink; mix them
well. Tie a rag to a small stick, and with that apply the shoe-
oil.

SHOE POLISH.—This can be made without much trouble
at home, and with less expense than if some one mixed it for
you. It will be found to answer the purpose equally as well as
that which is bought ready made. Take one-half of a pound of
gum shellac, one and one-half ounces of gum camphor, and two
ounces of lampblack. Dissolve the shellac in three quarts of
alcohol, then add the gum camphor, causing it to dissolve. At
last put in the lampblack, and mix them well together. Tie a
swab to a stick, and with that apply the polish.

WATERPROOF LEATHER.—Take one teaspoonful of
beeswax, one tablespoonful of mutton tallow, and melt them
together. Then add to them enough neatsfoot-oil to keep the
mixture in a pasty state. If neatsfoot-oil is not convenient,
then use castor-oil. Then add to the paste enough ivoryblack
to give a black color. Rub that on the shoes or other leather.
This paste makes leather proof against snow and rain.

KEROSENE ON SHOES.—Do not put your shoes near the
fire, but in a warm and dry room. When almost dry, brush
away the mud, and then rub them with a mixture of equal parts
of kerosene oil and glycerine. The kerosene alone will answer
if the glycerine is not at hand. Then let the shoes become perfectly dry, and repeat the oiling.

VASELINE FOR SHOES.—Patent dressings for shoes are
sometimes injurious to leather, making it dry and brittle. The
tops of men's shoes should be rubbed occasionally with a rag
moistened with vaseline. Rub hard, getting the vaseline well

into the leather. Should color be desired in the use of the oil, make it in this way: Melt the vaseline, and put into it enough good black ink to give color, and melt the two together.

CREAKING SHOES.—Put into a shallow pan, like a pie-pan, a small amount of linseed-oil, sweet-oil, or melted lard. Then put the soles of the shoes into that, and allow them to remain during the night. That will remove the noise, as well as make the shoes proof against the wet.

XXV—PLANTS AND GRASS

KEEPING FLOWERS

FLOWERS IN WATER.—To help keep flowers fresh, put a little salt in the water in. which they are placed, and it will keep them fresh for a long time.

TO KEEP CUT FLOWERS.—In order to keep cut flowers looking fresh for several days, treat them in this way. Mix sand with powdered charcoal, and with it fill a vase. Then wet it with water. Bury the stems of the flowers in the sand and charcoal. Water the sand now and then.

PARAFFINE KEEPS FLOWERS.—Flowers may be kept in their natural colors for a long time if treated with paraffine. The flowers should be as fresh as possible, and free from moisture, to obtain the best results. Take one pound of paraffine, and melt it. The paraffine should be only hot enough to remain in a liquid state. Dip the flowers into it, one at a time, holding them by the stem, and move them about for a moment, to get rid of air bubbles. Withdraw the flowers quickly, and let them harden.

TO CRYSTALLIZE FLOWERS

GRASSES.—Take one pound of alum, and dissolve it in one pint of hot water. Let it entirely dissolve. When the water is only warm, dip the grasses into the solution, and allow them to remain until the mixture is cold. Then it will be found that the alum has settled in crystals on the grass. The grass should be removed, and allowed to dry.

TO KEEP FLOWERS.—Flowers may be kept looking fresh and bright for many months in this simple way. The gum forms a complete coating on the stems and petals, which preserve their shape and color long after they have become wilted and dry. Take one tablespoonful of gum arabic, and dissolve it in a pint of water. When the gum is entirely dissolved, take a flower by the stem, and dip it into the solution. Allow them to drain for a few moments, then arrange them anywhere, and in any way you may wish to have them.

PRESERVING FLOWERS.—To preserve flowers in their original beauty, put them into a wire plate or holder. Dissolve one pound of alum in a gallon of water, and drop the plate of flowers into that. When there is a light but complete covering of crystals on them, remove the basket, and allow it to drip and dry for a day. Tie the flowers in the basket while dipping them.

TO DESTROY WEEDS

SALT.—Weeds and superfluous grass may be readily destroyed and removed. If around the garden-fence or outhouses, or springing up between the boards of the walk, apply common table salt, or fish brine if it is at hand. Apply the salt as thick as you can afford, and it will destroy all weeds and grass that are near it.

COPPERAS.—Brick walks often become infested with weeds. They grow up between the bricks. Any kind of garden walks that have spaces between the material are marred in that way. To remove the weeds and grass do this: Take two pounds of copperas and dissolve it in six gallons of water. Sprinkle that where the weeds grow along the walks.

TO DESTROY WEEDS.— If you are annoyed by weeds growing along the walks and paths, destroy them in this way. Take ten gallons of water and put into it two pounds of sulfur, twenty pounds of lime. Boil them. Let it settle, then take the clear water and sprinkle it upon the weeds. This application should kill them.

TO CLEAN BRICKS.—Brick and cement walks are often covered with a green growth that disfigures them. To remove this, take the water in which any vegetable has been cooked, only it must not be greasy. Let the water be boiling and pour it over the brick to be cleaned, repeating the process for a few times, and the green will disappear.

TO KILL BURDOCK.—Burdock is an annoying weed, as it grows so thick and large, and bears an ugly, adhering bur, getting into one's clothes, into the sheep's wool, into the pet dog's hair, and also into the horse's tail and mane. Cut it down, and then at once pour kerosene oil into the heart of the root; a small amount of oil will do. This will cause them to disappear entirely, not leaving any trace of their presence.

CARE OF PLANTS

AN INSECTICIDE.—Tobacco juice is better than any other remedy for insects. The juice must be made strong or adulterated, according to the nature of the plant it is to be used upon. Make a weak solution first, and spray that on the plant, and if it is found too weak, it can easily be made stronger. It is within reach.

WORMS IN FLOWER-POTS.—When flowers have been potted any length of time, little white worms appear in the soil, and feed upon the roots of the flowers, and bore up into the stem of the flowers. In order to get rid of them, stick matches, with the heads down, into the soil about the plants, and they will soon drive away the worms. There is no danger of the phosphorus injuring the plants; if it has any effect, it is to make the plants more vigorous. Put ten drops of carbolic acid in one pint of water, sprinkle that on the earth in the flower-pots.

PLANT WORMS.—This remedy may be used on any plant except azaleas. It will drive away those little white worms that pest almost every flower plant, and the plants are greatly benefited by its application. Take a piece of unslaked lime, enough to fill a pint cup, and slake it in two gallons of rain-water. Make the lime dissolve by stirring it around. When it settles to the bottom, pour off the water. Then use it as you would clear water on the soil about the plants, and the desired effect will be secured.

GROWING PLANTS.—There is a way to manage plants to make them healthy and growing. In watering plants it is a bad practise to give them little at a time, and apply it often. Never let the soil in the flower-pots get dry enough to cause the tender roots next to the sides of the pot to be injured. In order to prevent this, when the plants are watered apply enough to saturate the entire amount of soil in the pot completely. Give so much as to cause it to soak through and out at the aperture in the bottom of the pot. When the water has been applied in that way, do not water again until the surface of the soil looks dry. By following this method the plants will not be dwarfed by drouth, nor grow spindling and sickly from over-watering. There is no danger of applying too much at once, if applied as advised above.

XXVI—INSECTS

ANTS

TO GET RID OF ANTS.—Take oil of pennyroyal, and sprinkle it on the pantry shelves, and it will cause the ants to disappear.

ANOTHER WAY TO REMOVE ANTS. —Should your pantry or sideboard, or any place where food is kept, become infested with ants, and you do not wish to disfigure the shelves by smearing anything on them in order to get rid of them, saturate lumps of sugar with spirits of turpentine, and lay them about on the pantry shelves, or at the entrance where they find their way in. Put the lumps close enough together to touch, and completely surround the ants at the entrance with them. This will drive them away.

CAYENNE PEPPER FOR ANTS.—To dislodge ants from cracks in the wall, take cayenne pepper and sprinkle it into the cracks. If need be, blow the pepper into the crevices.

TO DESTROY ANTS.—If you can find where ants congregate at night, you may destroy them in this way: Pour on them, and into their haunt until saturated, pure carbolic acid, which will destroy them.

BIG BLACK ANTS.—These pests sometimes get in the habit of going to the pantry and getting into every article within reach. A good way to prevent that is to scatter pieces of tansy around over the shelves. This is not agreeable to them and they leave.

ANTS AND SWEETS.—In some places nothing sweet can be put down and left open without ants infesting it. A simple way to prevent this is to make several ridges in circles with common table salt. Then place the sugar-bowl or preserve-jar in the center of these ridges. The ants will not climb over them to get the contents of the vessel.

TO REMOVE RED ANTS.—Red ants will leave if you put sulfur in small sacks and place them in the cupboard or in the drawer where they frequent.

ANTS AND THE SUGAR-BARREL.—If ants trouble the sugar-barrel or box, take a piece of chalk and with it make a mark around the barrel or box, one-half inch in width; let the mark be continuous, leaving no gap in it. This will keep the ants back, as they will not cross it.

BORAX FOR BLACK ANTS.—In order to drive black ants from old houses, something disagreeable to them must be placed in the cracks through which they enter. Powdered borax is good for this, as they do not like it, and it is not good for them. Sprinkle the borax wherever they may be found entering.

TURPENTINE FOR SMALL ANTS.—Small ants of whatever kind may be gotten out of the cupboard if they infest it. Take spirits of turpentine, and with a rag apply it to the cupboard shelves. Rub it on as if painting the shelves. If one application does not drive them away, give the shelves another rubbing.

SAGE LEAVES FOR ANTS.—When ants of any kind begin to gather around and give trouble, gather a small amount of sage leaves, and while they are fresh and green, scatter them around where the ants frequent.

ANTS IN GENERAL.—Anything that has a pungent odor seems to be repugnant to ants. There are many simple remedies employed to drive them out of houses, and to keep them away from articles of food. They are especially bothersome about the pantry and where the cupboard is built into the side of a room. It is some little crevice where they enter. To effect a cure, take ordinary varnish and apply a coat of it all around the corners and joints of board, and so close every chance of entrance.

ROACHES

ONE CURE FOR ROACHES.—To get rid of roaches, one way is to keep the pantry and cupboard and sink perfectly clean. Pour boiling water into the cracks in the floors and all about the sink. Do not let any old scraps stand about. Scrub the pantry-shelves with a strong solution of concentrated lye, so that no old grease stains may attract them or supply food.

BORAX AND ROACHES.—To get rid of roaches, spread powdered borax in all corners, cracks, and places where the insects are in the habit of coming. Blow the borax into the cracks in the walls and floors, doing that thoroughly. Repeat the application three times at least. More may be needed.

HELLEBORE FOR REMOVING ROACHES.—It is a hard matter to drive away roaches. They should be destroyed. For that purpose take hellebore (get it at a drug store), and sprinkle it around the floor at night, and the roaches will eat it and die. Hellebore is a poison used in medicine on account of its great purgative qualities. It is also used to poison roaches, as they will eat it. If you are not near a drug store to obtain the powder, then get the root and powder it. Get the black hellebore root. When it is powdered, mix it with molasses, and place it where the roaches are apt to get it.

PLASTER OF PARIS FOR ROACHES.—To kill roaches take two tablespoonfuls of fine corn-meal and one tablespoonful of plaster of Paris. Mix well, and place where the roaches can get it. Put some water near it for them.

FLIES

TO DRIVE AWAY FLIES.—Get an ounce of oil of lavender. Put a little on a cloth, and with it rub the window-sill and sides of the window-frame. Also treat the door jambs the same way. The odor does not please flies, so they stay out of the house.

TO KEEP OUT FLIES.—Obtain a good-sized bunch of sweet clover, and lay that about the room where the flies are thickest, and they will leave. The clover may be put in small gauze sacks, and the sacks hung up out of the way about the room, or at the doors and windows where the flies find entrance to the house. They abhor clover.

LAVENDER BUDS.—Flies do not like the odor of lavender, and will keep away from it. If you live where lavender buds can be obtained, get two or three ounces of them and sew them up in sacks of porous material; then hang the sacks where the flies can come in contact with the odor.

TO DESTROY FLIES.—Take two tablespoonfuls of water and sweeten. Then add one teaspoonful of laudanum and mix all well. Put the mixture in a saucer, or several saucers, as you choose, and leave where flies can get it, and at the same time where children can not get it, as it is a narcotic.

SUGAR AND PEPPER FOR FLIES.—Flies may be effectually disposed of without the use of poison, if any one does not care to risk poison aroud where the children may get hold of it. Flies will soon disappear where this is used: Take one-half a teaspoonful of black pepper well powdered, one teaspoonful of sugar, two tablespoonfuls of cream, mix well together. Put it in a plate and place the plate where the flies are most abundant and annoying. Repeat when the plate is empty.

QUASSIA WILL KILL FLIES.—Quassia is poison to flies, but is used in medicines as a tonic. In a wineglass of water dissolve one dram of extract of quassia, add to it two tablespoonfuls of molasses, and put it on a plate. Then place it where the flies are troublesome.

MOSQUITOES

PENNYROYAL FOR MOSQUITOES.—Get an ounce of pennyroyal and put some of it on blotting-paper, using several sheets. Place them about the room, on the window-sill, the table, on the pillow. Leaving the bottle open in the room will answer in many cases.

TO DRIVE OUT MOSQUITOES.—There is no sleeping for a nervous person in the room where mosquitoes are buzzing about. The first thing to do is to clear the room of every insect. Take a teaspoonful of gum camphor, put it upon a small shovel or a tin plate, and hold it over a lamp-flame until it evaporates. Hold it far enough away to keep it from blazing, as the smoke is what is wanted. The smoke will fill the room and drive away the mosquitoes quickly.

LAVENDER FOR MOSQUITOES.—In order to keep mosquitoes from disturbing your sleep, put a little spirits of lavender on a handkerchief or cloth, and lay it on your pillow or across your forehead.

BED-BUGS

BUG POISON.—Take two ounces of gum camphor, four ounces of spirits of turpentine, one ounce of corrosive sublimate, and one pint of alcohol, and mix well together, causing the camphor and sublimate to dissolve entirely. A saturated solution of spirits of turpentine and corrosive sublimate will answer if other things are not at hand. Tie a rag to the end of a small stick, making a swab, with that apply the poison.

BLUE OINTMENT.—Take one tablespoonful of blue ointment, and one tablespoonful of kerosene oil, or more if it is required to thin the ointment sufficiently to spread it well. Mix thoroughly, and apply to the ends of the slats and sides of the bedstead.

HOT ALUM.—Hot alum water has been found to give satisfaction as a remedy for bugs, and many use it because it is easily obtained and applied. Make a saturated solution of alum and hot water, letting the water boil until the alum has completely dissolved. Then, while it is hot, take a painter's brush, and apply it thoroughly to the bedsteads, cracks in the walls, and any other places where the bugs are found.

WHITEWASH.—Sometimes bed-bugs get into the walls of a house, especially if it is built of logs, and has been standing a long time. In order to remedy this, take ordinary whitewash, and put into it a saturated solution of corrosive sublimate and water. Put enough of the solution with the whitewash to make it spread smooth. Whenever the whitewash needs thinning, use the solution instead of clear water. The corrosive sublimate is a deadly poison. Apply that with the usual brush, and as whitewash is used.

NAPHTHA FOR BUGS.—In many instances naphtha has proven of great value in getting rid of bed-bugs. Put it into a sprayer, and blow it into all the cracks and crevices where the bugs frequent. It may be used on woodwork and on the walls of a room. Saturate the places with it. Open the windows to let the odor escape. Be careful to have neither fire nor flame in the room when using naphtha, as it may ignite, causing fire.

FURNITURE VARNISH TO EXTERMINATE BUGS.—An experienced housekeeper, who had failed to get satisfaction from other remedies, resorted to this: Get furniture varnish, and apply it to the bedstead all over inside, taking care to fill the cracks well. Do that every spring, giving the bedstead a thorough coat. It is a sure cure.

QUICKSILVER.—Quicksilver, mixed with the white of an egg, and applied to the ends of the slats and the cracks of the bedstead with a feather, will kill bed-bugs.

RATS AND MICE

CAMPHOR AND MICE.—To keep mice out of the bureau drawers and wardrobe, and such places, get gum camphor and place it where the mice are in the habit of coming. Camphor is offensive to them.

PEPPER AND MICE.—Get an ounce of tincture of cayenne pepper, and saturate a cloth in it and stuff the cloth into the holes of these pests. Chloride of lime may also be used in this way.

BARYTES TO KILL RATS.—Kill rats so as to have them die only where there is water, and not under the floors in the house. Take one-half ounce of carbonate of barytes, and one-quarter of a pound of lard, and mix them. Put the mixture where rats can get it. It creates thirst, and when they drink it kills them.

CALOMEL FOR KILLING RATS AND MICE.—Another good way to kill rats and mice, and not have them die about the house, is: Take a level teaspoonful of calomel, three tablespoonfuls of corn-meal, or anything they will eat, and mix these well, and place it where rats and mice can get it. When they drink it kills them.

COPPERAS FOR RATS.—To get rid of rats in the cellar, use this simple method: Take two pounds of copperas, and dissolve it in enough water to mix sufficient lime to make a water-bucketful. With this lime whitewash the walls, partitions, and all over the cellar. The rats and mice will not return. Repeat the process every spring.

BLUE MASS TO EXTERMINATE RATS.—Take a lump of blue mass, about the size of a chestnut, and mix it with cheese three times the size of the blue mass, blending them thoroughly. Then put the mixture where the creatures can get it. Keep it out of the reach of children.

CARPET-BUGS

WHEN THEY COME.—Look for carpet-bugs early in the spring, February and March are not too early. They are apt to come to the windows in the few first warm days of spring. Any beetles seen on the window-sill and around the frame should be destroyed. Go over all woolen clothes at that time if they are not much in use. Examine the carpets that are not in constant use. Be careful of flowers that are brought into the house from the fields. The carpet-bug is fond of the flowers, meadow-sweet and hardhack, and with them is often brought into the house.

KILLING THE CATERPILLAR.—To prevent the caterpillar from attacking the carpet from beneath, treat the carpet in this way: Before it is put down after the spring cleaning, go over the floor and saturate the crevices with benzine. Then cover the floor with newspapers and put carpet paper on that.

PROTECTING THE CARPET.—The carpet that has been exposed to those bugs can be protected. Take sixty grains of corrosive sublimate, dissolve it in one pint of alcohol. Wash the spots with that. Be careful, as it is poison.

CHLOROFORM.—When you suspect carpet-bugs, put chloroform into a little soap-suds, and with it go over the carpet. Have the solution strong with chloroform.

MOTHS

CEDAR AROMA.—If one is afraid of the millers tha the moth eggs, some simple remedy may be used to keep them away. The aroma of red cedar is disagreeable to them, and will keep them away from the wardrobe and closet. Get red cedar chips and put them into the trunks and bureau drawers, wardrobe, and closets, and such places where the moths are likely to appear.

THE CEDAR CHEST.—In any place where cedar is found abundantly, a cedar chest could be obtained without much trouble or expense. And a chest made of that wood is one of the best places to store away furs of any kind, as moths do not bother around where there is an odor of cedar.

NEWSPAPERS.—Those who have tried many ways to prevent moths from getting into woolens and furs, find that newspapers answer the purpose. The printer's ink is offensive to moths. Large garments should be wrapped separately in two or three newspapers, then tied securely and marked. A few drops of oil of cedar would aid in keeping them.

PREPARED PAPER.—When the woolen goods are laid away in trunks or closets, take this precaution: Melt paraffine and dip good-sized pieces of paper in it, and when they are dry lay them between each layer of the garments. It is also good to lay among furs. The odor keeps off moths.

TURPENTINE.—Moths may be kept away by the scent of turpentine. Take sheets of newspaper or wrapping-paper and sprinkle them with spirits of turpentine. Lay those sheets among woolen goods or furs when they are packed away during the summer season.

TANSY.—Many have found tansy a sure preventative against the entrance of moths among furs and woolen goods. Sprinkle the tansy leaves freely about among the goods, then tie them in paper, or close them up in a trunk. That keeps the odor from evaporating.

TALLOW AND MOTHS.—A tallow candle or a piece of tallow has been found very satisfactory in keeping moths away from goods. It is equally good in preventing the attack of Buffalo bugs. Wrap the candle or a piece of tallow in tissue-paper, and lay it among the garments and furs. Several small pieces may be wrapped and used among the same goods.

MOTHS IN CARPET.—If there is reason to suspect that moths are in the carpet, remove the carpet and wash the floor with water that has been made strong with spirits of turpentine. Replace the carpet, then go over it with benzine or gasoline, and give it a good rubbing, saturating it with the fluid. Open the windows when through. Have no fire about when using the fluid.

MOTHS IN FEATHERS.—Moth is a pest that will sometimes attack the beds. When they get into the feathers use this method against them: Put the feathers into boiling water, and let them boil for an hour, then lift them out to drain, and put them into sacks to dry, placing them out in the air. While they are drying work them well, beating and stirring constantly. Replace them in the tick after it has been properly treated and cleaned.

A CASE FOR PACKING.—This is as good as a chest made of cedar wood, for the purpose of packing away clothes where moths can not attack them. This may be easily secured, and is a sure protection against moths. Get a barrel that has been used for whisky, wine, or alcohol, having been recently emptied, and still smelling strong with alcohol. Lay the woolen goods and furs in the barrel, pack them in as you please. Then secure the barrel head as tight as it was when removed. It may be placed away to remain undisturbed until needed again.

RUGS.—When about to leave the house closed for any length of time, take this precaution to protect the rugs. Wipe a floor with kerosene oil, then lay the rugs on that, and cover them with newspapers, and they will be rendered perfectly safe against the attack of moths.

CARBOLIC ACID.—Take small pieces of soft wood, and pour carbolic acid on them. the wood holds the scent. Let them dry before placing in contact with clothes or fur.

PERFUME AGAINST MOTHS.—Here is a good powder to be used in driving away the miller that lays the eggs from which moths are hatched. Take one ounce of powdered tonquin bean, one ounce of carraway seed, one ounce of cloves, one ounce of mace, one ounce of nutmeg, one ounce of cinnamon, and six ounces of florentine orris root. Let them all be well powdered, and then mix them together. Put the mixture into small sacks, and hang or lay them among the clothes and fur in the closet, trunks, or wardrobe.

CAMPHOR GUM.—Lay pieces of camphor gum between the folds of the garments, and also sprinkle black pepper between the folds, then wrap the goods in newspapers, which is an additional protection, besides they keep the odor from escaping. Exposure to the sun and air will take away the odor.

STEAM TO KILL MOTHS.—Take a coarse towel and wring it out of clear water, then put it over the place where the moths are, and iron it with a hot iron. The steam caused in that way kills the worm. It may be repeated as often as necessary or desirable.

MOTH MILLERS.—When the moth millers begin to appear, take some step to prevent their laying the eggs that produce the moth. Close the windows and outside doors, open the closet doors, bureau drawers, wardrobe, and such places where moths may hide. Then take a tablespoonful of gum-camphor, put it in a tin plate, and rest the plate on a brick, or stone jar, to keep from burning anything. Place it away from curtains, or anything that may catch the flame. Set fire to the camphor. The smoke will soon fill the room, and get into closets and bureau drawers. The miller can not live in that smoke. Let the smoke remain in the room for an hour. Choose a nice, sunny day for that purpose, so there will be no inconvenience in having the windows opened. The smoke will not soil anything.

FLEAS

BLACK-WALNUT LEAVES.—The odor of black-walnut leaves will drive fleas away, and if compelled to smell it, they die. Get the leaves and scatter them about the bedroom, under the bed, and even under the bedsheet. Use them plentifully and make sure work of the fleas.

LAVENDER AND FLEAS.—When ready to retire take oil of lavender and sprinkle it about on the bedclothes and under the bed, also rub some of it on your body if agreeable. It will drive the fleas away.

PENNYROYAL TWIGS.—If one is living where the oil of pennyroyal is not easily obtained, perhaps the plant can be secured. The fleas can be gotten rid of by throwing pennyroyal twigs around the room, under the bed, and about on the bed before it is made up, leaving it until the last thing before retiring to be made. If the odor is too strong for one, open the windows just before going to bed, and let fresh air into the room.

FLEAS IN WOOD.—Fleas often get into the wood pile, among the chips or in the sand in the cellar and other unexpected places. From that source they scatter everywhere, getting on people and into the house. On such places sprinkle quicklime quite thickly.

SASSAFRAS.—Almost any strong aroma is repugnant to fleas and drives them away. The way to get rid of them effectually is to thoroughly clean the premises and so dispose of the source from which they come. Then use some aroma, as the following: Get two ounces of oil of sassafras and two ounces of alcohol, and mix them until blended. Put that into an atomizer and spray it over the bedclothes, around the room, under the bed, and upon the body as well.

BUGS FROM VEGETABLES

BUGS IN BEANS.—Before the winter has gone, the beans are often infested with small bugs which feed upon them and soon destroy them. Cornfield beans are liable to be so eaten. When it is discovered that bugs are in the beans, put them in a basket and pour boiling water upon them. This will kill the bugs and help to keep the beans. The water runs through the basket. Hang it up where it may drip, and the beans will soon dry and be free from insects.

WEEVIL IN PEAS.—When weevil get into peas, and they are not intended for seed, the insects may be easily disposed of in this way: Put the peas in a tin pail and place the top on it, then put the pail on or in the cooking-stove. Let it remain there until the weevil are dead. In destroying them in this way none of them fly away as in the case when the weevil are left free, and the attempt is made to kill them.

XXVII—DYEING

DYEING IN GENERAL

SILK SCRAPS.—Silk scraps should be saved, cut into narrow strips, dyed any color desired, and then wound up like carpet rags and woven into portières on the carpet loom. Or, the strip could be dyed one solid color that would suit. They make very pretty ornaments.

RAG RUGS.—Pretty and useful rugs are made from all sorts of rags, silk and woolen. They are sewn together as in the making of rag carpet. The woolen rags may be sewn together, and the silk ones to themselves. Then dye them in any way that pleases. The rags may be knitted into any pattern desired, or they may be drawn through burlap or canvas, as in embroidery, mingling the rags as the work proceeds.

MAKING COLORS.—Experiment with small amounts of dyeing material in order to get new tints. For instance, mix gray and green to produce sage green. Mix pink with yellow in order to get salmon color. Blend gray with a little pink to get shell gray. Add red to brown to obtain a good mahogany Others that are not on the market may be gotten by experiment.

PREPARING TO DYE.—In redyeing silk garments, take them all apart; with woolen garments only take difficult pieces apart. The clothes of men and boys need not be ripped at all. Clean them well, and then dip into the dye. Let them dry, and then spread them out carefully, and moisten slightly. With a hot iron smooth and press them carefully. If they are to be made over, take them all apart and wash them, then dry, when they are ready for the dye.

HANDLING SILKS.—After silks are dyed, let them nearly dry. Then smooth them on the wrong side with a medium-warm iron. If the silk is flimsy after washing, it may be stiffened in this way: Dissolve an ounce of gum arabic in hot water. Into a little of the dye put some of the gum, if it does not change the color. Then add it to the body of the dye. Let there be just the suspicion of gum in thé dye. Try a little piece of the silk in that first to see if it will change the color or affect the dye.

TREATING WOOL DRESSES.—A woolen dress that is to be made into a new pattern may look like new. It is no more trouble to put it through a dye than it is to wash and rinse it. If the original color is liked, renew it by putting the dress through the same colored dye, which will freshen and brighten it admirably. It may be made a shade darker, if that should be desired. To make it lighter it must be bleached in oxalic acid or alkali, or boiled before dyeing.

SILK UNDERWEAR.—When a silk dress becomes too much soiled or worn to look well, it may be made into a nice petticoat, and it may be greatly freshened and changed by dye· ing it. If it is dyed black, it will always look well, and will not show dust.

BLACK STOCKINGS.—Prepared dyes are reliable, and can be easily secured. They are easily prepared for immediate use. Such dyes do not fade nor smut if used according to directions, and directions come with each package. Get good unbleached cotton stockings, and those that have undesirable stripes and colors, making them unsalable, and dye them in black, brown, blue, and such solid colors that are in good taste and wear well.

MUSLIN CURTAINS.—The various cotton materials, such as curtains are made of—like dimity and muslin—are made to look pretty by dyeing them in some pretty and prevailing color. This may be done as they are being washed and rinsed on the usual wash-day. The various shades of terra-cotta are pretty. They could be dyed the color of the window-shades—yellow or green, amber, primrose—anything in color that the times may suggest or require.

RIBBONS.—When the curtains have been dyed, then the ribbons that tie them back in place require renewing, and must be dyed also. Such ribbons as are used for decorating the best room may often be redyed, and made to look new and clean. Any ribbon that is good, but is only faded, may give good service by being dyed in attractive color. When almost dry, smooth them on the wrong side with a warm iron.

COLORING CARPETS.—If the color of your carpet does not suit, dye it the color desired. Take the carpet to pieces, and wash the strips, taking out all stains. Then let it dry, after which dip it into the dye, then replace it to the floor. If there are designs in the carpet, and it is thought best to brighten them, the proper dyes may be painted on with brushes. Where rugs are used, the carpet may be painted one color with a desirable dye, making it very pretty.

EMBROIDERY.—Pretty dyes may be used in helping to decorate by use on fancy work. Where the embroidery is done in outline, the dyes come in well. Dissolve a little of such dyes as will be needed, keeping each separate. Then with separate brushes paint the material between the stitching, imitating nature as nearly as possible, putting on the dyes with care. Such work should be very desirable, as well as original and artistic.

COLORING OVER

ABOUT DYES.—It is a mistake to think that any color that is desired may be dyed on any other color, no matter what. The depth and brilliancy of the new color will be modified by the original color of the goods. Light colors give the best effect on white goods, as on white goods stains and rough places do not show through the light colors. By dyeing on some of the obstinate colors, half colors are obtained, and they are some times very pretty. Here are some of the colors that will take a certain color when redyeing. If they do not take, boil the goods in strong lye-suds until the original color fades or comes out. The light colors show best on the bleached goods. It may be necessary to dye a darker color in order to get an even shade. When goods are worn, faded, or stained, it is best to use either black, dark brown, navy blue, or olive green for best effects. On white, or light shades of blue, use a light-blue dye. On light shades of drab and on all light shades use dark blue. On all colors except black, brown, plum, olive, cardinal, green use navy blue. On any color use black. On all colors except black use dark brown. On all light shades except blue and green use light brown. On yellow, orange, scarlet, and pink use cardinal. On orange, scarlet yellow, and pink use crimson. On white and light yellow use drab. On all colors except blue, purple, plum, brown, slate, green use garnet. On yellow, light blue, and very light drab use green. On blue, pink, yellow, and orange use dark green. On green, yellow, and very light shades of blue and drab use olive green. On pink and all light drabs use magenta. On all colors except navy blue, brown, and black use maroon. On all very light shades use orange. On white only use pink. On blue, drab, cardinal, and purple use plum. On drab, red, very light shades of blue use purple. On all the light shades use scarlet. On all colors except black, yellow, green, cardinal use slate. On red, light blue, yellow, and drab use wine color. On white only use yellow. Should any mistake be made in the use of the dyes, and a wrong color be obtained, which it is necessary to change that the goods may be redyed, then bleaching will have to be resorted to in order to partly or entirely get rid of the color that is objectionable. Make a strong solution of washing-soda, or take very strong soap-suds, put that in the wash-boiler, and put them upon the stove; when it comes to a boil, put the goods in and let them boil well, until the color is faded sufficiently or as much as it will. After such a process the dye will take better. The goods, of course, are thoroughly rinsed in clear water, and properly dried before being dyed again.

VARIOUS COLORS

YELLOW DYEING.—To make a pretty shade of yellow, and one that will wear well, use the following: Take red-oak bark, and break it into small pieces, or have it ground to a powder. Take a gallon of cold water and add to it enough bark to make strong dye. Put into this two ounces of muriate of tin, and mix them well together Then put the goods into that and stir them around, getting every part well under the dye Let the goods stand in the dye during thirty minutes. Let the goods drip, but do not wring them.

DARK PURPLE DYE.—When a dark purple dye is needed it may be obtained in this way, if no other dye is at hand with which to make the color. Take a peck-measureful of the bark of the hardwood maple, and break it up into small pieces, then cover it with water. Put it upon the fire and boil it until the desired shade of purple is obtained. After that strain it through something to get the bark out. Then in order to set the color in the goods, add one tablespoonful of powdered copperas. If it is an old garment that is to be dyed, have it clean, taking out grease spots that are large. Put the goods into that dye while it is warm, if it is woolen fabric. Thoroughly soak every part of it during thirty minutes. Let it dry by hanging up to drip.

GREEN DYE.—When it is not convenient to get other material with which to make a good green color for a dye, this will be found to suit perfectly. Put two gallons of water into the tin wash-boiler, and add enough red-oak bark to it to make a strong solution, boiling the strength out of the bark. Then strain the liquid. Add to it powdered indigo, put in a little at a time, watching the color closely, until the desired shade of green is reached. Let the goods boil in that for forty-five minutes or longer, if required, in order to get the color well into the fabric.

BLACK DYE.—This is a good black dye and is admirable to restore black goods that have become stained or faded. Take one pound of powdered oak-balls—they may be gathered and dried—two pounds of logwood chips and bark, break them up fine, one-half a pound of powdered copperas, five quarts of water. Put these ingredients into the water and let them boil during two hours. Strain and use.

CREAM-HUED LACE.—Laces may be given a beautiful creamy hue very easily in this way: Into the rinsing water put powdered saffron, adding a little at a time until the right ecru shade is obtained. Strained liquid coffee would give the same shade of ecru as the saffron.

RED DYE.—A good red dye may be made in the following way: Take one gallon of water and put it upon the fire. Add to it one-half an ounce of cream of tartar, and two and one-half ounces of muriate of tin. Boil together until blended. Then add cochineal until the desired shade of red is obtained. Put the goods into that and stir them into the dye until thoroughly saturated. Let the goods remain in the dye, and boil during one hour. Lift them out, letting them drain, and wash them well in clear water. Hang them out by the edge to drip until they are dry.

BROWN DYE.—This will dye a dark-brown color, and should be used where brown is indicated. This may be relied upon to hold fast and not smut. Take one pound of camwood and boil it fifteen minutes, put the goods into that and let them boil forty-five minutes. Remove the goods, add two and one-half pounds of fustic and let it boil ten minutes. Replace the goods for forty-five minutes, after which remove the goods again, and add one ounce of blue vitriol and four ounces of copperas, let them blend with the others. Replace the goods

again and let them boil during thirty minutes. If you wish the
dye to be darker, add more copperas. Remove the goods to dry.

BLUE DYE.—This makes a dark-blue color, and the dye
does not fade. Two pounds of wool, or the woven goods, may
be dipped into the alum and cream of tartar. Take five ounces
of alum and make a saturated solution in water. To it add
three ounces of cream of tartar. Put the goods into that and
let them remain for one hour. Take one gallon of hot water
and make it strong with indigo. Remove the goods from the
first mixture and put them into the indigo, letting them boil
during forty-five minutes. Then remove the goods, letting
them drain, and hang them up to dry.

PALE BLUE. — Some pale-blue goods may be recolored
without much pains being taken with them, and yet look bright
and new. Pale blue socks, stockings, and handkerchiefs may
be treated in this way. On washing-day when ready to rinse
them, take a basin of bluing water, and put into it a tablespoonful of alum, causing it to dissolve. Dip the stockings
into that water and thoroughly saturate them with it.

BLACK DYE.—Before dyeing old goods wash them clean,
and when they are yet moist dip them into the dye. This color
does not fade nor smut. Dissolve six ounces of blue vitriol in
one gallon of water, and let it boil during ten minutes. Let
the quantity be sufficient for five pounds of goods to be steeped
in thoroughly. Put the goods in and let them boil for forty-
five minutes. Then remove them and add this to the vitriol:
Three pounds of logwood and let it boil thirty minutes. Strain
out the wood. Dip the goods into this, letting them remain
forty-five minutes. Then take the goods out and air them a
few minutes. Replace them again for forty-five minutes or
longer, as necessity may require. Then take the goods out of
the dye and wash them in strong soap-suds. Put them out to
dry, hanging them up by the edge, turning the edges now and
then.

PINK DYE.—Should a pink color in dye be required, and it has to be mixed at home, then the following will be found useful: Take a gallon of water and make it strong with saffron powder, add to that one ounce of muriate of tin, letting it thoroughly blend. Then put into that cochineal, a little at a time, until the desired shade is obtained. Boil the goods in that until sufficiently colored.

PURPLE DYE.—This color may be made without much trouble, only exercise a little care in the proportion of elements used. Dip the goods in a strong solution of alum. Make a strong solution of indigo and water, and add to it powdered copperas until the desired shade is reached. Dip the goods in it.

SETTING COLORS

COLORED STOCKINGS.—It is a cause of annoyance to have the color of a piece of goods to fade and run, but it is especially so in the case of black or dark-colored stockings, as then the stain gets upon one's body. To prevent this in hosiery, calicoes, and cambrics of a black or dark color, before washing them put them to steep in a little water, into which put one tablespoonful of powdered black pepper, mixing it well with the water.

TO SET COLORS.—This has been tried by many experienced housekeepers with complete satisfaction. There is nothing better to be used in the matter of setting the colors of all washable goods. Soak the clothes in this the night previous to washing them. Put one tablespoonful of ox-gall into one gallon of water.

TO SET DELICATE COLORS.—If none of the articles recommended for setting colors are at hand, then you will find this will answer. It is to be used in setting pink, light blue, and all delicate shades. The clothes are to be soaked in this a few hours before washing them. Take a sufficient amount of water in which to soak the clothes, and make it quite salty, almost to a brine; when the salt has dissolved it is ready for use

BLEACHING STRAW HATS

A GOOD METHOD.—Straw hats that are in good condition, if not yellow, may be bleached, and made to give good service by this simple process. Take a clean barrel, and put the hat inside on the bottom, with the crown up. Put pins through the brim to hold the hat fast. Now turn the barrel bottom up. Put a handful of sulfur under it, and set fire to the sulfur. That bleaches like new. Leave nothing on the hat when bleaching.

TO WHITEN STRAW.—When a white hat becomes yellow it may be bleached in this way: Make a saturated solution of oxalic acid and water; dip a cloth into that, and with it rub the hat, as in the act of washing it. Let it stand a few minutes to whiten; then rinse with clear water and clean cloth. This is a perfectly safe method.

TO CLEAN HATS.—Leghorn hats may be cleaned in this way: Take all the trimming from the hat before submitting it to this process. Take the juice of one lemon, and add to it one tablespoonful of powdered sulfur. Mix them well. Dip a nail-brush into the mixture, and brush it well into the hat. When the straw is clean, throw clear water upon it to wash out the sulfur, and dry it in the open air in the shade.

TO BLEACH HATS.—If the hat is very dirty, take some simple cleaner, and clean it; then let it dry, after which use the following to bleach it: Take ten drams of hyposulphite of soda, five drams of glycerine, ten drams of alcohol, and fifteen drams of water, and mix them well. With the mixture rub the hat as if washing it. Then lay it in a damp place for twenty-four hours, after which apply the following: Take two drams of citric acid, ten drams of alcohol, ninety drams of water, and apply by rubbing it on the hat thoroughly. Let the hat almost dry, and then press it with a moderately hot flat-iron, laying something between the straw and the hot iron to prevent scorching and rusting, or imparting any particles of dirt.

OXALIC ACID.—In bleaching a Leghorn hat, take as much corn-meal as will lay thinly on the hat; then wet the meal into a thick paste with a solution of oxalic acid and water. Spread that on the hat, and let it remain until the hat is bleached, then brush it off.

CHLORINE WATER. — Chlorine is a powerful bleacher, and may be used to whiten a straw hat. Take chlorine water, and apply it with a cloth, rubbing it over the hat. When sufficiently bleached, wash the hat with clear water.

TO REMOVE SPOTS IN DYEING

SPOTS OF DYE.—In dyeing goods, care should be taken to have the color distributed evenly, for it often happens when in a hurry, and careless, that dyeing is done in such a manner that the dye appears in spots. Often the goods need to be treated so as to make the dye take alike all over the goods. When silk and woolen goods get spotted in dyeing, they should be treated in this way: Make a weak solution of lye and water. Let it be scalding hot. Put the goods into that, and let them stand for fifteen minutes, getting every part of the goods wet. This should cause the color to become even. Let the goods dry.

EVEN COLOR.—If about to dye a piece of goods, and there is any doubt about getting the color even, it would be well to treat the dye in this way: When ready for the goods, put into the dye a few tablespoonfuls of lye. Put the goods into that, and let them stand for five minutes. That makes the color even.

DYEING EVEN.—To have any goods dyed even, prepare the dye in this way: To one gallon of dye liquid, add one pint of a solution of oxalic acid and water. The acid does no harm, and makes the color spread evenly.

DYES FOR WOOLENS

ORANGE DYE.—In order to dye a nice orange color, use the following. It is the proportion for five pounds of goods, and the requisite amount of water for that amount of goods should be added to the dye. Six tablespoonfuls of muriate of tin, and four ounces of argol. Mix well. Put the goods in and let them boil one hour. Remove the goods, and add to the liquid one teacupful of madder root. Replace the goods, and boil one-half hour. For a brighter color, use two ounces of cochineal instead of the madder.

SCARLET DYE.—This is the proportion for one pound of goods: Take one gallon of water, one-half an ounce of cream of tartar, one-half an ounce of powdered cochineal, and two and one-half ounces of muriate of tin. Mix with the water, and let them boil well. Put the goods into that and stir them briskly for fifteen minutes. Then boil them for one hour and a half. Stir the goods while boiling. After that wash the goods in clear water, and dry them.

PINK DYE.—This is the proportion of dye for three pounds of goods: Take sufficient water for the goods. Add to it three ounces of alum. Boil the goods in that during one hour. Then add four ounces of cream of tartar, and one ounce of powdered cochineal, and boil well. Then replace the goods in that, and boil them, dipping them in and out of the dye while boiling. When the color suits, remove the goods.

BLUE DYE.—This is good and quick to dye a shade of blue: Take the proper quantity of water for two pounds of goods, and add to it five ounces of alum, three ounces of cream of tartar; let them dissolve. Boil the goods in this during one hour. Take clear warm water, and put into it a sufficient amount of indigo to make the shade of blue required. Put the goods into this, and boil them until the color has spread sufficiently.

CHROME BLACK DYE.—There is no better black dye than this. It will not fade by exposure to the sun. The proportion of dye is given for five pounds of goods. Use enough water to properly cover the goods. Then take six ounces of blue vitriol, and boil it a few minutes, then put the goods into it, to remain three-fourths of an hour, airing them often. Take the goods out, and add to the liquid three pounds of logwood chips, and boil them one-half an hour. Replace the goods to remain three-fourths of an hour, then air them, then replace in the dye during three-fourths of an hour more. Remove them, and wash in strong suds.

WINE-COLOR DYE.—Take enough water to cover five pounds of goods, add to it two pounds of camwood, and boil it fifteen minutes. Put in the goods to remain one-half an hour. Then air them, and boil again as before. Now add one and one-half ounces of blue vitriol; if that is not dark enough, add one-half ounce of copperas. Boil the goods until dyed.

PURPLE DYE.—Rinse the goods well in soap-suds. Then have some soap-suds hot, but not quite boiling. In those hot suds dissolve two ounces of cudbear for each pound of goods to be dyed. Put the goods into that, and let them remain until the desired color is secured. To brighten the color, rinse the goods in a moderately strong solution of alum and water.

YELLOW DYE.—This is a nice rich yellow shade. Take three ounces of bichromate of potassa, two ounces of alum. Boil them in enough water to cover five pounds of goods. Put the goods into that for one-half an hour while it is boiling. Lift the goods up to the air now and then. Take them out to cool and drain. Then take five pounds of fustic and put enough water on it to cover the goods. Boil it. Put the goods into it, and work them until well colored. Then wash the goods out and hang them to dry.

CRIMSON DYE.—Into enough water to cover the goods to be dyed, add the following: One pound of cochineal paste, six ounces of dry cochineal, one pound of cream of tartar, one pint of protochloride of tin. Bring them to a boil. Then put the goods into that dye and stir them well, getting the color thoroughly into the goods. Now rinse them well and hang up by the edge to dry.

SALMON DYE.—Rinse the goods in warm water, enough for the amount of goods. Take for each pound of goods one-fourth of a pound of annatto, one-fourth of a pound of soap. Put the goods into that, and boil them one-half of an hour. The shade is governed by the amount of the annatto used.

DOVE DYE.—Dove and slate colors of all shades are made in this way: Put into an iron boiler the amount of water needed. Then add to it one teacup of black tea, one teaspoonful of copperas. Dilute the dye until the right shade is secured. Then put the goods into that and stir them.

SNUFF-BROWN DYE.—This is a dark brown : Take water enough for five pounds of goods. One pound of camwood, boil it fifteen minutes, then put in the goods for three-fourths of an hour. Remove the goods. Add two and one-half pounds of fustic, and boil it during ten minutes. Replace the goods for three-fourths of an hour. Then add one ounce of blue vitriol, four ounces of copperas. Put the goods in again and let them remain during one-half an hour, stirring them all the time to get the dye well into the goods. If the color is not dark enough, add more copperas to the liquid. Wash the goods in good soap-suds, and rinse in clear water. Then hang them up by the edge of the goods to dry.

BROWN DYE.—This is to make any shade of brown: Take two ounces of alum, three ounces of copperas; dissolve them in sufficient water for the goods. Boil the goods in that. Make some water rich with madder, and rinse the goods through that. The tint will depend upon the relative proportions of copperas and alum. The more copperas used the darker the dye. Joint weight of both should not be more than one-eighth of the weight of the goods Mixtures of reds and yellows with blues and blacks, or simple dyes, will make any shade.

MADDER-RED DYE.—For each pound of goods use five ounces of alum, one ounce of cream of tartar. Put in the goods, and boil during one-half an hour. Air them, and boil again the same length of time. Fill a kettle with clean water, and add one peck of wheat bran; make the water milk-warm; let the bran rise to the top, then skim it off; then add one-half pound of madder. Put the goods into that, and heat it slowly until it boils. Then take the goods out, and wash them in strong suds. Dry them.

GREEN DYE.—For each pound of goods use one pound of fustic, three and one-half ounces of alum. Let the alum dissolve, and the fustic steep until the color is out. Soak the goods therein until a good yellow is obtained. Remove the chips, and add one tablespoonful of indigo at a time until the color suits. Put the goods into that, and stir until well colored with the dye. Then dry them.

DYES FOR COTTONS

YELLOW DYE.—For five pounds of goods add to the water seven ounces of sugar of lead. Put the goods into this for two hours, then take clear water, and add four ounces of bichromate of potash. Dip the goods in this until the color suits, then wring them, and let them dry. If not yellow enough, repeat the process of dipping in the bichromate of potash until it suits.

ORANGE DYE.—Into the water, for five pounds of goods, put four ounces of sugar of lead, boil it a few minutes; let it cool some, and put in the goods, letting them remain for two hours; then wring. Into clear water put eight ounces of bichromate of potash and two ounces of madder. Dip the goods into this until the color suits. Should the color be too red, take a sample of the goods and dip it into lime-water; then select between the shades of orange. Wring out the goods, and let them dry.

RED DYE.—Have enough water to cover the goods; add to it two thirds of a teacupful of muriate of tin. Bring to a boiling heat. Put the goods in for one hour. Stir them. Take them out. To clear water add one pound of nicwood. Steep it one-half an hour at moderate heat. Put the goods in, and increase the heat, but not to boiling. Air them, and dip for one hour, as before. Then wash the goods, using no soap upon them. Then dry them.

BLACK DYE.—This is a permanent black for five pounds of goods. Put into the water three pounds of sumach, and boil the goods in it for half an hour. Then let them steep for twelve hours. Dip them in lime-water for half an hour. Let them drip one hour. Put them into the lime-water again for fifteen minutes. Into clear water put two and one-half pounds of logwood, and boil for an hour. Dip the goods in this for three hours. Then add two ounces of bichromate of potash, and dip the goods one hour. Then wash them in clear cold water, and dry them in the shade.

SKY-BLUE DYE.—Take enough water for three pounds of goods, and add to it four ounces of blue vitriol, boil it a few minutes. Put in the goods for three hours. Then work them through strong lime water. Rinse in clear water, and dry them.

BROWN DYE.—Proceed the same as for sky blue, and when the goods leave the lime the last time, put them through a strong solution of prussiate of potash.

GREEN DYE.—Dip the goods in strong bluing water. Dry them a little. Into clear water put three pounds of fustic, three ounces of logwood, for each pound of goods. Boil them one hour. When tepid, add the goods, stir them well, and let them stand for one hour. Drain them. For each pound of goods, add one-half ounce of blue vitriol, return the goods for an hour. Wring them, and dry in the shade. Adding or diminishing the logwood and fustic makes any shade.

DYES FOR SILKS

BLACK DYE.—Take enough water to cover the goods, and in it put six ounces of blue vitriol. Boil for a few minutes. Put in the goods for three-quarters of an hour, airing them often during the time. Make a solution of bichromate of potash and heat it to a little below boiling point. Pass the goods through this. In clear water put three pounds of logwood and boil for half an hour. When a little cool, dip the goods in that for three-fourths of an hour, then air the goods and dip again for the same length of time.

ORANGE DYE.—Take enough water to cover one pound of goods, and add to it one pound of annatto and one pound of soda. Bring that to a moderate heat and dip the goods into it until properly colored. Then rinse them in moderately warm clear water.

LIGHT-BLUE DYE.—Take one gallon of water. In a teacupful of hot water dissolve one-half a teaspoonful of alum and put it into the gallon of water. Add to the water one teaspoonful at a time of indigo. Do that until the desired shade of blue is obtained. The more indigo added, the darker will be the shade. Put the goods into this, dipping them up and down until properly dyed.

THE END.

INDEX

A

Acid, oxalic stains, 77; acid, 77; carbolic, 256; acid in general, 78.

Alcohol and salt, to remove grease, 68.

Alpaca, to brighten, 71.

Alum water, for grease, 72; for clothes, 232; for bed bugs, 252.

Ammonia, as soap, 63; and blotting paper, 72; on carpet, 167; on walls, 177; on brushes, 187; to wash paints, 219; for sinks, 224; to disinfect, 230.

Ants, to get rid of, 247; and sweets, 248; in general, 248.

Aprons, pockets in, 94; goods, 95.

Asbestos, 107.

Ashes, removing, 36; wood ashes, 232.

B

Bags, for silver, 101; for soiled linen, 101; for shoes, 101; a dusting bag, 102; for traveling, 102.

Bath-tub, 224.

Beans, bugs in, 259.

Beater, a wire, 173; of wood, 174.

Bed Bugs, a poison for, 251.

Bed, stirring, 185; care of, 185; drapery, 181; the feather, 186; scour ticking, 186.

Bedsteads, creaking, 154.

Benzine, for grease, 72; stains of, 87.

Berry stains, 76.

Black goods, to remove gloss, 70; to remove mud, 71.

Blacking for hearth, 200.

Block, the chicken, 36.

Blood stains, 89.

Bluemass, for rats, 253.

Bluing, a good, 60; liquid, 60.

Books, oil on, 212; to extract grease, 212; a simple method, 212; dirt from, 212; torn pages, 213; to remove grease, 213.

Boots, rubber, to dry, 240.

Bottles, cleaning, 114.

Bowl, wooden, 32.

Box, for clothes, 110.

Brass, kettles, 138; kitchen vessels, 138; to brighten, 139; a cleaner, 139; clean old brass, 140; prevent tarnish, 140; a cleaning mixture, 140.

Bricks, wash for, 200; to clean, 245.

Bronze, to clean, 137; to wash, 137.

277

Brooms, to prepare, 191; new, 191; to keep, 191; not in use, 191; the ring, 192; two nails for, 192.

Brush, in washing, 43; borax on, 187; care of, 187; paint brushes, 188.

Buckets, to keep from shrinking, 32.

Buckskin, to clean, 234.

Burdock, to kill, 245.

Bureau draws, 154.

Byrates, for rats, 253.

C

Cake, to keep moist, 40.

Calico, to set black, 49; hold color, 50.

Calomel, for rats and mice, 253

Cane seats, to tighten, 152.

Canker, to detect in preserves, 33.

Canvas, to preserve, 158.

Carpets, to make last, 164; a cheap one, 164; selecting, 164; care of, 165; to beat, 165; shake often, 165; to mop, 166; to wipe, 168; remove grease, 169-90; a cleaner, 169; to clean ingrain, 170; soap on, 170; coloring, 262; to brighten, 168; to scour, 170; a good mixture for, 171.

Carpet bugs, when they come, 254; Caterpillar, 254; protection from, 254.

Camphor, for mice, 253; moths, 257.

Case, for packing, 256.

Cask, to sweeten, 32.

Cement, plaster, 203; acacia, 203; lime, 204; for metal and glass, 204; isinglass, 205; white lead, 205; colophony, 205; wax, 206; rubber, 206; for rubber and metal, 207; a good cheap, 207; litharge, 207; heat and moist proof, 208.

Chairs, willow, 153.

Chamois, to clean, 158.

Charcoal, 231.

Chimney, sooty, 223.

Chintz, to clean, 50.

Chloroform, for carpet bugs, 254.

Cinders, 36.

Cleanliness, 18.

Cleaning, a good mixture, 69, 73.

Clothes, to whiten, 46; to wash without rubbing, 46; resting, 100.

Coat, to clean old, 70.

Colors, making, 260; to set, 267; even, 269.

Combs, horn, 189; for cleaning, 190.

Composition, fireproof, 211.

Copper, vessels, to scour, 138, boilers, to clean, 140.

Copperas, on weeds, 244; for rats, 253.

Corks, 108.

Crocks, to clean, 114.

Cups and saucers, to remove stains, 114.
Curtains, muslin, 261.
Cushions, 104.
Cuts, to frame, 162.

D

Dampness, to absorb, 233.
Darn, a good, 97.
Dishcloth, caring for, 31; netting for, 106; cheesecloth, 106; gourd, 106.
Doilies, 105.
Door, stop, 108; creaking, 108.
Dress, at home, 17; set colors in summer, 50; to clean black, 68; to take stains out, 69; to clean silk, 75; making, 92.
Dusting, 25.
Dye, preparing to, 260; about, 262.
Dyeing, yellow, 264; dark purple, 264; green, 264; black, 265; red, 265; brown, 265; blue, 266; pale blue, 266; black again, 266; pink, 267; purple, 267; spots of dye, 269; make even, 269; orange on wool, 269; scarlet, 270; wine color, 271; pink, 270; blue, 270; chrome black, 270; purple, 271; yellow, 271; crimson, 271; salmon, 272; dove, 272; snuff brown, 272; brown, 272; madder red, 273; green, 273; yellow for cotton, 273; orange, 273; red, 274; black, 274; sky blue, 274; green, 274; black for silk, 275; orange, 275; light blue, 275.

E

Eggs, keep in liquid, 33; on shelves, 34; closing pores of, 34; in salt, 35.
Embroidery, 262.
Engravings, take stains from, 214; remove grease, 215; a bleacher, 215.

F

Fading, to prevent red, 50; in general, 50.
Feathers, to cure, 94; brushes, 107; to purify, 184.
Fish, keeping, 31; scale comb, 38; scale knife, 38.
Flannels, to bleach, 55.
Fleas, lavender for, 258; pennyroyal for, 258; in wood, 258; sassafras for, 258
Flies, to drive away, 250; to destroy, 250; lavender buds a remedy, 250; sugar and pepper for, 250; spots removed, 155; to keep away, 155.
Floors, grease from, 217; dry paint from, 217; chlorine for stains, 218; a good polish, 218; wiping, 218; musty floors, 221; the kitchen, 221; a fluid for, 221; uncovered, 221; waxed, 222.

Flowers, in water, 243; to keep, 244; preserving, 244.

Food, treat canned, 41; various articles fresh, 41.

Footstool, 104.

Frames, walnut, 157; plush, 160; ribbon, 160; canvas, 161; gilt, 161; ornaments, 161.

Fruit stains, 76; juice, 77; on hands, 79.

Fumigate, with salt and acid, 229; the process of, 229; to cellar, 230; nitrate of lead, 221.

Fur, white, 90; dark, 90; luster, 90.

Furnishing, with good taste, 11; poor taste, 11; the parlor, 13; the kitchen, 28.

Furniture, selecting, 15; to remove white spots, 145, 146; marks from, 146; ink stains, 146; a rub for, 146; a polish, 147; polish for table, 148; finger marks, 149; to clean, 149; to wash, 149; using polishes, 149; to renew, 150; to clean willow, 152; to remove scratches, 153; to remove bruises, 153.

G

Garters, perfumed, 93.

Gasoline, for paint stains, 87.

Gilt, to clean, 155; renew frames, 155; to restore frames, 156; to clean, 156; to retouch, 156; regilding, 157; to protect frames, 157; patch wall paper, 176.

Gingham, to set colors in, 49.

Glass, stopper removed, 106; cleaning cut glass, 113; in hot water, 113; wiping, 113; in cold water, 113; vessels cleaned, 115; seasoning, 120; cement for, 203.

Gloves, kid, 88; ink on, 88; suede, 88; mending, 98.

Glue, waterproof, 204; for glass, 204; wood, 208; liquid, 208; for all things, 209; photographs, 209.

Goatskin, rug, 90; cleaning, 91.

Grass, stain, 84.

Grease, to remove machine, 68; from child's dress, 68; a remover, 69; to remove candle grease, 72; wagon grease, 72; a general remover, 73; heat for, 74; magnesia for, 74; on china silk, 74; from silk, 74; brown paper for, 75; from satin, 75.

H

Hamper, of a barrel, 102; a box, 103.

Hands, a cleaner for, 55.

Heel, a protector for, 97.

Hinges, soap the, 108.

Holder, kitchen, 41; asbestos, 59; iron holders, 59; rose holder, 226.

House-cleaning, 25.

Housekeeper, the Expert, 18

I

Indicator, the pantry, 29.
Ink, on white goods, 80; on gingham, 80; and sour milk, 80; and salt, 80; on the tablecover, 80; on carpets, 81; on white linen, 81; red ink, 81; on colored cottons, 82; indelible, 82; on the hands, 82; on mahogany, 82; on wood, 82; and brine, 83; and pumice-stone, 83; a copying, 198; an indelible, 198, 199; for stamping, 199; for a pad, 199; good black, 200; a stencil, 200; ink stains, 213; a good eraser, 214; blots, 214; to erase, 214; remove from leather, 235.
Insecticide, 245.
Instruments, to clean of rust, 131.
Iodine, stains, 86.
Ironing, tablecloths, 60; ironing day, 97.
Iron rust, 84, 85; new rust, 85; on marble, 86.
Irons, wash flat-irons, 58; prevent sticking, 59; to make smooth, 59; care of, 59; the right kind, 60; to solder iron, 208.
Ivory, discolored, 112; bleaching, 112; stains on, 151.

J

Japaned ware, to wash, 137; to polish, 137.

Jars, to purify, 114; rose jar, 226.
Jewels, cleaning, 113; gold jewelry, 136; the common way, 137; laying away, 137.

K

Kalsomining, 198.
Keys, fitting, 106.
Knife handle, and hot water, 31; fastening, 205.
Knives, to remove rust from, 130; stains, 130; to clean, 130; a cleaner, 130; to polish, 130; ordinary cleaner, 131; a mixture for, 131; to keep polished, 143; care of, 143; soda on, 144.

L

Lace, to brighten, 47; cream hued, 265; silver lace, 47; black lace, 47; to renew, 47; to dry, 48; to whiten, 48; to wash Valenciennes, 48; white cotton, 48; white silk, 48; to renew delicate, 48; to clean, 49; edging, 49; curtains, 49; wrinkles in, 93.
Lamp chimneys, to clean, 115; smoke stained, 116; to anneal, 121; keeping, 121.
Lamps, the brass tops, 122; fitting tops, 122; the burner, 122; fixing the burner, 123; cleaning, 123; renew the brass, 123; to fill, 124; attend regularly, 124.
Lampblack, 194.
Laundry hints, 42.

Lawns, attractive, 12.

Lead, white, 211.

Leather, tan color, 234; to blacken, 234; restore luster, 235; cement for, 207; belts, 240; waterproof, 241.

Lifter, for stove, 37; of wire, 37; for cakes, 38.

Lime, chloride of, 231; quick-lime, 232.

Linen, laying it away, 52; starching, 57; sprinkling, 58.

Linoleum, 172.

Lounge, a cover for, 108.

Lye, in washing, 42; on paint, 219; vessels, 232.

M

Machine, the sewing, to clean, 150.

Making over, 96.

Management, 16.

Mantel, of wood, 15.

Manuscripts, to renew, 215.

Marble, to clean, 116; stains from, 117.

Mats, skins for, 236.

Meats, disinfect, 31; keep fresh, 31.

Mica, smoky, 112; cleaning, 112.

Mildew, stains, 83; on linen, 83; in general, 84.

Milk, to detect water in, 35; to keep sweet, 35.

Mind, cheerful, 27.

Mirror, choosing, 14; cleaning mixture, 111; care of, 111; paper for cleaning, 111; to scour, 111; to wash, 111; silvering, 112.

Mittens, children's, 95.

Mold, to prevent on preserves, 32; from vinegar, 33; from ink, 198; from books, 216.

Mosquitoes, pennyroyal for, 251; to drive out, 251.

Moths, cedar for, 254; a chest, 255; newspapers, 255; perfume against, 257; steam, 257; millers, 257; in feathers, 256; in carpets, 256; paraffine for, 255; tansy for, 255.

Mucilage, gum arabic, 209; government, 209; a good, 209; tragacanth, 209; white, 210.

N

Naphtha, on carpet, 167; for bed bugs, 252.

Neatness, 16.

Nickel, rubbing, 131; on stoves, 132; paste for, 132; to brighten, 132; to wash plate, 132; badly stained, 132; cleaning powder, 133; acid on, 133.

O

Odds and Ends, to be saved, 105.

Odors, from clothes, 93; onion, 233.

Oil-cloth, selecting, 15; to wash, 171; white spots from, 171; to make last, 172; grease on, 172; to polish, 173; clean with oil, 172.

Oil, kerosene, for dishes, 30; in washing, 45; on shoes, 241; on carpets, 168; cod liver oil stains, 71 ; kerosene stains, 89 ; lubricating oil, 107 ; an oil for shoes, 240; oil stains from paper, 176.
Oiling, the harness, 236.

` P

Packing, winter goods, 99 ; summer goods, 100.
Pad, a good, 174; more about, 174; copying pad, 199.
Paint, for kitchen floor, 30; on cloth, 87; a red, 193; acid proof, 193; a basis, 194; when to paint, 194; a black, 194; a green, 194; a good cheap paint, 195; fine paints, 195; water colors, 195; rule for quantity, 196; plain paint, 196; red stain, 201; ebonize pine, 201; to remove stains, 217; remove dry paint, 218; repainting, 219; before painting, 219; to wash paint, 220 ; fuller's-earth to wash, 220; to clean, 220; to remove paint odor, 230.
Paintings, to clean oil, 159.
Pan for dust, 109.
Pants, the knee of, 98.
Papers, family, 21; old, 22; oiled, 24; around ice, 24; bags, 24; for a pillow, 182; paper for a small room, 175; samples, 175; subdued colors

in, 175; broken on wall, 176; to clean, 177.
Paraffin, 206.
Paste, for walls, 178; stickfast, 210; a flour, 210; for walls, 210; simple, 211.
Pen, for marking, 109; prevent rust, 144.
Pepper, and mice, 253.
Perfumes, special, 227; geranium, 227; for the bath, 228; toilet water, 228; violet, 228; lavender, 229; floral, 229.
Piano, keys, 150; to bleach, 151; to clean, 152; care of, 152.
Pictures, in position, 162; a good effect, 162; in general, 162; arranging, 162.
Pillow, ticking, 183 ; cases, marking, 181; to clean feather, 185.
Pipes, drain, 224; sooty, 323; frozen, 225.
Plants, growing, 246.
Plastering, to mend. 177.
Plush, to renew, 75.
Pots, to clean, 125; to scour, 125; prepare new ones, 125; encrusted, 125; to clean, 126; to rivet iron pots, 127; the coffee pot, 128; paste to mend, 127.
Pottery, tempering, 120.

Q

Quilt, of eiderdown, 182; a warm one, 182; a pretty one, 183.

R

Rack for clothes, 61.
Razor, paste, 131.
Ribbons, to clean, 72, 262.
Rings, for poles, 108 ; for canopy, 181.
Roaches, a remedy, 249; borax for, 249; hellebore, 249; plaster, 249.
Room, The cozy, 14; model sleeping, 180.
Rug, to dust, 165; to clean, 171; rugs, 256; rag rugs, 260.

S

Sacks, flour, 104.
Salt, for the table, 35; on carpet, 166; on matting, 168; on weeds, 244.
Salts of lemon, on iron stains, 87.
Satin, to clean, 74.
Scorching, to prevent, 58; to remove, 73.
Screens, 110.
Screws, driving, 108.
Scuttle, for coal, 109.
Sheets that are old, 182.
Shirts, to polish, 55.
Shoes, ointment for, 238; tight, 238; lace, 93; coating for, 238; to freshen, 239; to soften, 239; for tan, 239; kid shoes, 239; to dry, 239; for ladies' shoes, 240; making waterproof, 240; polish for, 241; creaking, 240; vaseline for, 241.

Silk, to brighten black, 75; to renew, 94; to smooth, 94; silk scraps, 260; handling silks, 261; underwear, 261.
Silver, to polish, 133; a powder, 134; ink from, 135; egg stain, 135; medicine from, 135; putting away, 136.
Sinks, cleaned, 223; care of, 224; to brighten, 224.
Skins, to mount, 237.
Smoke, stains, 221.
Soap, a substitute for, 44; to clean soapsuds, 44; hard 62; to make soft, 22; borax curd, 63; good soft soap, 63; family soft soap, 63; catmeal, 64; white, 64; corn flour, 64; soap sacks, 64; scrap soap, 65; for all purposes, 65; coconut, 65; oatmeal bags, 66; small pieces for kitchen, 66; scouring soap, 66; to dry, 66; how to use. 67; to test, 67; with fuller's earth, 71.
Soda, to keep, 40; odd uses for, 41.
Sofa for the kitchen, 29.
Sponges, to clean with lemon, 189; for the toilet, 189.
Spots, to remove from wash goods, 70.
Starch, borax in, 56 ; gum arabic in, 56; salt in, 56; soap in, 56; good starch, 57; starching, 57; gloss starch, 56.
Stocking, guards, 97; pattern of foot, 98; black, 261; colored, 67.

Stove, mending, 107; a table, 109; heating, 141; to polish, 141; a polish, 142; prevent rust, 142, 143.

Straw hats, method to clean, 268; to whiten, 268; to clean, 268; to bleach, 268; oxalic acid on, 269; chlorene water on, 269.

Sweeping, 24; the stairs, 166; grass in, 167; paper in, 167.

T

Table cover, 105.

Tan, hides with hair on, 237; wool on, 237.

Tanin, stains, 78.

Tar, from clothes, 69.

Tapestry, to clean, 171.

Tea leaves on carpet, 166; tea for varnished paints, 220; save cold, 40; stain, 78; on table cloth, 79; clean tea-kettle, 126; incrusting, 126.

Thread, red stains, 77; shrinking, 108.

Tin, when new, 126; to clean, 126; mending, 126; patching, 127; milk cans, 127; salt on tin, 128; to polish, 128; greasy tins, 128; when to wash, 128; prevent rusting, 128; to wash, 129; scouring material, 128.

Towels, mended, 96; material for, 106.

Transfer, made, 159.

Tricot, to prevent spotting, 71.

Turpentine, for grease, 72; on carpets for cleaning, 168.

V

Varnish, from the hands, 87; for the stove, preventing rust, 144; to restore, 145; discolored, 145; to remove scratches, 146; brown, 201; turpentine varnish, 202; mahogany, 202; black, 202; for bronze, 202; for bed bugs, 252.

Velvet, to renew, 93; to clean, 93.

Verdigris, to remove, 139.

Vessels, to sweeten, 232.

W

Walls, grease on, 177; to clean, 177; to cover black parts, 178; preparing, 178; walls in general, 179; damp, 233.

Walnut, leaves for fleas, 258.

Wardrobe, a good one, 110.

Wash, the usual, 46; the family, 46; special goods, 50; silks, 51; silk dress, 51; china silk, 51; silk handkerchiefs, 51; embroideries, 52; about linen and white goods separately, 52; embroidered linen, 52; tidies and doilies. 52; lawn, 53; flannels, borax for, 53; flannels, 53; blankets, 53; worsted goods, 53; challis, 53; ordinary woolens, 54; flannels in general, 54; a wash for woolens, 54; fluid for washing, 44; wash for silks, 73.

Water, to clean cistern, 38; to clarify 39; make pure, 39; soften, 39; and chalk, 39; soften with ashes, 39; borax in, 39; make fit to drink, 40; to settle, 40; boiling water for stains, 76; destroy weeds, 244; water, cologne, 227.

Wax, red sealing, 206.

Weavel, in peas, 259.

Whalebone, 95.

White goods, mending, 97.

Whitewash, spots removed, 71; on carpet, 89; for vermin, 196; a fast, 196; a good, 197; a superior one, 197; for bed bugs in wall, 252.

Wicks, good, 123; care of, 123; to improve, 124.

Windows, cleaned of paint spots, 118; polishing, 118; washing, 118; corners, 118; oil on, 118; cleaning, 119; soda on, 119; wiping, 119; tea on, 119; to keep flies away from, 119.

Wine stains, 76.

Woolen dresses, treated for dye, 261.

Woolens, to clean, 70.

Work, How to slight, 20.

Worms, in flower pots, 245; plant worms, 246.

Wrappers, 95.

Z

Zinc, for the stove, 133; to wash, 133.